Website Hosting and Migration with Amazon Web Services

A Practical Guide to Moving Your Website to AWS

Jason Nadon

Apress®

Website Hosting and Migration with Amazon Web Services: A Practical Guide to Moving Your Website to AWS

Jason Nadon
Kingsville, Ontario
Canada

ISBN-13 (pbk): 978-1-4842-2588-2   ISBN-13 (electronic): 978-1-4842-2589-9
DOI 10.1007/978-1-4842-2589-9

Library of Congress Control Number: 2017941339

Managing Director: Welmoed Spahr
Editorial Director: Todd Green
Acquisitions Editor: Susan McDermott
Development Editor: Laura Berendson
Technical Reviewer: Matt Dilts
Coordinating Editor: Rita Fernando
Copy Editor: Mary Behr
Compositor: SPi Global
Indexer: SPi Global
Cover image designed by Freepik

Distributed to the book trade worldwide by Springer Science+Business Media New York, 233 Spring Street, 6th Floor, New York, NY 10013. Phone 1-800-SPRINGER, fax (201) 348-4505, e-mail orders-ny@springer-sbm.com, or visit www.springeronline.com. Apress Media, LLC is a California LLC and the sole member (owner) is Springer Science + Business Media Finance Inc (SSBM Finance Inc). SSBM Finance Inc is a **Delaware** corporation.

For information on translations, please e-mail rights@apress.com, or visit http://www.apress.com/rights-permissions.

Apress titles may be purchased in bulk for academic, corporate, or promotional use. eBook versions and licenses are also available for most titles. For more information, reference our Print and eBook Bulk Sales web page at http://www.apress.com/bulk-sales.

Any source code or other supplementary material referenced by the author in this book is available to readers on GitHub via the book's product page, located at www.apress.com/9781484225882. For more detailed information, please visit http://www.apress.com/source-code.

Printed on acid-free paper

Dedicated to those I wish were still here.

Contents at a Glance

Contents

About the Author

Jason Nadon started creating web content back in the days of bulletin board systems (BBS). His interest eventually lead him to join a company providing complex Internet-hosted tax and accounting applications, and he has enjoyed growth with that same company for the past 17 years. He has held positions as a Web Analyst, Web Services Administrator, Web Project Lead, IT Project Manager, Customer Systems Infrastructure Manager, and is currently the Lead Analyst on the Development Operations team. He has been the technical reviewer for six web-related book titles published by Apress. He founded the Ann Arbor, Michigan Macromedia User Group and participated in the Macromedia/Adobe MAX conferences from 2001–2005. Most recently Jason's focus has shifted to Amazon Web Services and Cloud Infrastructure, and he is helping extend on-premise data center environments to better serve customers.

About the Technical Reviewer

Matt Dilts is currently a Senior Development Operations Engineer in a large multi-national corporation. He has spent more than 15 years in the IT industry, largely developing and maintaining highly-available enterprise-class solutions to host applications for customers. He is currently in the process of designing and implementing highly-available solutions in AWS and migrating existing infrastructure to AWS.

Acknowledgments

This work would not have been possible without the support of many project team members. First and foremost, thanks to Susan McDermott for believing that this idea had merit and talking me into writing this book. I'd like to acknowledge Rita Fernando for doing her best to keep me on track in terms of delivery; I do know how challenging this can be. Thank you to my Technical Reviewer Matt Dilts for adding value and keeping me honest. Lastly, thanks to the many creators of software and systems referenced and brought together to bring this book to life. Their hard work and innovation have given us the opportunity to become more efficient and productive.

Introduction

Welcome to *Website Hosting and Migration with Amazon Web Services* and thank you for picking up this book. I'm excited to be your guide for this adventure in web hosting in AWS. The adoption rate of cloud services for startups and enterprises alike has been astounding. It reminds me of another time in my IT career when a major shift happened to move software architecture from desktop, stand-alone applications to web-based, interconnected applications. As with other disruptive movements in technology, cloud services offer a way for more control over resources used and much greater choices of self-service managed services. This shift means that it is possible for everyone to take control and deliver a highly available, scalable, cost-effective infrastructure to host their application or websites, which results in a better experience for end users.

As I was thinking about the best format for delivering a book that offered an introduction to hosting in Amazon Web Services, the leading cloud services provider, I wanted to make sure that the book was both accessible and interesting for those who perhaps have never managed the hosting of their own website as well as valuable to those looking at Amazon Web Services as an option for migrating their existing website. The most effective way for me to deliver on both of these goals was to organize the book into "scenarios" that offer you the choice of working through from start to finish or using it as a "choose your own adventure" style book and focusing on the content that is most relevant to you. It should be noted that if you're new to AWS, starting with the first scenario and working through to the last will give you a progressive experience that offers the most exposure to services offered in AWS, and each scenario does build on knowledge gained in the previous scenario.

This book has three web hosting scenarios. First, in Chapter 1, you'll look at the simple static website: a simple, multi-page site that is used by many companies to provide an online presence for their goods and services, complete with a simple contact form. In Chapter 7, you'll look at the second scenario where I'll show how to host popular content management systems in the AWS platform using dedicated compute, database, and storage resources. Lastly, in Chapter 14, you'll take a look at a much more complex website scenario that will have additional challenges and more complex features to be supported such as staff logins, email services, and ecommerce requirements. You'll also look at how to extend your enterprise website with AWS managed services.

In each scenario, I'll describe the type of website that you'll be working with as well as give you sample files that can be used to follow along and host the content in your very own AWS account. I'll give you the tools and knowledge needed to host the sample files that are provided for your use and, wherever possible, I'll put in tips that are related to how to migrate existing content that you may have over to AWS.

One of the many benefits of Amazon Web Services is being able to easily set up environments and resources that allow you to learn the AWS platform and deliver a proof of concept: a functional service with very little investment upfront. This enables you to use the sample files provided, or your own content in a functional environment, and to monitor billing costs before committing to AWS as your new hosting provider. Since the hosting cost is a major factor in most people's decision to use a given hosting provider, I'll provide a section on hosting cost considerations in the summary section of each hosting scenario that will be based on billing data outside of the free-tier hosting period so that you can make an informed decision in regard to whether to move to AWS for your web hosting needs.

■ ■ ■

Hosting a Static Website in Amazon Web Services

CHAPTER 1

■ ■ ■

Static Content Scenario

In this chapter, you'll explore your first web hosting scenario: the static content website. A static website is one that consists of files and web pages that do not change based on user interaction. When a user visits the website, the content displayed to them is static in nature, meaning that it doesn't change unless the author of that content updates the files with new content to be displayed.

This type of website is the least complex architecture to work with since the assets that make up the site are limited to files. As you progress through future chapters you'll learn how those asset lists will include files and also application dependencies such as web servers and databases.

In this scenario, you will be setting up web hosting in Amazon Web Services (AWS) for a fictional local law office. This small law firm employs less than five staff members but realizes the importance of having a "web presence" for potential customers to learn about their services, read past client testimonials, and get contact information for the office.

It is important to understand a bit more about the content and the file assets that you'll be working with in the next several chapters. Laying this foundation will allow you to see parallels in working with your own website content and how you will be able to migrate it to AWS.

Website Content Overview

This hosting scenario will consist of a static website made up of five pages. You will be using a template provided from www.templated.co; this site offers an excellent selection of responsive, clean HTML/CSS templates for use with your website. The web pages that you'll be working with are described below.

- **Home:** The home page will be the landing page for the website. This page will hold basic information about the law firm, a high-level overview of services provided, and important contact information.

- **Services:** The services page will hold detailed information about the services offered by the law firm.

- **Testimonials:** The testimonials page will hold the best of the feedback and testimonials that the firm has collected from previous and existing clients. As you progress through this web hosting scenario, I'll show you how you can use page templates to add new testimonials and update this page over time. This same process can be used if you want to do the same with a page for the latest firm news or blog posts (more on this later).

- **About Us:** The "About Us" page will hold information about the history of the firm, the founding partners, and other firm-specific information.

© Jason Nadon 2017

J. Nadon, *Website Hosting and Migration with Amazon Web Services*, DOI 10.1007/978-1-4842-2589-9_1

- **Contact**: The contact page will hold contact information for the firm. This will include the full address and an embedded map, which will illustrate how you can still use external resources even though this is a static website. In addition, you see how other AWS services such as Lambda can be leveraged from your static files to process information. This will be your first exposure to the power of Amazon Web Services Managed Services offerings. This one will dive a bit deep, so I'll save it until you work through some of the other foundational services.

Website Asset Overview

The file assets that will be used in this web hosting scenario are listed in Figure 1-1.

Name	Date modified	Type	Size
css	8/28/2016 2:57 PM	File folder	
images	8/28/2016 2:18 PM	File folder	
js	8/28/2016 2:18 PM	File folder	
about_us	8/28/2016 2:18 PM	Chrome HTML Do...	9 KB
contact	8/28/2016 2:18 PM	Chrome HTML Do...	9 KB
index	8/28/2016 2:18 PM	Chrome HTML Do...	8 KB
services	8/28/2016 2:18 PM	Chrome HTML Do...	9 KB
testimonials	8/28/2016 2:18 PM	Chrome HTML Do...	9 KB

Figure 1-1. *The directory listing with the file structure for your static content website scenario*

As you can see, you have an HTML page for each of the pages described in the previous section. You have a folder to hold your CSS content files (which control the styling of your website), a folder for your image assets, and a folder for any JavaScript that will be used. You can download these sample files from www.apress.com/9781484225882.

Relevant AWS Services

Let's briefly go over the services that I will be introducing in this website hosting scenario. The services listed below are some of the core Amazon Web Services infrastructure service offerings that will be used throughout the rest of the book:

- **AWS S3**: Amazon Web Services Simple Storage Service is Amazon's core object-based storage service, and you'll be using it in this hosting scenario. I'll cover all of the fundamentals and I'll give you some tips for working with this service when hosting static web content.

- **AWS Route53**: Amazon Web Services Route53 DNS service is a fully managed domain name system that resolves domain names to IP addresses. This service offers so much more, though, and while working with this hosting scenario you'll explore some of the basics, such as domain registration and working with DNS record sets. In later chapters, you'll extend your knowledge by using some of the more advanced features available with this service.

- **AWS Lambda**: Amazon Web Services Lambda is managed service that enables you to leverage AWS infrastructure to process compute workloads. Think of it as a process factory. If you have work to be done, you can have it done on your dedicated web servers or you can outsource the workload to AWS Lambda. A service like this comes in very handy when trying to handle simple tasks without the need to invest in full server architecture. You'll learn a bit about this service when you use it to process data input from your visitor's input on your Contact web page. It is important to note that AWS Lambda is not available in all AWS regions at the time of writing. To learn more about regional service availability, go to https://aws.amazon.com/about-aws/global-infrastructure/regional-product-services/.

Summary

This chapter provided the big picture of what you're going to accomplish in the first part of this book. I'm eager to get started and I hope you are too! Let's begin with an introduction to the AWS Free Tier Account and show you how to get started using Amazon Web Services.

CHAPTER 2

Introduction to AWS Free Tier

In this chapter, you'll register for an account. After setting up your AWS account, I'll walk you through how to secure your account and I'll give you a high-level overview of how to access your account resources.

For new customers, Amazon offers a 12-month period where you can try out many of the features of AWS at a minimal cost. They call this offer period the *AWS Free Tier*. The free tier allows for a certain set of AWS resources to be run under your account at no cost. When choosing to start resources within AWS, Amazon will highlight whether the resource or service is covered under the free tier usage terms. I'll also highlight whether a service or resource is included in the free tier as you look at each service in future chapters. For a current list of what is covered within the free tier usage terms, go to https://aws.amazon.com/free/.

This link is also the place where you sign up for the AWS account that you'll use throughout this book. When you visit the link, you will see information about which resources and services are covered under the free tier usage agreement. From this page, click the "Sign in to the Console" button and that will bring you to the login page (see Figure 2-1).

Sign In or Create an AWS Account

What is your email (phone for mobile accounts)?

E-mail or mobile number:

jae@thinknadonmedia.com

○ I am a new user.

● I am a returning user
and my password is:

Sign in using our secure server ▶

Forgot your password?

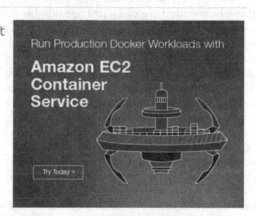

Learn more about <u>AWS Identity and Access Management</u> and <u>AWS Multi-Factor Authentication</u>, features that provide additional security for your AWS Account. View full <u>AWS Free Usage Tier</u> offer terms.

Figure 2-1. *The AWS Login screen with options to sign into an existing account or to create a new one*

© Jason Nadon 2017
J. Nadon, *Website Hosting and Migration with Amazon Web Services*, DOI 10.1007/978-1-4842-2589-9_2

From here you can log into your account if you already have one, or you can choose the "I am a new user" radio button, enter your email address, and click the "Sign in using your secure server" button. When you've done that, you will see the screen shown in Figure 2-2. Behind the scenes, Amazon will verify that this is indeed a unique email address and will require you to fill out your name and email address and have you choose a password to be used with your new account.

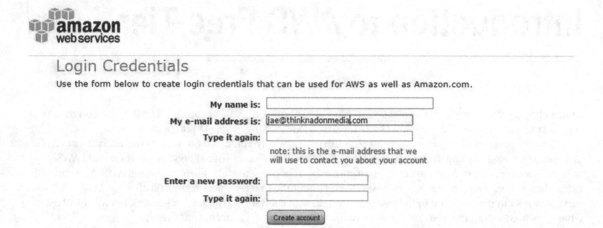

Figure 2-2. *The first step of a new AWS account setup consists of entering your full name and a valid email address, and choosing a password for your new account*

After entering your name, email address, and new password, you will walk through the New Account Setup Wizard where additional personal information will be collected and where you will specify your billing information. Although the free tier allows for a limited amount of free usage per month for a period of 12 months, a valid credit card is required to complete the new account process. During the new account setup process you will also be required to give a telephone number where you can be reached and an automated verification can be performed. This automated verification will call the phone number that you provide and will deliver a verification code that you will then enter into the New Account Setup Wizard to complete the verification process.

Although this sounds like a lot of information gathered, it is important to understand that Amazon Web Services is a pay-as-you-go platform that offers flexibility and control over the resources that you use. It also gives you the option of trying services without locking you into a long-term contract like you find at other web hosting services or Internet service providers.

As part of the setup process you also have the opportunity to select the level of AWS support that you would like to have associated with your account. The Basic Support plan is included with all AWS accounts; however, you do have the option to pay for a higher level of support and engagement based on your operating requirements. For this first web hosting scenario example, you will use a limited amount of services, and I believe that the Basic Support plan is sufficient at this time. As you start to use more resources and have a need to receive answers to your questions in a more expedited fashion, you do have the ability to upgrade the support plan associated with your AWS account at any time.

Once the new account setup process is complete, you will receive an email welcoming you to AWS and giving you a plethora of information about how to get started using their services. You can now return to the link above, or to http://aws.amazon.com and click the "Log in to the Console" button and, when prompted, enter your new account email address and password. Once logged in, you'll be presented with the AWS Console (see Figure 2-3), the central location for accessing all of the AWS resources and services. Up next I'll dive into a Console overview and introduce AWS IAM (Identity and Access Management), a service used to control access to your AWS Account and resources.

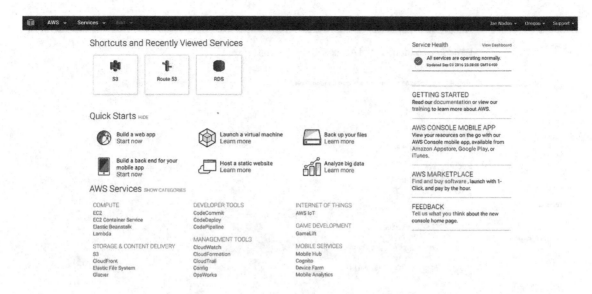

Figure 2-3. *The AWS Console, a central management web interface for all AWS resources and services*

Now that you have an account and are able to log into the Amazon Web Services Console, the first thing you need to do is to protect that account. The account that you just used to sign up for AWS and to sign into the console is known as the *root* account. This is the administrative account and it has full access to all of Amazon's services within AWS. Although it may seem quite convenient to continue to use this account for day-to-day administration, I suggest that you follow AWS best practices and lock this account down and create a new account that will be used for creating resources within AWS. To do this, let's take a look at your first AWS managed service, IAM.

Introducing IAM and Securing the Root Account

To access AWS IAM from the console screen, search for the category "Security and Identity." Underneath this category you will see a link for IAM, so click it. When you access IAM, you'll be presented with a screen similar to Figure 2-4.

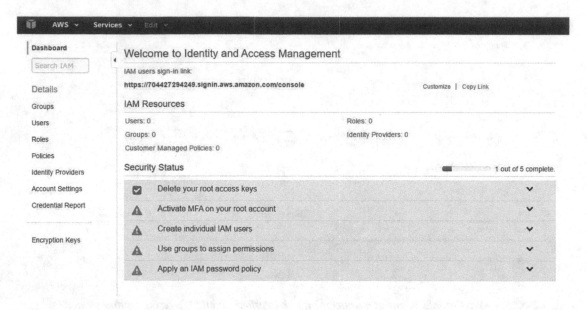

Figure 2-4. *The AWS IAM Welcome screen, which is accessed under the "Security and Identity" category from within the AWS Console*

As you can see from Figure 2-4, you will be presented with the IAM Management screen. From here you can view the IAM user sign-in link, which is a direct link to your AWS account sign-in page. This can be shared with others whom you wish to have access to your account, or bookmarked for direct login access for future visits.

You will notice that you currently have zero users, groups, policies, roles, policies, and identity providers set up. These five areas cover what you can manage within IAM. You can create users, who can access resources in your AWS account. You can create groups, which are a collection of users. You can create roles, which are a type of account that can be assumed by other AWS resources (this may seem a bit confusing right now, but I'll explain it in greater detail in later chapters). You can create policies, which are permissions that can be assigned to users, groups, or roles, and you can utilize identity providers to allow for integration with third-party identity providers (think corporate domain account or your Facebook login), but this is a topic outside the scope of this book.

In this section, you will focus on securing your root account as best as you can and creating a new group and account for day-to-day use. The root account information should be stored away for safekeeping and only accessed if the new administrator account that you're going to create is lost. After you perform these steps, you will also see all the Security Status items shown in Figure 2-4 marked as complete with the green checkmark.

Steps to Secure Your AWS Root Account

The following steps are needed to secure your AWS root account:

- Step 1: Implement a strong password policy

- Step 2: Create an Administrators group

- Step 3: Create a user and add it to the Administrators group

- Step 4: Secure your root account with multi-factor authentication

In Step 1, you will implement a strong password policy to be used in your AWS account. This password policy will apply to all accounts created, which is why you want to do this step first. From the IAM home screen, click the drop-down arrow next to "Apply an IAM Password Policy" and then click the "Manage Password Policy" button. After clicking this button you'll be presented with a screen similar to Figure 2-5.

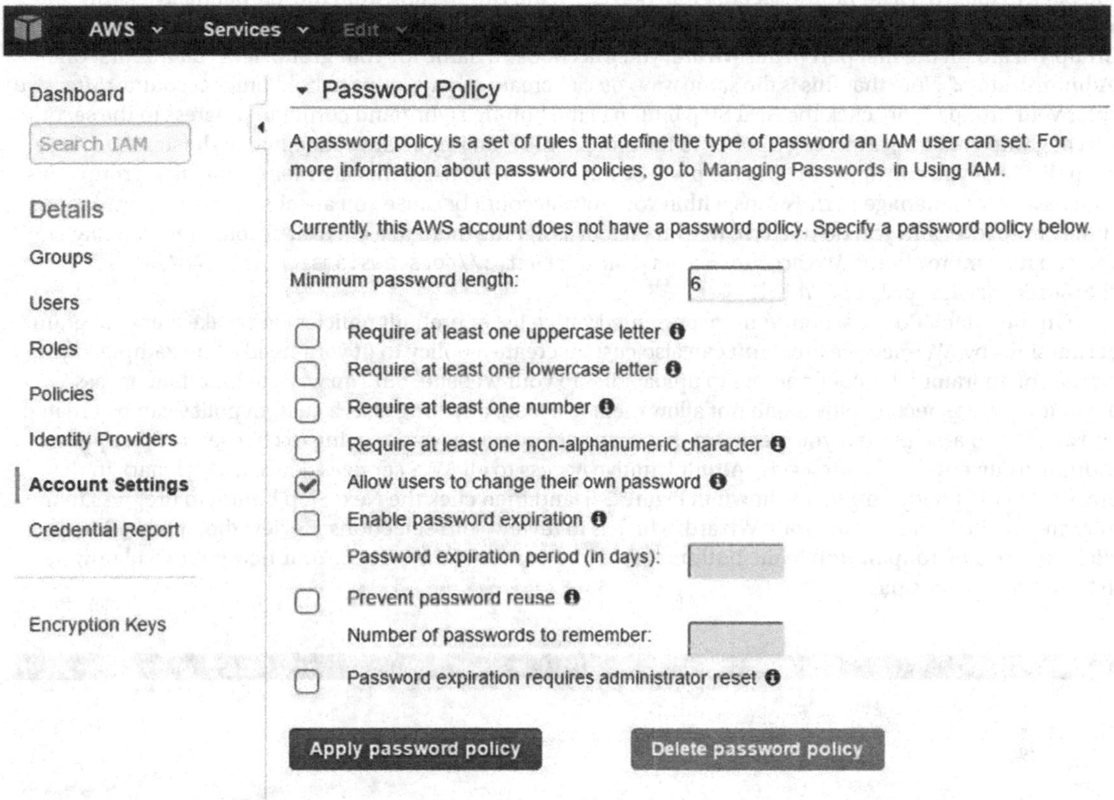

Figure 2-5. *The AWS IAM Password Policy screen allows for management of the options for requiring strong passwords for all IAM accounts*

From this screen you can customize a policy that will enforce all accounts created to meet certain minimum requirements as it relates to passwords used. My recommendations for choosing settings for a strong password policy are the following:

- Require at least one uppercase letter.

- Require at least one lowercase letter.

- Require at least one number.

- Require at least one non-alphanumeric character.

These settings are what I recommend for the majority of accounts. For accounts that will have Administrative Account access, I also recommend adding the additional security options available on this screen to increase the level of security on the account.

Once you have selected the features you would like to enable on your password policy, click the "Apply password policy" button to save your changes. The dialog box at the top of the screen should indicate "Successfully updates password policy."

Now you'll move to Step 2 and create your first group to hold the user that will be created in Step 3. From the password policy screen, click the Dashboard link in the top left-hand corner; this will bring you back to the AWS IAM home screen. From here, click the Groups link from the left-hand navigation and you will go to a screen where you can click the "Create New Group" button to launch the Create New Group Wizard. In the first part of this wizard, you will choose a name for your group; let's call this first one "Administrators." Note that this is the same way you can create other groups to hold other accounts. After you enter your group name, click the Next Step button in the bottom right-hand corner to progress to the second part of group creation, attaching a policy to the group. This is an important concept to understand because the policy that you will apply to this group will be inherited by all users that are members of that group. This is an easy way to manage permissions within your AWS account because you are able to assign permissions at the group level and you do not have to worry about assigning them to each user account individually. You can read more about AWS account access policies at http://docs.aws.amazon.com/IAM/latest/UserGuide/access_policies.html.

On the Attach Policy screen you are presented with a list of prebuilt policies that make it easy to grant permissions by AWS service area. You can also custom create a policy to fit your needs; for example, if you have a collaborator who needs access to upload files to your website, but you want to lock their access down to a list of specific folders and not allow them to access anything else, a custom policy can be created and applied to a group that you create for that user. For your case, you're going to choose the first option, "AdministrativeAccess," which gives Administrative Access to all AWS services. Place a checkmark in the box next to the policy option, as shown in Figure 2-6, and then click the Next Step button to progress to the final step of the Create New Group Wizard, which is to review your selections. Review the information and click the Create Group button in the bottom right-hand corner of the screen. Your new group will now be listed on the Groups page.

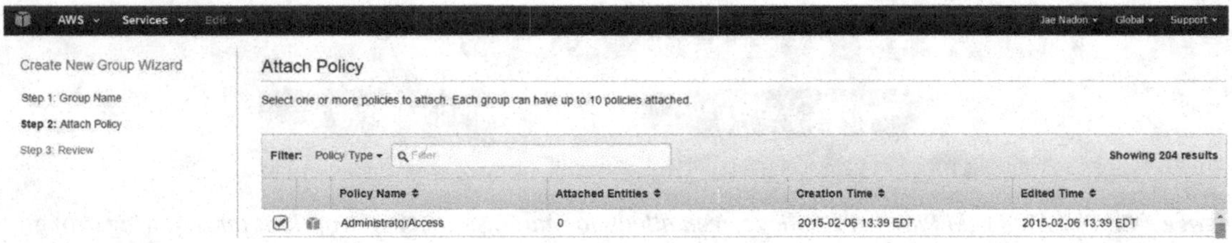

Figure 2-6. *The AWS IAM Create New Group Wizard showing the Attach Policy step with "AdministrativeAccess" selected*

Now you'll move on to the third of four steps to secure your AWS root account. Step 3 involves creating your first user and making them a member of the Administrators group that you just created. Click the Users link in the left-hand navigation and then click the "Create New User" button to start the Create User Wizard. The creation of users is a pretty straightforward process: enter the username to be used and click the Create button to create the user. For your first account, I recommend using the format firstname.lastname for your user account, but feel free to use any formation that you find easy to remember. There is an important option in this process, which is enabled by default, to generate access keys for each user. You want to make sure that you do this for any account that will need access to the AWS Console (logging in via your IAM users sign-in URL, shown on the IAM Dashboard) as well as through other tools or integration points. You will be using an integration point that will require these access keys in the next chapter, so be sure to download the credentials after the user is created and keep this file in a very safe place that you will be able to access when the time comes. After the user is created, you will be prompted with the screen shown in Figure 2-7. The Download Credentials button can be found in the bottom right-hand corner of this screen. Once you have downloaded the user credential files, which will be in CSV format, you can click the Close button to exit out of the New User Wizard.

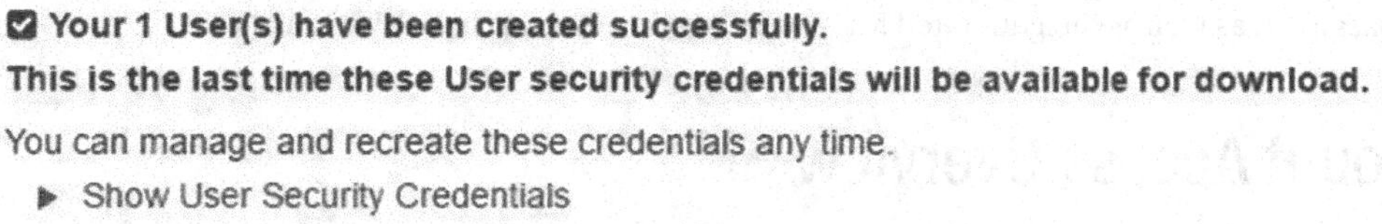

☑ **Your 1 User(s) have been created successfully.**

This is the last time these User security credentials will be available for download.

You can manage and recreate these credentials any time.

▶ Show User Security Credentials

Figure 2-7. *The AWS IAM Create User Wizard after the Create button has been clicked. At this point, you can download or view the user security credentials. These credentials are needed for tool or integration access such as the AWS Command Line Interface.*

Although you have now created your user, by default the account does not yet have a password, so you'll set it up. You should be back at the AWS IAM Users screen with the new user you just created listed; if not, just click the Users link in the left-hand navigation. From here, place a checkbox next to the user account you would like to manage, and then choose the User Actions drop-down menu near the top of the user list. From the drop-down list, choose "Manage Password." You will have the option to have AWS generate a password (based on the password policy you created in Step 1) or to assign a custom password that you will deliver to the new user. You will also have the option to force the user to change their password upon first login. This is recommended because it allows the user to create their own password to be used when logging into your AWS account, but don't worry; even the one that they generate will be forced to comply with the password policy that you created in Step 1. Select a password option and click "Apply." You will want to log this password in a safe location because this first account will be the one that you will be using to do the majority of your tasks moving forward.

The last step in securing your AWS Root Account is to enable multi-factor authentication (MFA). To do this last step, let's head back to the IAM Dashboard/Home screen by clicking the Dashboard link in the left-hand navigation. At this point, your Security Status section should be looking much better, with four of the five items listed with a green checkbox next to them showing that they have been completed. The last item listed with a caution symbol is to enable multi-factor authentication on the AWS root account. MFA by design requires more than one authentication factor to access your account. This means that in addition to a username and password, another factor of authentication will be required for you to log into your AWS root account. This may seem painful, but securing your AWS root account is an important thing to do; if someone compromises this account, they have the keys to the kingdom and can start using resources and services that could end up costing you a lot of money.

The easier of the two ways to use and enable MFA on your root account is to use a virtual MFA device loaded on a cell phone. Google Authenticator is an MFA application that can be downloaded from the Apple or Android App Store and can be used with AWS. If you do not have a mobile device to use as a virtual MFA device, you do have the option of ordering a hardware device from Amazon. In addition to these options, there are desktop applications that can be loaded on your PC to act as a virtual MFA device. Installation and configuration of specific MFA applications goes beyond the scope of this book, but you can find more information about the MFA setup options at `https://aws.amazon.com/mfa`.

After you've downloaded Google Authenticator on your mobile phone or installed an MFA application on your PC, click the drop-down arrow to the right of "Activate MFA on your root account" and then click the "Manage MFA" button. Choose the "A virtual MFA device" radio button and click the "Next Step" button. At this point, you will be reminded that you need a compatible MFA software application on your mobile phone or computer to continue. Click the Next Step button when you're ready to proceed. From the next screen you can use your smart phone to scan the QR code presented or use the secret keys for manual configuration. Once this information is entered into your MFA application, you'll be presented with your first 6-digit MFA code, so enter it in the first text input field. You will then wait 30 seconds until the MFA 6-digit code refreshes and enter that next code in the sequence into the second text input field and click the "Activate MFA Device" button and then the Finish button. Once you do this, your AWS root account will now have MFA enabled; each time you log in with this account you'll need to use your AWS root account username and password as well as the generated MFA code to gain access to the AWS Console.

AWS Account Access Overview

Now that you have set up your root account and an administrative user account in your AWS account, it is time to talk a bit about the access methods and concepts for using your AWS resources. The first method of accessing your AWS account and resources is by logging into the AWS website and using the web interface, which is referred to as the AWS Console. You can log into the AWS console with your root account, or any other account that you create within AWS IAM.

As you also learned when you set up your first user account earlier in this chapter, each user has not only a username and password but a set of security credentials called keys that can be used to access account resources programmatically. These keys are used to identify your user account through various tools or software integrations.

An example of a tool that implements the use of these keys is the AWS command-line interface (CLI). This tool can be installed on your desktop PC and can be used to interact, from the command line, with your AWS account and resources. Everything that can be done via the AWS Console can be done via command-line commands using the CLI. This makes the CLI a great resource to use when performing tasks that are repetitive in nature. You can read more about the CLI in the AWS documentation at http://aws.amazon.com/cli/.

Third-party software is another example of an integration that will use your IAM user account security credential keys for access to resources within your AWS account. In the next chapter, you will walk through setting up Cloudberry Explorer, a client interface that allows you to access AWS S3 like an FTP client or File Explorer. This software will use your credential keys to impersonate your user account as it accesses your AWS S3 resources.

The three methods presented here will be the main forms of access that you'll use throughout this book when accessing and working with your AWS account resources.

Summary

In this chapter, you signed up for an AWS account, secured your root account to minimize the risk of it falling into the hands of evil-doers, created an administrative user account that you'll use for the rest of this book, and briefly explored the different options that you'll use to access your account resources and services. AWS IAM is an important managed service and is one that you will get to use in later chapters when you create additional accounts for collaborators, staff members, and more. You're now prepared to jump into the most important service that will help you with hosting your first web scenario: AWS Simple Storage Service (AWS S3). Grab a cup of coffee, log into your AWS Console with the new administrative account you created in this chapter, and let's proceed.

■ ■ ■

CHAPTER 3

Your Content Solution: An Introduction to AWS S3

In Chapter 1, I discussed the files that will make up your static content website scenario; in Chapter 2, I introduced AWS Identity and Access Management, the service that is used to control and manage your Amazon Web Services account and access to it and all of the resources in AWS. In this chapter, I'm going to introduce Amazon Web Services Simple Storage Solution, known as AWS S3. I'll give a brief introduction and then you'll prep your website scenario content for uploading. I know you're eager to get started hosting your static content in AWS so in this chapter you'll use the sample files discussed in Chapter 1 and get the content uploaded to AWS S3 in the most effective manner first, so that you can see how easy it is to host content in S3 using the AWS Console (which was introduced in Chapter 2). Then I'll spend more time on an overview of the AWS S3 service and all the options you have for managing and controlling access to your content.

Later in the chapter I'll cover how to set up the AWS command-line interface (CLI) and give examples of how to interact with your content in S3 via the CLI. I'll also show you an example of a third-party application that makes interacting with your S3 files as easy as using an operating system file explorer.

Amazon Web Services: S3 Overview

AWS S3 is Amazon's highly redundant, highly available storage solution for the AWS Platform. The easiest way to think of it is as a file system that allows for the organization and storage of files. In contrast to an operating file system, AWS S3 is object-based. This is an important concept to understand: S3 allows for the storage of *objects* and these objects have properties that control information about them. I'll give you a good summary of these properties later in this chapter and you'll dive much deeper into using object properties in later web hosting scenarios.

Objects stored in AWS S3 can be organized into folders, and folders are organized into buckets. A bucket is a collection of objects. An object can't exist outside of a bucket, so a bucket is the top-level storage unit within AWS S3 and the first thing that you'll create to hold your website content.

As mentioned, Amazon S3 is highly available, meaning that data stored in S3 is replicated to all other AWS regions. A region is a geographical area that holds a minimum of two availability zones. An availability zone can be thought of as a data center location. In AWS, some services have a scope of a given region, such as Oregon or North Virginia, but the two services that you've been introduced to, IAM and S3, are global in scope. This means that when you upload data to S3, it is replicated across Amazon's infrastructure to allow for extremely fault-tolerant storage. In terms of service level agreements (SLA), Amazon promises 99.99% (also known as "four nines") for S3 durability and they promise 99.999999999% availability. This can be summarized by saying that the data you store in S3 will be there when you need it and loss of data is very rare.

© Jason Nadon 2017

J. Nadon, *Website Hosting and Migration with Amazon Web Services*, DOI 10.1007/978-1-4842-2589-9_3

Accessing AWS S3 via the Console

Now let's see how to access S3 via the console. In Chapter 2, you created an administrative user account that you can use for day-to-day console access and management. Go ahead and log in as that user.

After you successfully log into the console, you will be presented with the main page, which lists all of the Amazon Web Services resources sorted into categories. You will find S3 listed under the "Storage and Content Delivery" category heading.

Click the S3 link under that category to be brought to the S3 landing page. Since you have not yet done any work in S3, the landing page will present you with an introduction to the AWS S3 service, and link to full documentation for all the features of the service. Most of the AWS platform services have a similar landing page that explains the service, offers links to documentation, and gives you a call to action to get started. On this landing page, the call to action is to create your first bucket.

■ **Tip**   Bookmark frequently used AWS services by clicking the Edit link near the top of the AWS Console. A list of all services will be displayed, and you can click and drag a service to the top to bookmark it for easier access in the future. An example of the activated Edit link is shown in Figure 3-1. Figure 3-2 shows it with bookmarks added to the navigation bar.

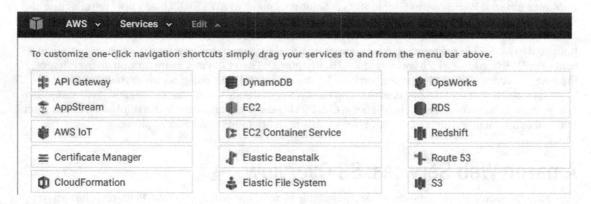

Figure 3-1. *After the Edit link at the top of the AWS Console is clicked, all services are listed and can be dragged to the top of the screen for easier access in future visits. Click the Edit link again to hide the list of services.*

Welcome to Amazon Simple Storage Service

Amazon S3 is storage for the Internet. It is designed to make web-scale computing easier for developers.

Amazon S3 provides a simple web services interface that can be used to store and retrieve any amount of data, at any time, from anywhere on the web. It gives any developer access to the same highly scalable, reliable, secure, fast, inexpensive infrastructure that Amazon uses to run its own global network of web sites. The service aims to maximize benefits of scale and to pass those benefits on to developers.

You can read, write, and delete objects ranging in size from 1 byte to 5 terabytes each. The number of objects you can store is unlimited. Each object is stored in a bucket with a unique key that you assign.

Get started by simply creating a bucket and uploading a test object, for example a photo or .txt file.

Create Bucket

Figure 3-2. *The top navigation bar after shortcuts for IAM and S3 have been added and the "call to action" to create your first bucket*

Creating a Bucket for Web Content

As mentioned, a bucket is the top-level organization structure for S3 content. It can hold folders and file objects within it. In this section, you'll create a bucket to hold your static website content files and then you'll upload your content files. You'll also examine some of the properties and settings of file objects and S3 buckets.

After clicking the Create Bucket button, you'll be taken to a screen similar to Figure 3-3 where you will enter your bucket name and choose an AWS region where the bucket will be created. The home region for your bucket should be the one that is closest to the majority of your website visitors to minimize latency. If you are unsure about where your visitors will be coming from, simply choose the default AWS region selection that is presented. S3 content is replicated to other regions as part of the service; there is nothing you need to do to other than upload your content to provide high availability and access.

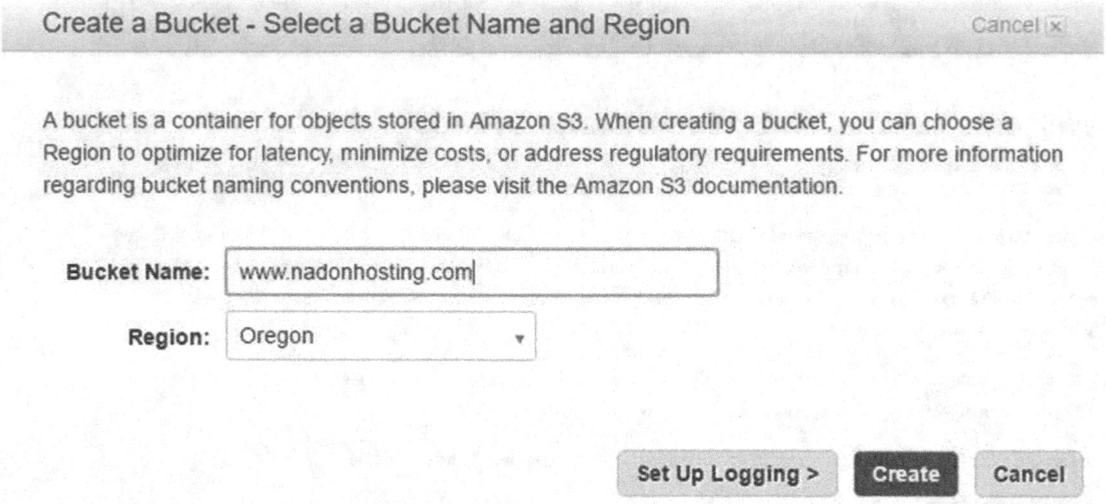

Create a Bucket - Select a Bucket Name and Region   Cancel ⊠

A bucket is a container for objects stored in Amazon S3. When creating a bucket, you can choose a Region to optimize for latency, minimize costs, or address regulatory requirements. For more information regarding bucket naming conventions, please visit the Amazon S3 documentation.

Bucket Name: www.nadonhosting.com|

Region: Oregon   ▾

Set Up Logging >   Create   Cancel

Figure 3-3. The "Create a Bucket" screen, asking for the bucket name and AWS region

You are going to name your bucket the exact name of the website that you want to host. In Figure 3-3, I use the website `www.nadonhosting.com`; you will choose a bucket name that is unique to you and to all other AWS accounts. I know this may sound a bit unorthodox, but this will help you in later chapters. As mentioned, S3 is a global platform service, so each bucket name must be unique across the platform. This means that once any AWS account creates a bucket with a specific name, that name is unique to that account and can never be used again, in any other account, even if deleted. Click the Create button once you have entered your bucket name and chose an AWS region. Your bucket will be created and you'll be brought to the S3 main administration page, shown in Figure 3-4.

Bucket: www.nadonhosting.com

Bucket: www.nadonhosting.com
Region: Oregon
Creation Date: Sun Sep 11 09:21:47 GMT-400 2016
Owner: jae

▸ Permissions

▸ Static Website Hosting

▸ Logging

▸ Events

▸ Versioning

▸ Lifecycle

▸ Cross-Region Replication

▸ Tags

Figure 3-4. The S3 main administration page showing the newly created bucket and properties for that S3 bucket

From this page you can see that the current bucket is `www.nadonhosting.com` and the properties of that bucket are displayed to the right-hand side of the screen (and shown in Figure 3-4). From here you can manage all aspects of this bucket you just created. You can see the bucket name and the AWS region that is resides in; you can set permissions and enable logging and versioning and much more. You'll dig into these bucket properties soon, but for now, let's upload your static website content. Click the bucket name to navigate to that bucket.

The next screen is the bucket home screen for this specific bucket. It will tell you that the bucket is empty, but you will see that there are new buttons available such as Upload, as seen in Figure 3-5.

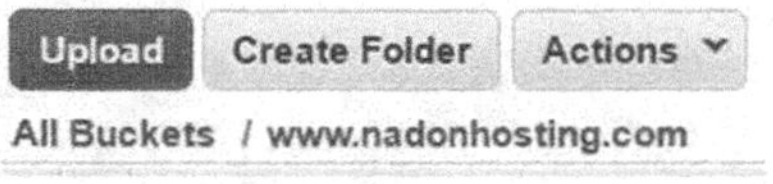
Upload
Create Folder
Actions
All Buckets / www.nadonhosting.com

Figure 3-5. *The S3 Bucket home page buttons are shown. From here you can create folders, upload files, and more.*

You can upload your content by clicking the Upload button, which will bring you to the Upload - Select Files and Folders wizard. S3 objects must have a minimize size of 1 byte and can support a maximum size of 5 terabytes! The wizard allows you to select files by clicking the Add Files button or by dragging them from a File Explorer window onto the wizard window. I've included sample files with this book that can be used to follow along. Once you have downloaded them and unzipped them to a folder on your local computer, you can use them as the content to upload to S3. I recommend the drag-and-drop method because this will allow for the upload of folders and files in the same operation. Select the folders and files, and click the Start Upload button. The upload process will start; when completed, you will be presented with a screen similar to Figure 3-6.

All Buckets / www.nadonhosting.com
Name
Storage Class
about_us.html
Standard
contact.html
Standard
contactForm
--
css
--
download
--
images
--
index.html
Standard
js
--
services.html
Standard
testimonials.html
Standard

Figure 3-6. *An S3 bucket holding your static web content assets*

Congratulations, you now have content hosted in AWS S3! Because you took a look at S3 bucket properties earlier, let's investigate the object-level properties of a file you uploaded. Click the `index.html` file and then click the Properties tab in the top right-hand corner of the screen. This can be seen in Figure 3-6.

When an object is selected in S3 and the Properties tab view is enabled, you will see all of the information related to that object. Figure 3-7 shows the object name, the S3 bucket in which it resides, and additional details such as object size, last modified date, and more. This should feel pretty familiar to the information you can get from a file's properties in an operating system's File Explorer window.

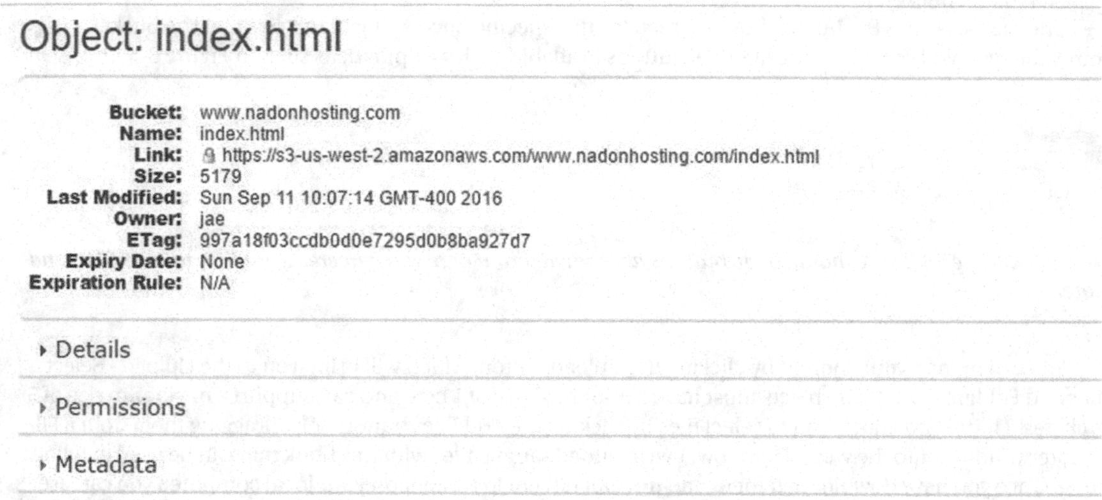

Object: index.html

Bucket:	www.nadonhosting.com
Name:	index.html
Link:	https://s3-us-west-2.amazonaws.com/www.nadonhosting.com/index.html
Size:	5179
Last Modified:	Sun Sep 11 10:07:14 GMT-400 2016
Owner:	jae
ETag:	997a18f03ccdb0d0e7295d0b8ba927d7
Expiry Date:	None
Expiration Rule:	N/A

▸ Details

▸ Permissions

▸ Metadata

Figure 3-7. *An S3 object properties dialog box. Above is the property information for the index.html object.*

One difference that you will notice is that each object has a unique link property, which is the HTTP endpoint that this specific file is available from. By default, uploaded files become objects that have no permissions and are not publically available. As part of making these objects available on the Internet, you will perform a step in the next chapter to change a property to make them "public." If you were to copy the object link property of index.html and paste it in a browser, you would not be able to resolve the page since it is currently set to "private." In fact, you would receive an error, as illustrated in Figure 3-8. Don't worry; you'll fix it in Chapter 4 when you enable these files to be accessed over the Internet.

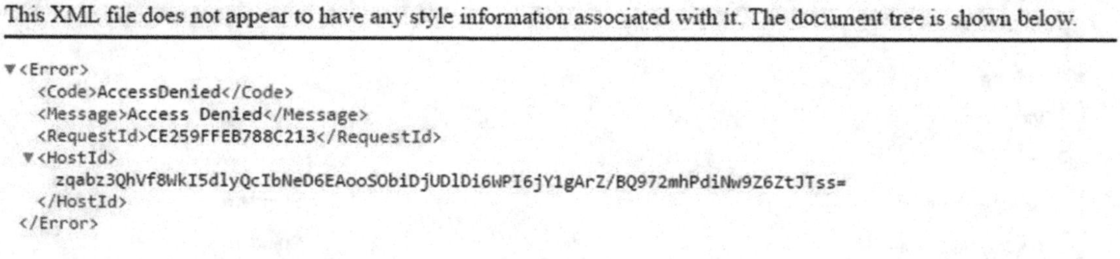

This XML file does not appear to have any style information associated with it. The document tree is shown below.

```
▼<Error>
    <Code>AccessDenied</Code>
    <Message>Access Denied</Message>
    <RequestId>CE259FFEB788C213</RequestId>
  ▼<HostId>
      zqabz3QhVf8WkI5dlyQcIbNeD6EAooSObiDjUDlDi6WPI6jY1gArZ/BQ972mhPdiNw9Z6ZtJTss=
    </HostId>
  </Error>
```

Figure 3-8. *An S3 object link error when trying to be accessed in its default state through a web browser*

Accessing S3 Resources via the AWS CLI

Until this point in the chapter you have only accessed your AWS S3 resources via the AWS Console. Although this is the most effective way to get started using S3, once you have resources (buckets, folders, and objects) in S3 you may want to interact with these resources in other ways. Some of you are very familiar with using command-line interfaces (CLIs) to complete tasks, and AWS has a CLI that can be installed on your local computer and can give you access to all of your AWS platform resources (IAM, S3, and more).

The installation of the CLI is a bit outside of the scope of this book, but Amazon offers excellent documentation on how to get this handy tool installed here: http://docs.aws.amazon.com/cli/latest/userguide/installing.html.

Once you have installed the CLI, open a shell window or command prompt, enter the following command, and you should see a response similar to Figure 3-9:

```
aws --version
```

```
Command Prompt
Microsoft Windows [Version 10.0.14393]
(c) 2016 Microsoft Corporation. All rights reserved.

C:\Users\thinkNadon>aws --version
aws-cli/1.10.22 Python/2.7.9 Windows/8 botocore/1.4.13
```

Figure 3-9. *The AWS CLI response from issuing a version command*

The AWS CLI allows you to perform any action that you can perform through the AWS Console via the command line. It relies on the secret key and access ID of a given AWS IAM account to authenticate and access AWS platform resources. When you installed the AWS CLI, you used the credentials for the day-to-day account that you created in Chapter 2. As you'll remember, you created that account as an administrative account with full access to all AWS platform resources. To verify that the account is set up correctly, let's issue a command to get a view of available buckets in your S3 account:

```
aws s3 ls
```

This command first calls aws, and then it states that you want to use the s3 resource. The last part of the command lists available resources. A full command reference for AWS S3 can be found at http://docs.aws.amazon.com/cli/latest/reference/s3/. You'll just focus in on what I feel may be of the most use to you when needing to update your static website content. The output of this command can be seen in Figure 3-10.

```
▓▓ Command Prompt
Microsoft Windows [Version 10.0.14393]
(c) 2016 Microsoft Corporation. All rights reserved.

C:\Users\thinkNadon>aws s3 ls s3://www.nadonhosting.com
                          PRE contactForm/
                          PRE css/
                          PRE download/
                          PRE images/
                          PRE js/
2016-09-11 10:07:13        5126 about_us.html
2016-12-04 15:59:31        4455 contact.html
2016-12-18 15:16:03        5670 index.html
2016-09-11 10:07:15        5126 services.html
2016-09-11 10:07:16        5126 testimonials.html
```

Figure 3-10. *AWS CLI command output for a list of S3 resources*

In the response of that command you'll see a listing of the single S3 bucket that you created. If you'd like to see a listing of all files in that bucket, you can add the name of the bucket to the command by using the following command (replace my website name with yours):

```
aws s3 ls www.nadonhosting.com
```

This command will list all objects and folders in the www.nadonhosting.com bucket. Other useful commands for finding out what resources are in S3 are the --summarize, --recursive, and --human-readable options with the command. The output of these commands can be seen in Figure 3-11.

```
C:\Users\thinkNadon>aws s3 ls www.nadonhosting.com --summarize --recursive --human-readable
2016-09-11 10:07:13       5.0 KiB about_us.html
2016-12-04 15:59:31       4.4 KiB contact.html
2016-12-03 14:37:11        0 Bytes contactForm/
2016-09-11 10:07:04      16.7 KiB css/LICENSE.txt
2016-09-11 10:07:09      40.1 KiB css/ie/PIE.htc
2016-09-11 10:07:09       2.3 KiB css/ie/html5shiv.js
2016-09-11 10:07:10      494 Bytes css/ie/v8.css
2016-09-11 10:07:11      255 Bytes css/ie/v9.css
2016-09-11 10:07:12      545 Bytes css/images/mobileUI-site-nav-opener-bg.svg
2016-09-11 10:07:13      352 Bytes css/images/toggle.svg
2016-09-11 10:07:05       3.5 KiB css/skel-noscript.css
2016-09-11 10:07:05      479 Bytes css/style-1000px.css
2016-09-11 10:07:06       4.1 KiB css/style-desktop.css
2016-09-11 10:07:07       5.0 KiB css/style-mobile.css
```

Figure 3-11. *AWS CLI output of a bucket listing with the summarize, recursive, and human readable options included*

The last command that I'd like to cover is one of the most useful commands for managing your static website content: the sync command. The command will synchronize a local folder with your S3 bucket and can be used as a very simple way to push any content changes that you've made to your local files up to S3 without having to log in to the AWS Console. In addition, the sync command can also sync content between S3 buckets, making it an easy method for moving files around in AWS. In the following code, I have my local directory named the exact same name as my S3 bucket and I changed my working directory to be the one that has the content that I'd like to sync. Doing this allows me to just pass the "." in the command to reference the current working directory as the source of the sync process. I've also made an update to the about_us.html file and run the sync command with the --dry run option. This option will tell you what would happen, but won't actually do it; it's good for testing the sync before actually performing it. The output of the command can be seen in Figure 3-12.

```
aws s3 sync . s3://www.nadonhosting.com --dryrun
```

```
c:\www.nadonhosting.com>aws s3 sync . s3://www.nadonhosting.com --dryrun
(dryrun) upload: .\about_us.html to s3://www.nadonhosting.com/about_us.html
Completed 1 part(s) with ... file(s) remaining
```

Figure 3-12. *AWS CLI output of a bucket sync process using the working directory as a source and the S3 bucket as the destination. Used with the --dryrun option so that you know what tasks will be performed before actually doing the sync process.*

In this CLI output, I can see that there is only one file that has been changed and needs to be updated. When I'm OK with this process happening, I can rerun the command without the --dryrun option and it will sync my content and update the object in my S3 bucket.

This process makes it very easy to update your website content via a single command rather than logging into the AWS Console, navigating to the S3 service, navigating to your bucket resource, and uploading the file manually.

In these code examples, you were accessing the default credential profile by not specifying the profile option in the command. It is worth noting that the CLI can support multiple named profiles. Once these are set up in the credentials file, using the profile option in the command will allow you to switch between profiles. More information on this topic can be found at http://docs.aws.amazon.com/cli/latest/userguide/cli-chap-getting-started.html#cli-multiple-profiles. This is useful when you have multiple AWS accounts that you want to manage with the CLI. Another example is if you want to switch between users within a specific account, such as one user that has read-only access vs. one that has the ability to create, update, or delete resources.

Accessing S3 Resources via Third-Party Applications

You've now learned how to access your S3 resources through the AWS Console and the command-line interface. Let's briefly talk about another way that you can access your AWS S3 resources: third-party applications that can use AWS IAM credentials in a similar way to how the CLI uses them. One application that I have found particularly helpful for managing S3 content is CloudBerry Explorer for Amazon S3. It can be downloaded from www.cloudberrylab.com/free-amazon-s3-explorer-cloudfront-IAM.aspx. There are two versions: a freeware version and a Pro version. My recommendation is to use the freeware version, and if you find it to be valuable, you can upgrade when you are ready. The configuration of the client software will ask you for your AWS account access keys and secret keys, so be sure to have them handy from your work in the last chapter.

Figure 3-13 shows the interface of this application with my local computer directory on the left and my AWS S3 bucket on the right.

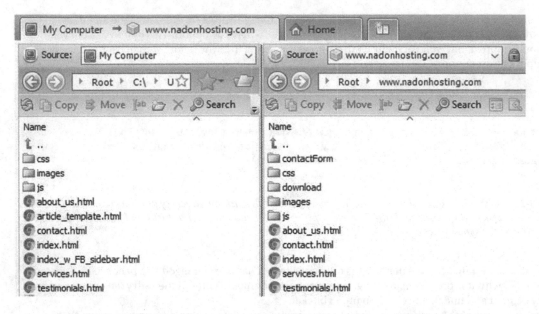

Figure 3-13. *CloudBerry Explorer for Amazon S3, a graphical user interface for working with S3 resources*

This interface should seem pretty familiar to you in that it is a graphical user interface (GUI) that feels very much like an FTP client application or File Explorer. CloudBerry has built in all of the functionality that is exposed through the AWS CLI into this interface, enabling you to create and delete resources, sync locations, and work with your resources in an easy way.

As you can see, although the AWS Console is an effective way to work with all of the AWS platform resources, in certain cases, such as with S3, there are many other ways to work with your resources.

I also want to mention that although I have specifically talked about using AWS S3 to host your website content, the platform is a highly available, highly durable, inexpensive solution for all of your storage needs. Personally, I use this platform for backing up personal data, photos, music, and other files in addition to using it to host website content.

Summary

In this chapter, you gained confidence and experience in storing data in S3. You learned about the basic organizational structure of S3 and created a bucket that will host your static website content. You now know how to upload content to AWS S3 in three different ways and how to keep files in sync between your local computer and your AWS S3 environment. You are now ready to set up your domain and enable the website content uploaded in this chapter to serve as a functional website, which is what I'm going to cover in Chapter 4. Onward and upward!

■ ■ ■

Setting Up Your Website Content and Domain

This chapter picks up where the previous chapter left off. Now that you know how to store your content in AWS S3 and you have been introduced to several ways to access that content, it is time for you to walk through the final steps of setting up a static website in AWS, which includes making the content of the buckets public, creating policies to control access, and making the bucket publically available by enabling website hosting on the S3 bucket. From there I'll show you how to set up a domain name in your third core AWS service, Route53, to front your new static content. We have quite a bit to cover to get your static website content ready for delivery to your customers, so let's get started.

Making Your Content Public

The first thing that you need to do is to make your content available for your visitors to view. As you may remember from Chapter 3, I mentioned that content has no permissions set on it when you upload it. When you try to view it in a web browser, you received an error. You're going to fix that by using a S3 bucket policy that will allow all content in the bucket to be viewed publically. When an S3 bucket is created, the only person that is granted any permission to that bucket is the account that created it. You can see an example with the main grantee shown in Figure 4-1. This account has full permissions on the bucket and can read the contents of the bucket (list), write to the bucket (upload), delete objects in the bucket, view objects in the bucket (though not until the object is made public), and edit the properties of objects within the bucket.

© Jason Nadon 2017

J. Nadon, *Website Hosting and Migration with Amazon Web Services*, DOI 10.1007/978-1-4842-2589-9_4

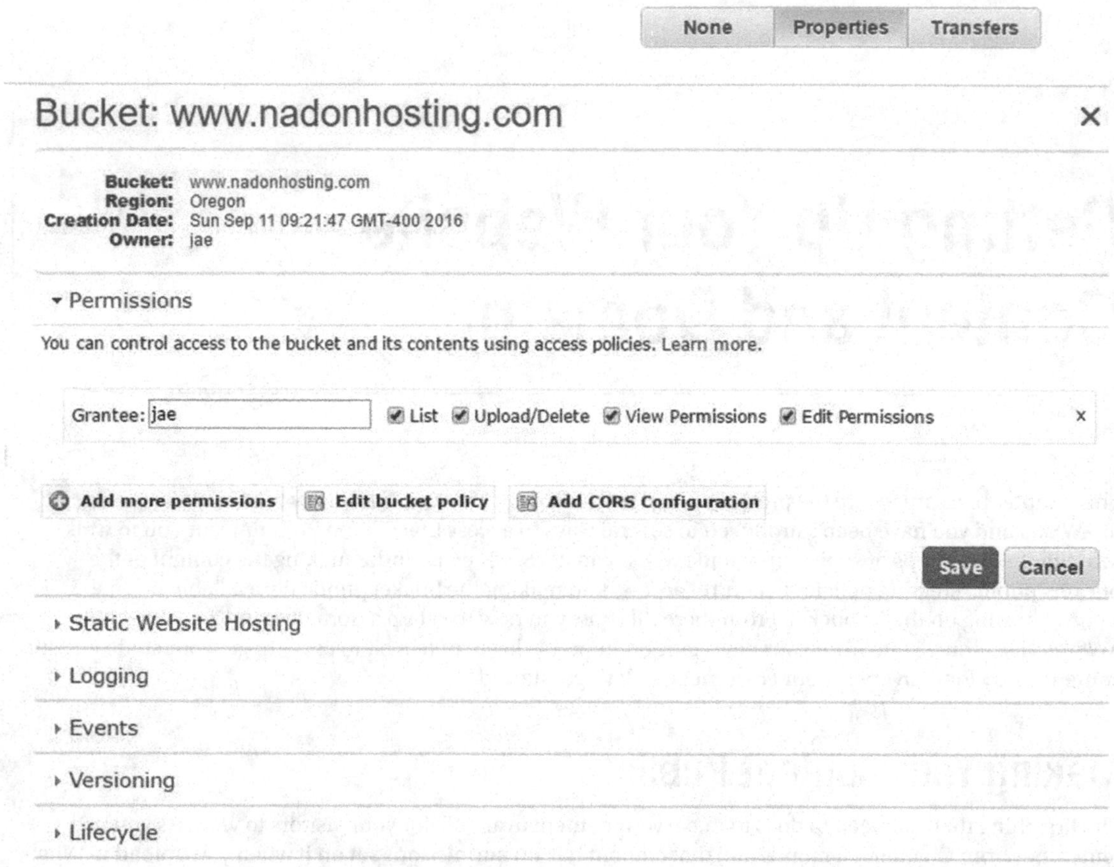

Figure 4-1. *S3 properties listing for the* www.nadonhosting.com *bucket showing the default grantee under the* **Permissions** *tab*

An important concept to understand is that control can be set at the bucket level and at the object level. At the bucket level, access to the resources within the bucket is controlled through the ACL (access control list). Each object within the bucket, excluding folders, can have their own object level permissions set. This allows for fine-grained access control to the content that you host within S3. There are multiple ways to grant users, visitors, and other AWS accounts permissions to S3 resources. The first way is to add additional grantees. As you recall from above, a grantee can be given list, view, upload/delete, and edit permissions at the bucket level. You could make your content public by granting the Everyone grantee the list and view permissions, but doing this would allow all visitors to view a listing of your bucket and all objects within it. This would be a security concern, so rather than doing it that way you will make use of setting permissions/rights to the content in your bucket via a bucket policy.

Bucket Policies and Permissions

A *policy* is a JSON-formatted document that can be applied to an AWS resource such as an S3 bucket to control access to that resource by defining actions, resources, and effects. *Actions* are predefined work that can be performed against a resource. For in-depth information about using S3 actions, AWS has a resource available at http://docs.aws.amazon.com/AmazonS3/latest/dev/using-with-s3-actions.html.
An example of an action is the ability to list an S3 bucket's contents. *Resources* are AWS resources and can be things like an IAM account or, in this case, an S3 bucket. An *effect* is the end result of the permission or control that you are looking to enforce, such as Allow or Deny. The policy that you will apply to your bucket is listed as follows (and is also included in the Chapter 4 sample code, named s3bucket_policy.json):

```
{
        "Version": "2012-10-17",
        "Statement": [
                {
                        "Sid": "PublicReadForGetBucketObjects",
                        "Effect": "Allow",
                        "Principal": "*",
                        "Action": "s3:GetObject",
                        "Resource": "arn:aws:s3:::www.nadonhosting.com/*"
                }
        ]
}
```

In this policy code, you set the Effect to be "Allow," the Principal value of "*" is a wildcard meaning *everyone*, the Action lists the predefined method that includes the request of an S3 object, and Resource is set to the S3 Bucket Name that is holding your static web content. In this example, you should update the code to list the name of the bucket that you created to host your static web content rather than the resource www.nadonhosting.com.

To apply the bucket policy, select your bucket in S3 and view the bucket properties. From this page, drop down the Permissions tab and click the "Add bucket policy" button to open up the Bucket Policy Editor. In this dialog box, you will paste your edited text content from the JSON sample file. The result should look like Figure 4-2.

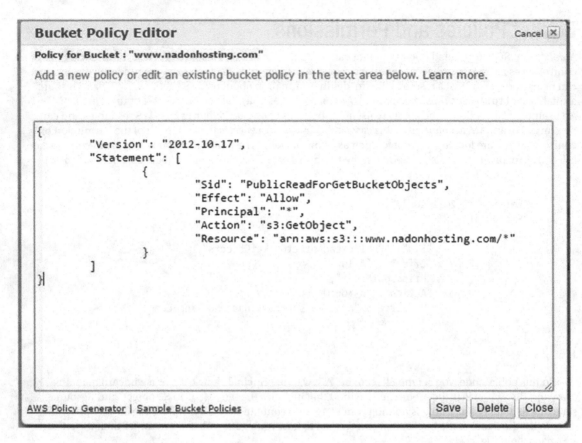

Figure 4-2. *S3 properties listing of the* www.nadonhosting.com *bucket showing the default grantee under the Permissions tab*

Once completed, click the Save button and your bucket policy will be applied. Applying this policy will mean that everyone can perform the Get Object method against any content in the www.nadonhosting.com S3 bucket. If you click your bucket name, explore your content, and choose the link, you should now be successful in accessing the object endpoint via a web browser and no longer receive the error message you experienced previously. Figure 4-3 shows one of the objects being accessed via the S3 object endpoint URL.

Figure 4-3. *Accessing a static image from the S3 endpoint URL in a web browser*

Controlling Object Access/S3 Lifecycle Management

Since you have applied the policy at the bucket level, this means that any object within that bucket will inherit the control set forth in that policy. This is fine for your static web content because you want all the HTML files, image files, and associated content to be available to the public via the Internet, but what if you have files that you don't want to be accessible? One way to tackle this is to create a separate bucket and apply a specific policy to that content.

In future chapters, I'll cover more advanced topics on locking down S3 content, including creating links to objects that are available for just a specific amount of time and are not available after that time period has passed. I do want to show how easy it is to create a similar concept using S3's lifecycle management features for buckets.

Let's use an example of your law firm wanting to offer clients a 10% discount coupon for services. Using S3 policies you can create a bucket called "nadonhostingpromotions" (remember that S3 buckets must be unique, which is why you're using a very specific bucket name) and use Lifecycle rules for content that reside in that bucket.

S3 has an excellent Lifecycle feature that can be used with the service to archive infrequently accessed data to lower cost storage options such as AWS Glacier or, in your case, set expiration on content that is created in this folder.

For this example, you will apply the same bucket policy so that content within this new bucket can be accessed by everyone on the Internet and can be linked from one of your static pages. Figure 4-4 shows the addition of the policy to the nadonhostingpromotions folder. Note that the policy looks very similar to what you used on your static web content bucket, but has the updated bucket name listed in the resource key value pair.

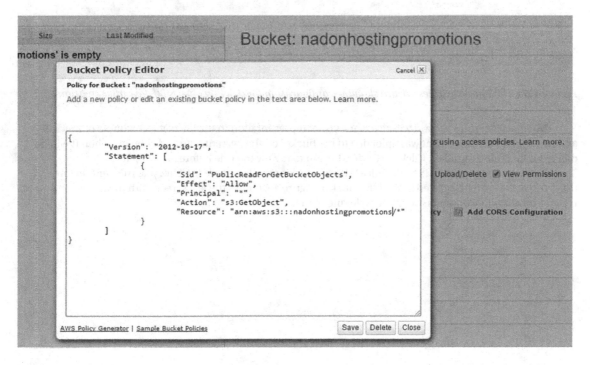

Figure 4-4. *Applying a policy to your new S3 bucket to allow the public read access to the bucket's contents*

Now that you know that the public will be able to access content created in the bucket, let's add a Lifecycle rule to have any content that is created in this bucket expire in 30 days.

To do this, select the bucket in the S3 management console and be sure that the Properties tab is selected. Open the tab labeled Lifecycle and click the Add Rule button to start the Lifecycle Rules Wizard.

On the first page of the wizard you need to select how the rules will apply. It's important to note that you can apply a Lifecycle rule against a subset of a bucket. The subset can be defined with the use of a folder, or a prefix by selecting the A Prefix method. You're going to keep things simple and apply the rule to the entire bucket. After selecting the radio button to apply the rule to the whole bucket, click the Configure Rule button.

The second page of the wizard asks you what actions you want to perform on the objects in this bucket. You will choose the Permanently Delete option by marking the checkbox to select that option. In the "Days after the object's creation date" option, enter the number 30. The configuration of this screen is shown in Figure 4-5 for reference.

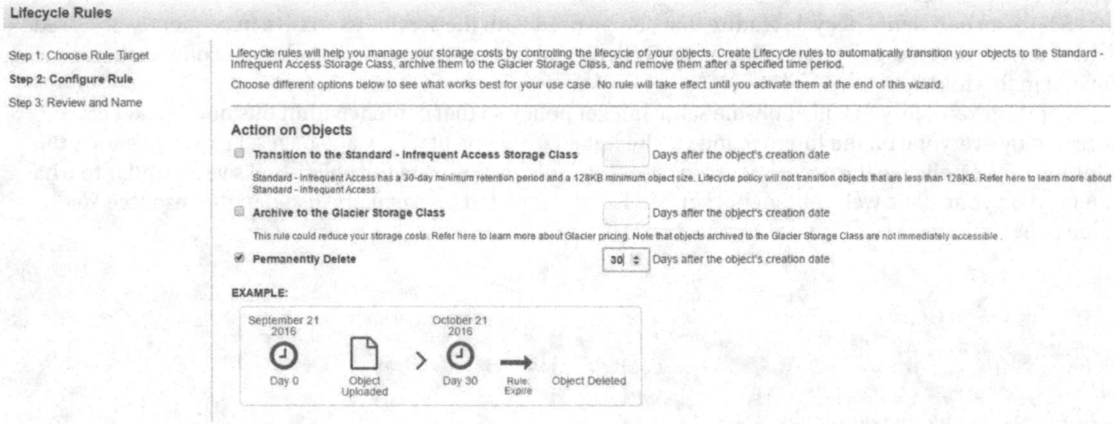

Figure 4-5. *The Lifecycle Rules Wizard showing configuration for deleting objects 30 days after creation*

The Lifecycle Rules Wizard will give you a visual representation in the form of an example of this rule and its effect on an object that was uploaded to the bucket on the current date and showing when it will be deleted if this rule is applied. Click the Review button to review the rule before applying it.

On the last page of the Lifecycle Rules Wizard you are asked to name the Lifecycle rule and review the settings that will be applied against this bucket. Figure 4-6 shows the last screen with the name DeletePromotionalContent as your Lifecycle rule name.

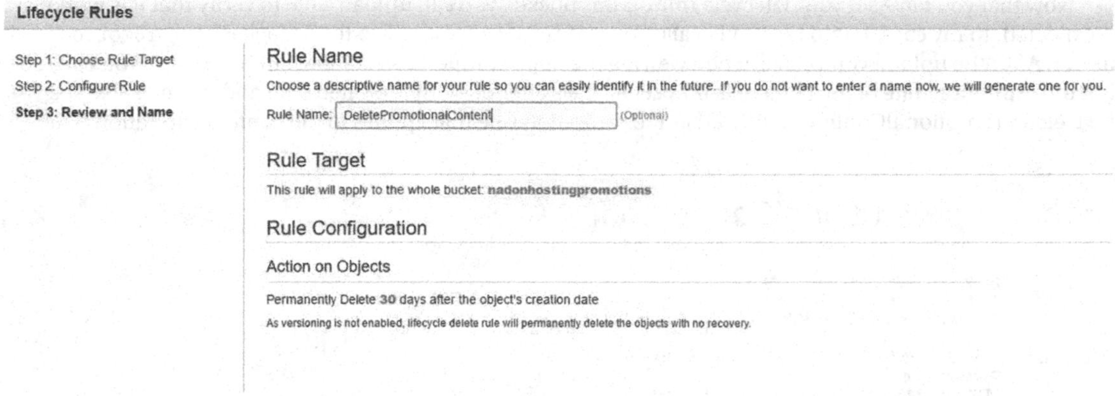

Lifecycle Rules

Step 1: Choose Rule Target
Step 2: Configure Rule
Step 3: Review and Name

Rule Name

Choose a descriptive name for your rule so you can easily identify it in the future. If you do not want to enter a name now, we will generate one for you.

Rule Name: | DeletePromotionalContent | (Optional)

Rule Target

This rule will apply to the whole bucket: **nadonhostingpromotions**

Rule Configuration

Action on Objects

Permanently Delete 30 days after the object's creation date
As versioning is not enabled, lifecycle delete rule will permanently delete the objects with no recovery.

Figure 4-6. *The last page of the Lifecycle Rules Wizard showing your defined rule name*

Once reviewed, click the "Create and Activate Rule" button to create the Lifecycle rule. Figure 4-7 shows your newly created Lifecycle rule under the Lifecycle tab of the Bucket Properties screen.

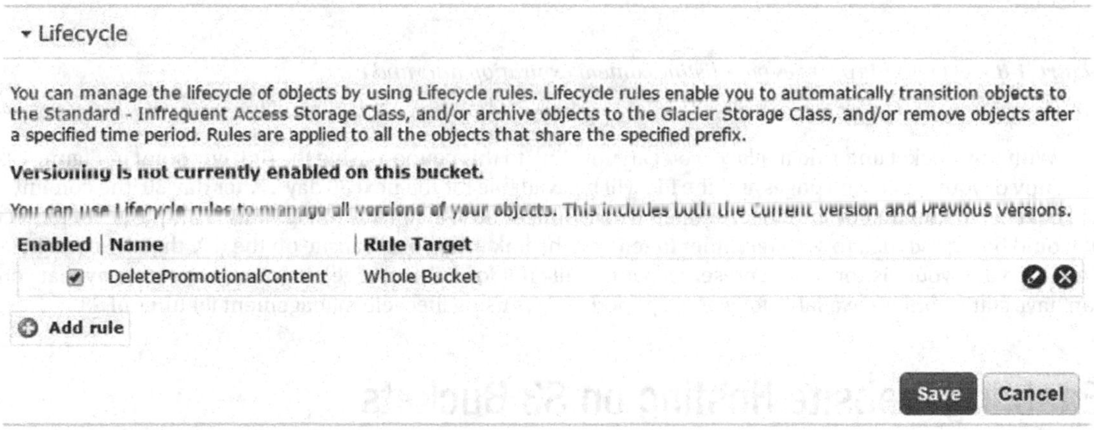

▼ Lifecycle

You can manage the lifecycle of objects by using Lifecycle rules. Lifecycle rules enable you to automatically transition objects to the Standard - Infrequent Access Storage Class, and/or archive objects to the Glacier Storage Class, and/or remove objects after a specified time period. Rules are applied to all the objects that share the specified prefix.

Versioning is not currently enabled on this bucket.

You can use Lifecycle rules to manage all versions of your objects. This includes both the current version and previous versions.

Enabled	Name	Rule Target	
☑	DeletePromotionalContent	Whole Bucket	🖊 ✖

⊕ **Add rule**

[Save] [Cancel]

Figure 4-7. *S3 Lifecycle rules listed on your Bucket Properties page*

Now that you have set your Lifecycle rule on this bucket, you can upload a file to verify that it is working as expected. In my case, I uploaded a file called `promotionalCoupon.pdf` to the `nadonhostingpromotions` bucket. After the upload completed, when viewing the object properties, as shown in Figure 4-8, you can see that the expiration date of the content is now set 30 days after the Last Modified date and you can also see the DeletePromotionalContent rule listed as the expiration rule that applies to the content expiration date.

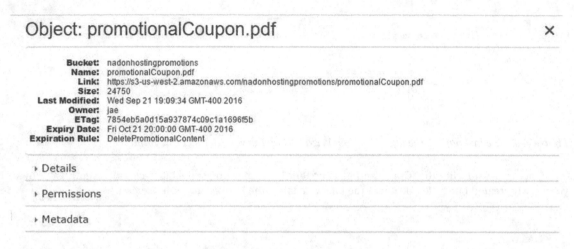

Figure 4-8. *S3 Object Properties page listing content expiration date and rule*

With this bucket and rule in place, you can now link to this coupon using the link endpoint in Figure 4-8 from any of your static web pages and the file will be available for the next 30 days. After day 30, the content will be deleted and that promotional coupon will no longer be available. Although this example is not perfect (it would be a good idea to set a reminder to remove the link from your website on the day that the content expires so that your visitors aren't presented with a "file not found" message), it does illustrate a way that you can have static content available for a given period of days using lifecycle management features of S3.

Enabling Website Hosting on S3 Buckets

I have talked quite a bit about S3 and the basics of managing content within buckets as well as how to access this content via each individual object's web endpoint. You know that your content is accessible from the Internet, but only an object at a time. Although you could link from one object to another using each public object's endpoint, this would be a nightmare for managing the collection of content as a website. AWS S3 has a feature that makes this task easier: static website hosting. The feature can be found in the Properties screen of any S3 bucket. Figure 4-9 shows the Properties screen of the bucket holding your static content with the Static Website Hosting drop-down expanded to show the configuration options.

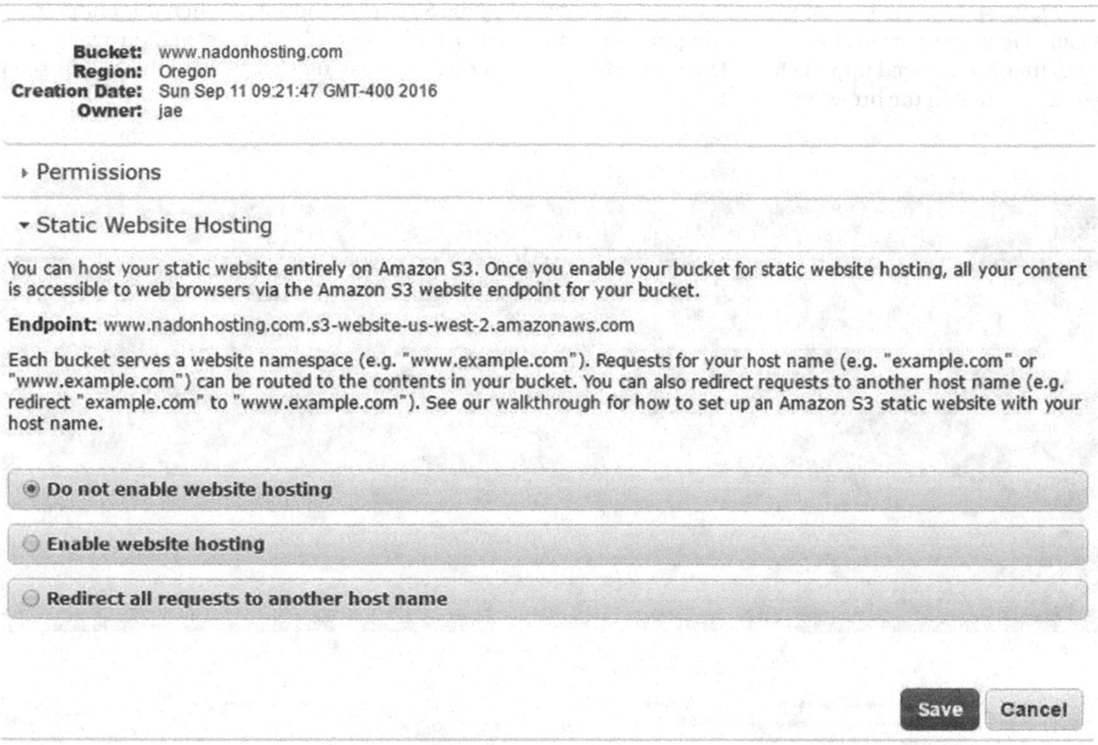

Bucket: www.nadonhosting.com
Region: Oregon
Creation Date: Sun Sep 11 09:21:47 GMT-400 2016
Owner: jae

▸ Permissions

▾ Static Website Hosting

You can host your static website entirely on Amazon S3. Once you enable your bucket for static website hosting, all your content is accessible to web browsers via the Amazon S3 website endpoint for your bucket.

Endpoint: www.nadonhosting.com.s3-website-us-west-2.amazonaws.com

Each bucket serves a website namespace (e.g. "www.example.com"). Requests for your host name (e.g. "example.com" or "www.example.com") can be routed to the contents in your bucket. You can also redirect requests to another host name (e.g. redirect "example.com" to "www.example.com"). See our walkthrough for how to set up an Amazon S3 static website with your host name.

⦿ **Do not enable website hosting**

◯ **Enable website hosting**

◯ **Redirect all requests to another host name**

Save   Cancel

Figure 4-9. *S3 Bucket Properties page with the Static Website Hosting option expanded*

After a brief description of this feature you are presented with three options for configuration. By default, all S3 buckets created have this feature configuration set to "Do not enable website hosting."

The third radio button, which is labeled "Redirect all requests to another host name," can be used to redirect website traffic bound to this S3 bucket endpoint to another location. I'll discuss this configuration option in a bit, so let's just move forward by choosing the second radio button option of "Enable website hosting" for your S3 bucket.

When you choose this option, you need to fill in at least one additional piece of information and that is the name of your main page to be served at your S3 bucket endpoint. In my case, I'm going to enter index. html; however, if you have a different name for your landing page, you can enter it here. Once you enter your home page name in the Index Document field, click the Save button to complete the configuration.

Browsing Your Website

Now that you have enabled static website hosting on your S3 bucket you can open a web browser and point to the S3 bucket endpoint domain name listed in that section on the S3 bucket's Properties page. The URL is shown in Figure 4-9; it has the bold text "Endpoint" in front of it.

Figure 4-10 is the view of your website being delivered by the S3 bucket endpoint. When this endpoint is called in a browser, S3 checks the configuration that you set up and issues a `GetObject` method against the value that you entered into the Index Document field. In your case, this was `index.html` and this can be seen being returned in the browser.

Figure 4-10. *Using the S3 bucket endpoint address in a web browser, you see the content of the index.html page returned*

At this point, your static website is fully functional. HTML is being delivered by S3 and rendered in your browser. You have a URL that your visitors can access, but it is not a "friendly" URL. I don't know about you, but I don't want to print `http://www.nadonhosting.com.s3-website-us-west-2.amazonaws.com/` on my business cards, nor do I want to say that mouthful of words when telling potential customers how to access my site. The logical next step is to set up a domain name to point to this S3 bucket.

Setting Up a Domain with Route53

Amazon Web Services offers a highly available DNS managed service called Route53. The name comes from the port used for DNS services. AWS backs this service with a 100% service level agreement (SLA). This means that the service is guaranteed to be up at all times, which is a very rare thing to find in the information technology industry. DNS servers are used to map IP addresses to domain names and are the backbone of what allows you to type www.google.com into a web browser and have the Google website resolve before your eyes. In the background, a series of calls are being made to DNS servers to find out the IP address for a server that hosts the content for the given domain name. Route53 is very easy to use and supports the registration of new domains, transfer of existing domains, and full DNS management of your domain name. There are some charges for using the service that I'll talk about in Chapter 6, where I'll discuss cost considerations for hosting a static website in AWS.

Registering a New Domain

The most straightforward way for you to get started is to register a new domain name to use with your static website. If you recall, I had you name the S3 bucket the exact same name as your website domain name. In the example I've been using in this section, mine is www.nadonhosting.com.

To register this domain name, you'll first login to the AWS Console, click the Services drop-down, and choose Route53. As a reminder, you could also click the Edit link at the top of the console screen and add this shortcut to your Console for easier access in the future.

Once you've clicked the Route53 service, you'll be presented with a familiar AWS Getting Started screen that you'll see on most services the first time that you start using them. Figure 4-11 shows the Getting Started with Route53 splash screen when being accessed for the first time.

Figure 4-11. *The AWS Route 53 Getting Started splash screen*

Since you are going to first go through the steps of registering a new domain name, let's choose the domain registration option. When you click this link you are brought to the Registered Domains page on your Route53 Dashboard. You don't have any domains registered yet, so it will be blank.

At the top of the screen are buttons named Register Domain, Transfer Domain, and Domain Billing Report. For this section, you will choose the Register Domain option. Clicking this button will start the Domain Registration Wizard. You will first be prompted for your domain name and top-level domain (TLD) type such as .com, .org, .edu, etc. There are different requirements for each TLD and you may want to research this first if you want to use something different than .com. Once you have entered your domain name and chosen which TLD you want to register, click the Check button to see if that domain name is available. Figure 4-12 shows the result of my domain name registration search with alternative domain names and pricing below.

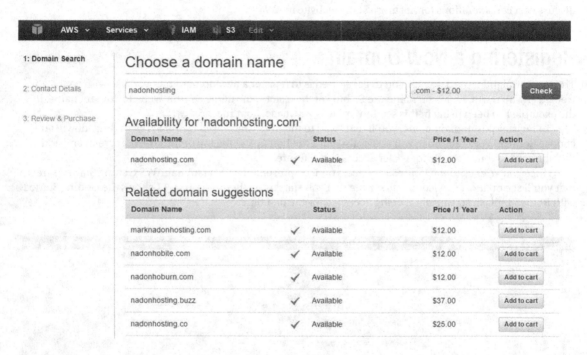

Figure 4-12. *AWS Route 53 Domain Registration Wizard with the availability status for a new domain to be registered*

If the domain status is "Available", click the Add to Cart button to add the domain to your shopping cart. If not, you may need to search again for a more specific name or use a different TLD.

Once the domain has been added to your cart, click the Continue button at the bottom of the screen to proceed with the next step in the Domain Registration Wizard.

The second step in the Domain Registration Wizard is where you add your contact information for the domain. Fill in all relevant details and be sure that you have access to the email address that you use here because this will be the address contacted for renewals and if any changes are made to the domain or associated DNS records. Once your information has been entered, click the Continue button to move on to the final step of the Domain Registration Wizard.

In the final step, you review your domain contact and order information. If all of the information looks correct, read and accept the terms by clicking the Accept Terms checkbox and then click the Complete Purchase button.

After you click the Complete Purchase button, a request to register the domain will be sent to the AWS Domain Registrar and your billing credit card will be charged the domain registration fee. In addition, you will receive an email at the email address you specified in the domain contact details. You must acknowledge this email or the domain will go into a suspended state with the registrar and will not be available for use until resolved.

Figure 4-13 shows a domain registration status as "In Progress" while waiting for the registrar to process the order and for me to acknowledge the email sent to my administrative contact email address. Figure 4-14 shows the email asking for me to acknowledge that I am the domain contact.

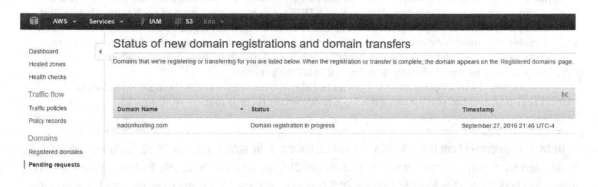

Figure 4-13. *The Pending Requests screen with the newly registered domain in a status of "Domain registration in progress"*

Figure 4-14. *The email received after registering a new domain name. The call to action is to click the enclosed link to verify ownership of this email address.*

When the domain registration has completed, it will move from the Pending Requests screen into the Registered Domains screen. Once the domain has been registered, a default zone file with DNS records will be created. I'll talk more about this in the "DNS Zone File Basics" section later in this chapter.

Transferring an Existing Domain

If you already have a website, chances are you already have a custom domain name. You may have registered the domain name through one of the popular domain registrars such as GoDaddy, Network Solutions, or Register.com. The domain registrar is the entity that manages your domain record and metadata on the Internet. This is the vendor that will let you know when the domain record is expiring and will collect fees to renew the use of the domain name. If you want to use AWS Route53 DNS servers, you have a couple of options. The first is to keep the domain with the current registrar and update the DNS name servers to use AWS Route53. The second option is to transfer the management of the domain from the current registrar to AWS and, once the transfer is complete, use AWS DNS services. Before I go over each option below, the important point is that you don't specifically have to change the domain registrar to use AWS Route53 to host your DNS, but you must have access to your current registrar in order to manage the DNS name servers.

To illustrate the two options that I've described above, I'll use an existing domain called heritagematters.ca that I currently have hosted at GoDaddy.com.

Let's discuss the first option that was presented above. This option keeps the domain at GoDaddy, the current registrar, and has you updating the DNS name server records to use AWS Route 53.

■ **Note**   The domain I am using for this example is not currently active on the Internet. If you wanted to do these steps for an active domain, you must replicate all DNS hosted zone file records that exist at your current registrar in AWS Route53 before updating the DNS name servers used. Not doing so would result in a disruption of service for the website. See the "Zone File Basics" section below for more information on record types and their function before updating the name servers on an active website domain.

Step 1: Add the domain to your Route53 account as a hosted zone. In the AWS Console Route 53 Dashboard, you'll see a Hosted Zones navigation link. Hosted zones are a collection of DNS records associated with your domain. As you'll notice from Figure 4-15, you currently only have one hosted zone, which is automatically created when you register a new domain name with AWS Route53.

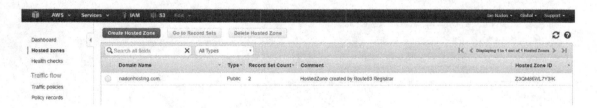

Figure 4-15. *AWS Route53 Dashboard with hosted zones showing*

For this first step you need to add a hosted zone for the heritagematters.ca domain name to Route53; doing this will create DNS name servers that will host your hosted zone and serve as the source for your DNS records for the domain.

Click the Created Hosted Zone button to expand the single-step wizard to create the hosted zone. Figure 4-16 is a screenshot of the details I entered to create the hosted zone for `heritagematters.ca`.

Create Hosted Zone

A hosted zone is a container that holds information about how you want to route traffic for a domain, such as example.com, and its subdomains.

Domain Name: heritagematters.ca

Comment: Domain Hosted at GoDadd

Type: Public Hosted Zone ▼

A public hosted zone determines how traffic is routed on the Internet.

Create

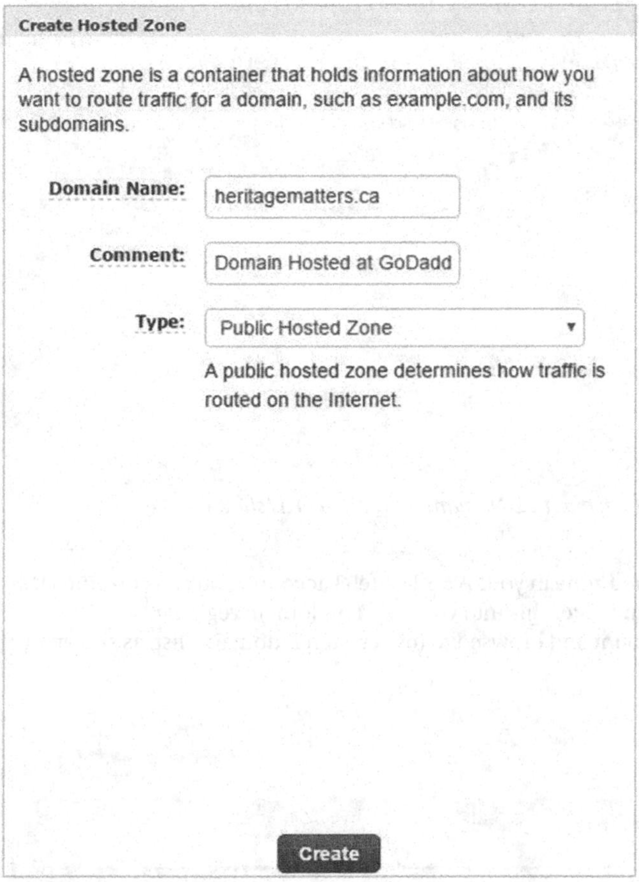

Figure 4-16. *AWS Route53 hosted zone creation input data*

Once you have entered your details, click the Create button at the bottom of the screen to create your new hosted zone.

When the hosted zone is created, by default AWS moves you to the detail page for the hosted zone. This page, shown in Figure 4-17, lists the DNS recordsets for that hosted zone. AWS automatically creates NS records, which are the DNS name servers that are hosting the DNS record information for your domain. This is the information that you'll need to enter in your current registrar (recall that mine is GoDaddy for `heritagematters.ca`).

AWS Route53 uses highly available DNS name servers that are spread across the globe on their regional infrastructure. You will see evidence of this in Figure 4-17 as one of the name server record values has the UK TLD in the domain name (ns-1548.awsdns-01.co.uk).

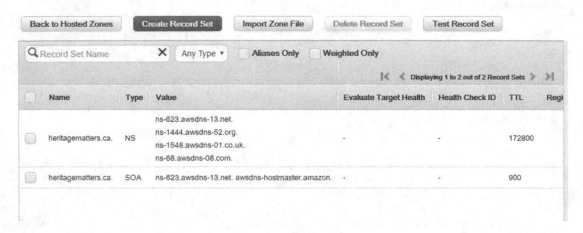

Figure 4-17. *AWS Route53 Hosted Zone detail screen with DNS name server records shown*

Step 2: Now that you have created the hosted zone in your AWS Route53 account, you can copy the DNS name server information listed in Figure 4-17 and enter this into your current domain registrar.

In my case, I logged into my GoDaddy account and browsed to my registered domains list, as shown in Figure 4-18.

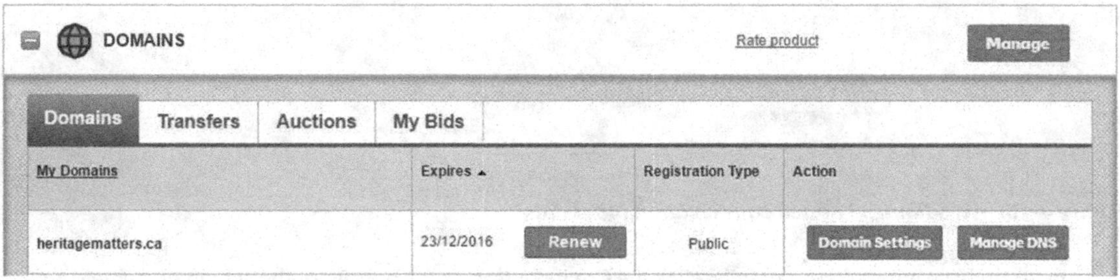

Figure 4-18. *GoDaddy.com Domain Summary screen showing the heritagematters.ca domain*

Click the Manage DNS button to go to the Domain Detail page. Once here, click the Change button under Name Servers. This will open up an input screen allowing you to change your DNS name server settings. As explained briefly earlier, name servers are used to find information specific to your domain. You set up a hosted zone in AWS Route53 and by doing so create information on AWS Route53 name servers. This allows you to update your domain name server records to point to AWS Route53 for domain-specific information. Figure 4-19 shows the input of the new Route53 name server records into the GoDaddy Domain Management Name Server fields.

Nameservers

Choose your new nameserver type

Custom	▾

Nameserver

ns-623.awsdns-13.net	

ns-1444.awsdns-52.org	

ns-1548.awsdns-01.co.uk	🗑

ns-68.awsdns-08.com|	🗑

Save	Cancel		Add Nameserver

Figure 4-19. GoDaddy.com Domain Management Nameservers input screen with newly added AWS Route53 name servers added

Once you have entered in the name servers to be used, click the Save button to update the domain information at GoDaddy. This update can take as little as an hour or as long as 48 hours. The timeframe depends on your current registrar.

Now that this change has been made, I can use Route53 to manage my DNS records, which will allow me to set up the records needed to point the domain name at content hosted on AWS S3. I'll talk more about this in the "DNS Zone File Basics" section below.

Now that I've covered the first option for using the AWS Route53 Managed DNS service, which is to keep the current registrar but use AWS Route53 name servers, let's talk about the second option: to transfer the domain control and management over to AWS.

As you may have noticed from Figure 4-18, the domain expiration for heritagematters.ca is coming up later in the year. As part of the AWS Route53 domain transfer process, in which you move from your current registrar to AWS, the domain is renewed for another period of one year automatically. This means that evaluating the move makes sense for me now, since the process will include the renewal of the domain name at the new registrar, AWS. This also means that if your domain still has a long time before expiration at its current domain registrar, you may want to wait to do the transfer of the domain since doing so will add another year renewal when it's really not a requirement. The domain transfer process can be broken down into the following steps:

1. Unlock the domain at the current registrar.

2. Obtain the authorization code needed to transfer the domain (not a requirement with all registrars).

3. Submit a transfer domain request to initiate the domain transfer.

4. The Domain Administrative Contact must approve the domain transfer request.

5. Finalization of the domain transfer to the new registrar.

The full process can take as little as two days and as long as several weeks to complete. One important detail is to make sure that you have your domain updated with current contact information. Doing so will ensure that step four in the above list can be completed as quickly as possible. Figure 4-20 shows the domain at my current registrar with the domain lock setting set to disabled.

Figure 4-20. *GoDaddy.com Domain Management Overview input screen with newly added AWS Route53 name servers added*

Since my domain is unlocked and ready to be transferred, I can click the "Email my code" link to have the registrar email me the authorization code needed to complete the transfer process.

Now I'm ready to move on to step three in the above list: requesting the domain transfer from within the AWS Route53 Dashboard. Once I've logged into the AWS Console and after I've navigated to the Route53 service, I click the Registered Domains navigation link. From here I can see my currently registered domains and buttons named Register Domain and Transfer Domain. Clicking the Transfer Domain button will start the Transfer Domain Wizard.

You will need to fill in detailed information about the domain that you want to transfer. In my case, I need to make sure that I select the correct top-level domain as well since it is a country-specific domain name. Figure 4-21 shows information on the first screen of the Domain Transfer Wizard.

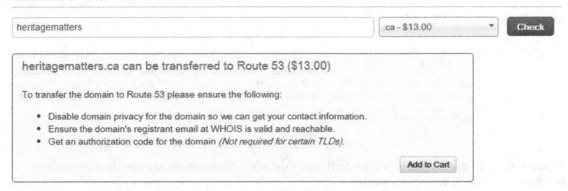

Figure 4-21. *AWS Route53 Domain Transfer Wizard page one input screen with details about the transfer*

Once you review your domain information, you'll click the Add to Cart button to continue with the transfer process. You will then be prompted to put in the authorization code for the transfer, as shown in Figure 4-22, and you will have the choice to transfer the domain but keep the name servers the same or update them to the new domain's name servers. If the website that you are transferring is currently serving customers, an outage may be unavoidable, but to minimize the risk be sure to copy over all DNS records into the Route53 hosted zone that you created earlier and then choose to use those new name servers during the transfer process.

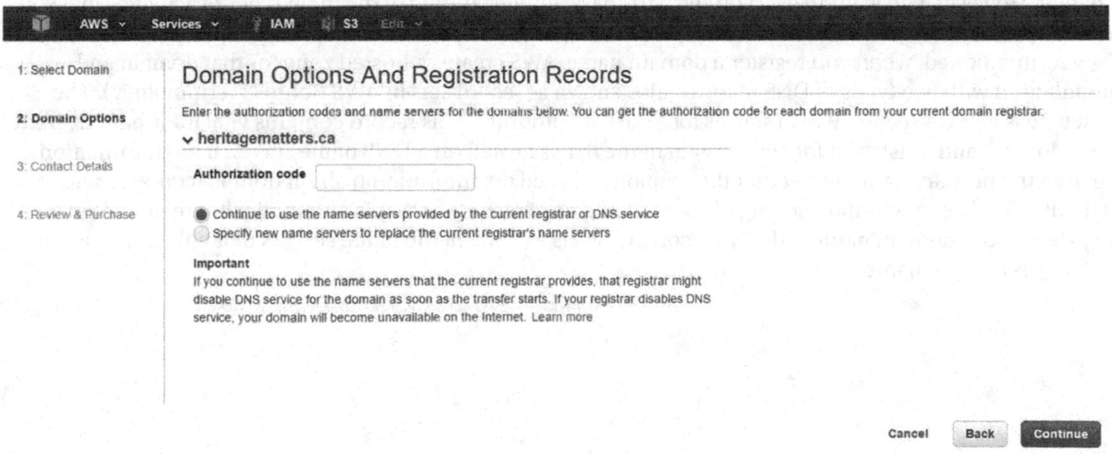

Figure 4-22. *AWS Route53 Domain Transfer Wizard page two input screen with prompts for the domain transfer authorization code and name server prefrences*

After entering the authorization code and your name server preferences, click the Continue button to move on to the next step of the process, which will have you confirm your contact information for the domain name. Once verified, click the Finish button to finalize your order and start the domain transfer process. You will be presented with the information shown in Figure 4-23, which sets the expectation for the timeframe and next steps of the transfer process.

Thank you for transferring your domain to Route 53

Your transfer request for following 1 domain is in progress.

- heritagematters.ca

Transferring a domain to Route 53: what happens next?

- We'll send email to the domain registrant when the domain transfer is approved. The email will come from noreply@domainnameverification.net or noreply@registrar.amazon.com.

  Important! When you receive this email, the transfer is not complete. You must click the link in the email to verify that you want to transfer the domain, or your transfer request will be canceled after 6 days.

- Transferring the registration for your domain to Route 53 might take **up to 11 days** to complete.
- You can view the current status of your transfer request on the dashboard in the Route 53 console.

[Go To Domains]

Figure 4-23. *AWS Route53 Domain Transfer Wizard final page with expectations for the next steps and timeframe to complete the domain transfer*

Once the transfer process has been completed and all approvals have been fulfilled, you will find that your domain moves from the "Pending Requests" section of the Route53 Dashboard to the "Registered Domains" section. Now that you have full control over a domain that you have registered and transferred, let's talk about how you manage DNS settings in Route53 and the various types of records that you can create and how to instruct your domain name to front your S3 static website content.

DNS Zone File Basics in Route53

An introduction to DNS is a topic that could fill a book on its own, so I can't go too deep into this topic in this chapter. However, I do want to give you the bare, basic understanding of the main types of activities that you will be able to do within Route53 when it comes to working with your domain.

As mentioned, when you register a domain name, AWS creates a hosted zone for that domain and populates it with two types of DNS records (also known as record sets in AWS Route53 terminology). The first type is an SOA record, which stands for "Start of Authority." This record contains vital information about your domain and must exist for any domain name that is hosted on a DNS name server. It has information such as the primary name server that the domain is hosted on, information about domain contacts, and default domain configuration settings. The second type of record set that is automatically created when you registered your domain name is the NS record, which is a listing of the name servers that hold information about this domain name.

In addition to these two types of domain record sets, you may end up using a combination of one or more of the following three types:

1. A Record: This type of record points a domain name or sub-domain resource to an IP address. An example is nadonhosting.com > 192.168.2.100. The IP address is usually that of a web server.

2. CNAME Record: Also known as a canonical name, this type of record points a domain name or sub-domain resource to another name. An example is www.nadonhosting.com > nadonhosting.com (using this same example from the A record above, if both of these records exist in the same hosted zone, the www.nadonhosting.com address would resolve to nadonhosting.com, which in turn would resolve to 192.168.2.100).

3. MX Record: Also known as a mail exchange record, this type of record points a domain name or sub-domain resource to an IP address where the source is a mail server. These are used when you have domain-specific email addresses, such as jason@nadonhosting.com.

Although these are not the only types of DNS record sets that you'll be working with, they are the most frequently used for setting up a domain name to front web content and mail services. Other record set types are shown in Figure 4-24.

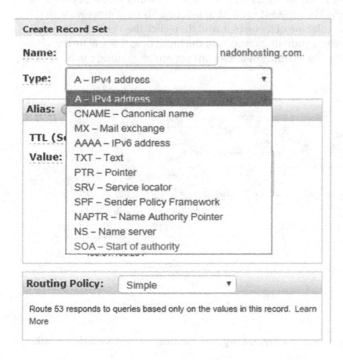

Figure 4-24. *The Type drop-down, available after selecting "Create Record Set" from within a Route53 hosted zone*

In terms of AWS, there is an additional configuration option when using Route53 that allows for the routing of domain names to sources of content: the alias. I'll talk a bit about this next as you finish setting up your domain DNS settings to point to your AWS S3 content.

Route53 Alias Records

Route53 allows for the use of what is referred to as an alias record to point to AWS-specific resource endpoints such as elastic load balancers, CloudFront distributions, or S3 static website content. This term/functionality does not exist in standard DNS; it is available only within Route53 and allows for simple routing in the same hosted zone. In the next section, you will use the alias record to direct website traffic to your root domain, also known as the *apex* to your S3 static website endpoint.

Adding DNS Records to Point to the Static Website Content

From within the Route53 Dashboard, choose the Hosted Zones link from the left-hand navigation menu. Once presented with the list of hosted zones, select the one that you want to add DNS record sets to; for this example, choose the nadonhosting.com hosted zone. By default, there are currently only two record sets listed in your hosted zone, as previously illustrated in Figure 4-17.

To create a new record set in this hosted zone, click the Create Record Set button at the top of the screen. An input area will display to the right of the screen and will collect details about the record set to be created, as previously illustrated in Figure 4-24.

You must first create a record set to handle the "www" sub-domain. You will need to have your S3 static website endpoint handy because you will be entering this as the alias value for your record. As you may recall, in your example, the website endpoint is found in the S3 Bucket Properties window and in your case is formatted as www.nadonhosting.com.s3-website-us-west-2.amazonaws.com. You will enter www in the Name input box, leave the A - IPv4 Address default type of record set, and then click the Yes radio button for the Alias option. Once selected, you can then enter your alias target into the input box; this will be the value of your S3 website endpoint noted above. A filled-in example of the record set you're creating can be seen in Figure 4-25.

Figure 4-25. *AWS Route53 record set creation for* www.nadonhosting.com *pointing to your S3 static website endpoint using the Alias type*

Review the data on the record set to be created, and click the Create button at the bottom of the screen to create the record set.

This takes care of any visitors that enter www.nadonhosting.com into a browser. They will see the S3 static website that you have hosted due to the alias record routing the traffic to that specific resource. What about those that enter the domain name without the www sub-domain? Those visitors will be greeted with a DNS error. To address this, perform the following steps:

1. Set up a new S3 bucket with the same name as the root domain name, nadonhosting.com.

2. Enable static website hosting on the S3 bucket, but choose the "Redirect all requests to another hostname" radio button.

3. Enter the value of the host name to redirect to in the input field. In your example, it is www.nadonhosting.com.

4. Take note of the newly created S3 static website hosting endpoint for this new bucket. Figure 4-26 shows the newly created S3 bucket with properties.

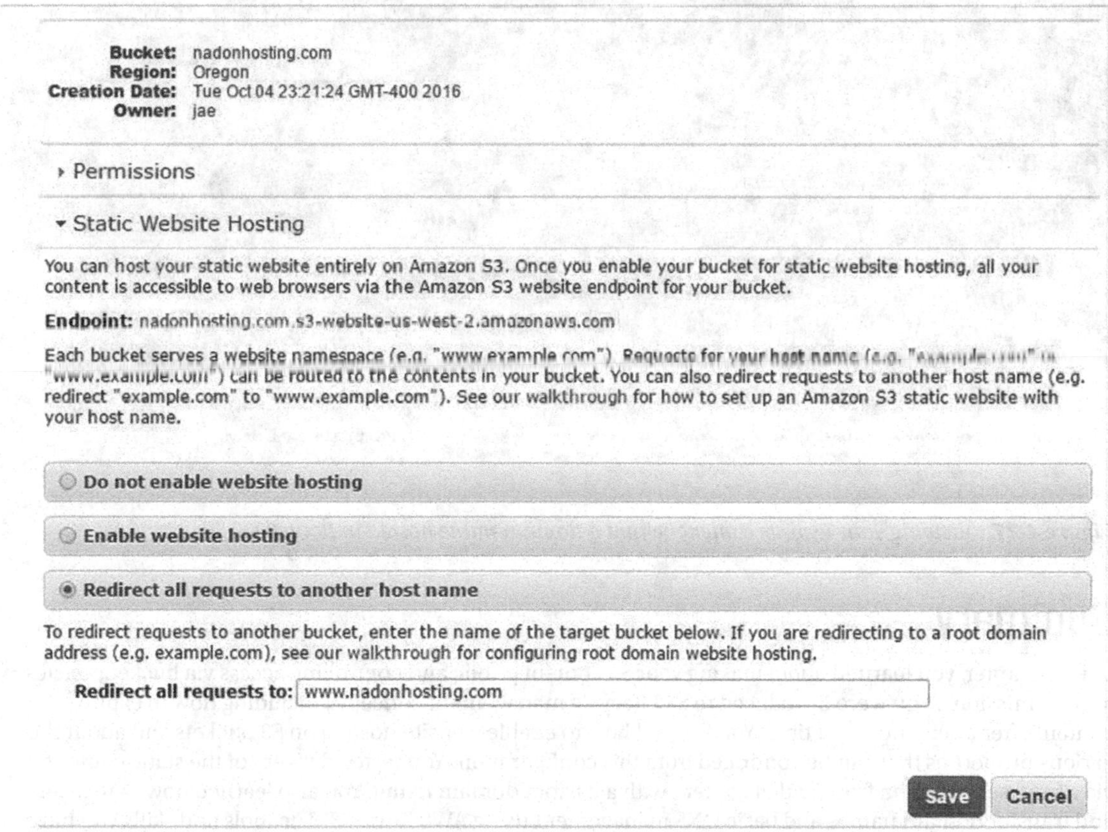

Bucket: nadonhosting.com
Region: Oregon
Creation Date: Tue Oct 04 23:21:24 GMT-400 2016
Owner: jae

▸ Permissions

▾ Static Website Hosting

You can host your static website entirely on Amazon S3. Once you enable your bucket for static website hosting, all your content is accessible to web browsers via the Amazon S3 website endpoint for your bucket.

Endpoint: nadonhosting.com.s3-website-us-west-2.amazonaws.com

Each bucket serves a website namespace (e.g. "www.example.com"). Requests for your host name (e.g. "example.com" or "www.example.com") can be routed to the contents in your bucket. You can also redirect requests to another host name (e.g. redirect "example.com" to "www.example.com"). See our walkthrough for how to set up an Amazon S3 static website with your host name.

○ **Do not enable website hosting**

○ **Enable website hosting**

◉ **Redirect all requests to another host name**

To redirect requests to another bucket, enter the name of the target bucket below. If you are redirecting to a root domain address (e.g. example.com), see our walkthrough for configuring root domain website hosting.

Redirect all requests to: | www.nadonhosting.com |

[Save] [Cancel]

Figure 4-26. AWS S3 bucket properties showing static website hosting enabled with the redirection option set to redirect traffic

5. Browse to Route53 and select the hosted zone that you want to edit.

6. Create a new record set, leave the Name field blank, leave the default type as IPv4 Address, and select the Yes radio button for the Alias option. In the input field, enter the newly created S3 website endpoint from Step 4. Click the Create button.

The steps above will create a new S3 bucket with website hosting enabled, but with the option to redirect that traffic to the host/domain name of www.nadonhosting.com. In addition, you've created a new record set for the apex or root domain so that any traffic received there will be directed to your S3 bucket, which then redirects to www.nadonhosting.com.

Testing Your New Website

Now that you have created DNS records for the root and www sub-domain, your site is ready for viewing in your favorite web browser. Figure 4-27 shows the new website content as viewed after entering the domain name in the browser.

Figure 4-27. *Viewing your website content behind a domain name hosted in Route53*

Summary

In this chapter, you learned about making your S3 content public and controlling access via bucket policies and permissions. You were introduced to S3 Lifecycle management concepts, including how to expire content after a set amount of time. You learned how to enable website hosting on S3 buckets and about the various properties that can be controlled from this configuration. You tested delivery of the static content via a browser and then fronted that content with a custom domain name. You also learned how to register and transfer domain names and basic DNS management using AWS Route53. The tools and skills you have learned to this point will help you as you move forward into the next chapter, which is all about thinking outside the box when it comes to what defines a "static" website. I'll show you some ways to make your static website feel dynamic and how to enable visitors to interact with your website even though you don't have a web application server!

CHAPTER 5

■ ■ ■

Next-Level Static Content Hosting

In the last chapter, you finished getting your files hosted in AWS S3 and then you worked through getting your static content set behind a domain name using AWS Route53 to register a domain and to add DNS entries to point to the static web content hosted in S3. In this chapter, you'll switch your focus from setting up resources in Amazon Web Services to some of the management challenges that come with hosting a website that has only static content. You'll take a look at how you can use HTML templates to give you an easy way to update parts of your static website. Next, you'll use embedded content in your website content to give a more dynamic feel. Finally, you'll end this chapter thinking very much outside the box by looking at technologies like client-side scripting and serverless architecture that will allow you to extend your static content and interact with your website visitors.

Limitations of Static Content Websites

The term *static* is used to define something that does not change at any regular interval. The Internet started with only static websites. These websites were usually text-based in nature and may have used some images, text formatting, and colors to make them more visually appealing, but they were quite limited in terms of the type of information that could be displayed and how visitors could interact with that information. Fast forward a bit and you started to see websites that had an element of server-side processing happening that allowed for a website/web page to be assembled using static elements as well as dynamic elements (information that could be updated and read from data storage). This server-side processing gave birth to systems referred to as content management systems (CMS) that allowed you to dynamically manage and display content. An example of a very popular CMS platform is WordPress. I'll cover how to host such a platform using AWS in the second section of this book, but as you're in this section dedicated to the static content website, I want to focus on how you can deal with the challenges and limits of static files.

Static files are just that: static. The content in these files does not change at runtime; they are delivered to the website visitor as they sit on disk. So if you want to update your website, you need to update the static content on your pages. If you want to update a section on each page of your website and you happen to have five web pages, this means that you must update five separate pages. I would classify this as the first limitation of a static website: the need to manually update content. The time that you have to dedicate to these updates could be a key factor when deciding if you want to choose static content as your main type of website content. Since there is a time commitment involved in updating the content, the likelihood of you doing it often is low. This brings me to another limitation: the chance that the content will be out of date or irrelevant. Having out-of-date information displayed on your website, in my opinion, is worse than having no website presence at all. Think of the frustration and lost time that bad information can cause visitors who come to your site. Losing a potential customer's trust is not a good way to start a long-term relationship.

A final factor that could be considered a limitation is that you may need to learn some HTML and other technologies to be able to update your content efficiently.

With all this said, static hosting requires no server-side processing because the rendering of the static content takes place on the client side, meaning the browser and device of the person visiting your website. This also means lower resource requirements from a hosting perspective, which means lower hosting charges in general. A static website is also the least complex of the types that I'll be covering in this book and for these reasons I felt it was worth dedicating this chapter to discussing how to overcome some of these limitations.

Extending the Boundaries of Static Content

Through the rest of this chapter I am going to talk about a few ways that you can manipulate your static content to give it a more dynamic feeling. I think it is important for me to set a proper expectation before getting started: updating your website is something that your visitors want you to do and it takes effort. I'll cover a few tricks to make things easy to update, but the actual updating is fully on you. You will only get out of your website what you are willing to put into it. Now let's talk about the first way to extend your static website to make it feel like a dynamic website: by using web page templates.

As you may recall, your static website is made up of five pages. The home page uses a sidebar layout on the right to highlight your firm's latest news, as shown in Figure 5-1.

We are **Williams and Sons Law Firm**, a responsive and caring firm that is dedicated to serving the legal needs of customers in our community and surrounding areas. Founded in 2016, we have been practicing law and specializing in Family Law for more than 6 months!

We are a full service law firm that treats each customer as family. We work with you to understand your needs and custom fit a legal solution to deliver results.

LEGAL ISSUES AND NEWS

AUGUST 11, 2016 | (8) COMMENTS

Government launches new provisions to track income over a longer period.

AUGUST 1, 2016 | (10) COMMENTS

Williams Law launches new web portal for client document exchanges.

Figure 5-1. *The sample home page with the sidebar content displayed on the right-hand side of the screen*

Although this sidebar content looks like it has been updated recently because the date of the article is listed along with how many comments have been made, this is a bit of an illusion. This is just HTML text; when a visitor clicks one of these images or article titles, they will be taken to a static web page template that has been used to create the content.

Updating this part of the site with new content is a two-step process. First, you will want to use a page that you have defined to use as a template to create the new article content. Second, you update the index. html page to add a new article on top of the existing ones. I've included a file called article_template. html to give you the shell of an article page that you can use or edit to fit your needs. Figure 5-2 shows the rendered HTML of the web page template complete with the areas to be updated called out.

LEGAL ISSUES AND NEWS

UPDATE ARTICLE DATE HERE

Update Article short description of the content here.

AUGUST 1, 2016 | (10) COMMENTS

Williams Law launches new web portal for client document exchanges.

UPDATE ARTICLE TITLE HERE
Update Article Date Here

Update article body content here

Figure 5-2. *The sample article_template.html file rendered in a web browser showing areas to update*

In the template file I used the text "Update" in each area to be updated. This means when you're in the editor of your choice you can search for the term "Update" and you can easily find all the locations that need to be updated. You can see from Figure 5-2 that in addition to the main article content there is also a sidebar layout similar to the home page, but this time it's on the left-hand side of the screen, and it will need to be updated as well. Once updated here, it will be an easy copy-and-paste to update the home page. The following code is from the article_template.html file and shows the main areas to be updated:

```
<!-- Sidebar -->
<div id="sidebar" class="4u">
    <section>
    <header>
        <h2>Legal Issues and News</h2>
    </header>
    <ul class="style">
        <li>
        <a href="article_template.html">
        <p class="posted">Update Article Date Here</p>
        <img src="images/pic04.jpg" alt="Update Article Image Here" />
        <p class="text">Update Article short description of the content here.</p>
        </a>
        </li>
        <li>
        <a href="080116.html">
        <p class="posted">August 1, 2016  |  (10 )  Comments</p>
        <img src="images/pic05.jpg" alt="" />
        <p class="text">Williams Law launches new web portal for client document exchanges.</p>
```

51

```
        </a>
        </li>
        <li>
        <a href="071916.html">
        <p class="posted">July 19, 2016 | (4 ) Comments</p>
        <img src="images/pic06.jpg" alt="" />
        <p class="text">Free Family Will Kits are now available for pickup at your head
          office location</p>
        </a>
        </li>
      </ul>
    </section>
</div>

<!-- Content -->
<div id="content" class="8u skel-cell-important">
    <section>
      <header>
          <h2>Update Article Title Here</h2>
          <span class="byline">Update Article Date Here</span>
      </header>
          <img src="Update.jpg" style="visibility:hidden">
          <p class="">Update article body content here</p>
    </section>
</div>
```

The main areas to be updated are in the sections that are marked Sidebar and Content. In the Sidebar section, updates should be made to the link to the article template (to be made after you've decided what to save this file as described below), article date, the small image to be used, and the short description of the article. In the Content section, updates should be made to the article title, article date, and article content. You may also notice that I've placed a holder for an image that is currently set to `"visibility:hidden"` so that the image won't be displayed by default. There may be times when you want an image at the top of your article, and a simple update to point the image source of the image to be used and removal of the style definition will make the image visible in the article.

Once you have updated these sections with your new content, the next step is to save this template as a new page that you can link to from the home page. My suggestion here is to either name the page with an abbreviated title of the article or with a filename based on the date of the post, such as `112016.html`.

From here you'll head to the home page, `index.html`, and open it for editing locally in your favorite editor. The relevant code to be updated is in the Sidebar section and is listed below for reference:

```
<li>
<a href="article_template.html">
<p class="posted">August 11, 2016 | (8 ) Comments</p>
<img src="images/pic04.jpg" alt="" />
<p class="text">Government launches new provisions to track income over a longer period.</p>
</a>
</li>
```

You will want to copy this section from the page you updated earlier and then paste this new entry right on top of the existing ones. Depending on how many articles you would like to display, you may want to remove the oldest entry. Personally, I think having the three most recent articles is sufficient on the home page.

Once you have pasted the information for the new article page, remember to save the file. Now that you've updated these two files locally on your system, you'll need to push them up to AWS S3 so that your website will use the updated content. My preference is to use the AWS S3 Sync command as described in Chapter 3, or to use Cloudberry Lab S3 Explorer to copy the files up to the S3 bucket. Another option is to use the Console to upload the updated files. Any of the choices are fine; it is really your preference for which one to use.

Although this may not seem like the easiest way to update content, once you have done it a couple times you will see that it can be an effective way of keeping content fresh with minimal effort.

There is another option for pulling in content from other sources to your static website: embedding content. Next, I'll talk about how you can embed your latest posts from Facebook on your home page in that same sidebar section.

Embedding Content from Other Sources

In the previous section, I discussed how to manually update a section of your static website to give the appearance that this section was being updated automatically or in a dynamic fashion. The process was quite manual and would fit certain use cases, such as a website that has a few content updates a month. You also have the ability to bring in content from other websites to be displayed on your static website. The content from these other sources could be content that is updated frequently, which means that your static website would also have the updated content on it, ensuring that your website doesn't feel stale.

There are many methods for displaying content from other sources on a HTML-only based website. I'll discuss a few of the most accessible options next.

JavaScript/Client-Side Scripting

JavaScript or other client-side scripting languages process code during runtime using the processing resources of the client machine. In short, this means that you can include JavaScript code in your HTML web page that will be run when the visitor to your website opens that page with their browser.

The benefit of client-side scripting is that it can use resources on the visitor's computer and interact with their session in a way that feels like a lightweight, positive experience for the visitor. Many web-based forms use JavaScript to validate data that is being entered into a form by a web visitor and interact with the visitor as they are entering the data. An example is validating that an email address is entered in the proper format before accepting the input.

In your use case, JavaScript can be used to load content from another source. To give an example of this type of content embedding, you will pull in some information from Facebook using code that is available from within the Facebook UI.

For your example, you will update the "Legal Issues and News" sidebar with content that pulls from a public Facebook post. The important part to note here is that the post has to be public to be able to be displayed without any form of authentication being required. You'll use a public post that has relevant data that could be listed in your sidebar section, but if you already have a Facebook page with content on it, you may choose to link to that content instead.

The first step is to open in a browser the Facebook post that has the content that you would like to display on your page. Once opened, click the Settings drop-down in the top right corner, as illustrated in Figure 5-3.

Figure 5-3. *The settings drop-down menu is exposed from an existing Facebook public post*

Click the Embed option to open up a window that will provide you with the code that you need to add to your page. Let's bypass this code for the moment and click the Advanced Settings option. This will bring you to Facebook's Code Generator wizard, as shown in Figure 5-4.

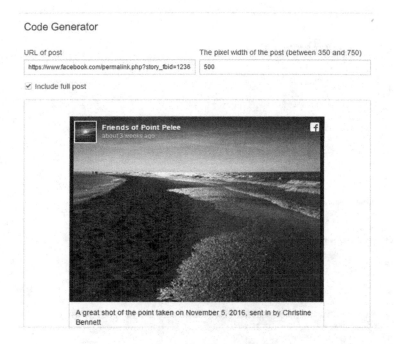

Figure 5-4. Facebook's Code Generator Wizard is shown with configuration options for your embedded content

Here you have the option to change some of the characteristics of how this post will be shown on your page, such as the width of the post. By default it will be 500 pixels wide. Let's go with the defaults and then click the Get Code button. This will present you with the window shown in Figure 5-5 where you can copy and paste the JavaScript code from here into the sidebar area on the webpage where you would like to embed the content. It is worth noting that the code displayed in both sections will be needed on your page. The first code snippet, listed in the Step 2 area of Figure 5-5, is used to call to the necessary libraries for the JavaScript code to work on your page. The code snippet in Step 3 must be placed on the page where you would like the content to be embedded and displayed.

Figure 5-5. *JavaScript created by the Facebook Code Generator is shown. This will be used on the page where you would like to embed this content*

Once this has been added to the page, when loaded in a browser the HTML page runs the JavaScript and reaches out to Facebook for the content to be displayed and then displays it in your browser, as shown in Figure 5-6.

We are **Williams and Sons Law Firm**, a responsive and caring firm that is dedicated to serving the legal needs of customers in our community and surrounding areas. Founded in 2016, we have been practicing law and specializing in Family Law for more than 6 months!

We are a full service law firm that treats each customer as family. We work with you to understand your needs and custom fit a legal solution to deliver results.

Figure 5-6. *An embedded Facebook post is shown on the home page of the sample site*

JavaScript can be used to do many things on your website, such as adding scripts to the page that can alternate through a set of featured images. An effect like this enhances the user's experience on your website.

As you can see, embedding content using JavaScript is a viable way to add content to your static website. There is, however, a potential drawback. Since this is run within the client-side browser, if the visitor has disabled the use of JavaScript, your script will not work and the content will not be loaded. There are ways to prepare for this and to show content in the place of something that doesn't load. I have a resource in the Appendix that can be helpful in testing whether JavaScript is enabled or disabled and how to display content based on the feedback from that test.

Using an IFrame to Display Content

You may have noticed in the Facebook example above that there was an option to copy IFrame code. An IFrame (Inline Frame) is an HTML tag that can be used to embed external content into an HTML web page. The properties of the tag are very simple; the only required property is the source property, as shown below:

```
<iframe src="http://www.google.com">
  <p>Your browser does not support iframes.</p>
</iframe>
```

This code will result in the Google website being displayed in a rather small window inside your page. For a more relevant example, review the following code. You'll see that I'm setting the width and height properties of the IFrame and pointing at the sample website for this book, www.nadonhosting.com.

```
<iframe src="http://www.nadonhosting.com" width="600" height="400">
  <p>Your browser does not support iframes.</p>
</iframe>
```

This code results in the page shown in Figure 5-7. As you can see, setting the width and height of the IFrame will cut off some content since the page content on www.nadonhosting.com is much larger than 600x400 pixels in size.

Figure 5-7. *A rendered view of the www.nadonhosting.com website in an IFrame element*

Note the scrollbars on the bottom and right of the IFrame element. These can be controlled by setting another property in the tag. To see a full list of supported properties for HTML tags, I highly recommend the W3 Schools website located at www.w3schools.com/.

The IFrame tag is supported by most major browsers, but you have added in the paragraph tag so that it will be displayed in the event of someone visiting your website via a browser that does not support the IFrame tag.

You may be asking yourself why you would want to use the IFrame tag, and in short, it is just another tool that can be used to bring in content from another site to make your site more dynamic without having to update your website frequently.

As you saw earlier in the chapter, Facebook offers the use of the IFrame tag to embed content provided by them into your webpage. Google Maps is another useful example. Figure 5-8 shows the Embed option with IFrame code that can be used on your website to embed a Google Maps Street Image. This can be useful if you want to allow a visitor to interact with Google Maps to find your business location.

Figure 5-8. *An example dialog box from Google Maps Embedded Content Wizard*

The IFrame lets you embed content on your website in a way that makes it look like it is part of your site, but it is actually a "window" into content on another website. As such, there are some limitations, and the main one to warn you about is that the content you are displaying in the IFrame tag is being delivered by the external source website. So if they have a disruption in service or content changes, your IFrame implementation will display the changed content or perhaps may show nothing. This could result in a negative experience for your website visitors.

API and Hosted Services Content Embedding

The last type of embedding that I'll talk about in this chapter is application programming interface (API) and hosted services content embedding. This type of embedding is usually implemented by using a client-side scripting language such as JavaScript in your HTML code. This makes the implementation a bit similar to the JavaScript example above, but since APIs are hosted applications that are designed to deliver content and services to those who are utilizing them, they are much more robust and can be thought of as a more dependable way to deliver content on your website over IFrame or link-based embedding.

Although APIs are more dependable, they are a bit more of an advanced implementation, and using external APIs that are not related to Amazon Web Services is outside the scope of this book. However, here is a link to the Google API so that you can see how you can use it to deliver maps, images, and other web content via the API on your website: https://developers.google.com/maps/web/. Implementation on your website involves signing up for a Developer account, requesting an API key for the services you would like to use, and enabling and testing code deployment.

In the next section, I will discuss a way to extend your website well past its static foundation using AWS Services. The first one you'll need to set up and utilize is the AWS API service, so you will get some experience working with an API.

Using AWS Serverless Architecture to Empower Your Static Website

In this section, I will show you how to use the power and benefit of the Amazon Web Services platform to extend your static web content to do something that would not be as easy or elegant if you were hosting this content outside of the AWS platform.

As you are aware, you have a page in your sample code called `contact.html`. On this page you want to add a form to allow your website visitors to leave a comment or ask you a question. Although this sounds like a very simple thing to do, on a normal website the form would be filled out by your visitor and when the visitor clicked the Submit button, your web server would process the request. Since you are hosting your static files in S3, you don't have a web server to do the processing. Thankfully, you can use other services in the AWS platform to help you process the request.

First, you'll set up AWS API Gateway to have your form code call that service upon visitor submission of the form data. You'll then have the AWS API Gateway call to AWS Lambda to accept the form data submitted and to store it in S3 for you to review. Finally, you'll set up the AWS Simple Notification Service (SNS) to let you know when someone has filled out and submitted your contact form. The process flow is show in Figure 5-9.

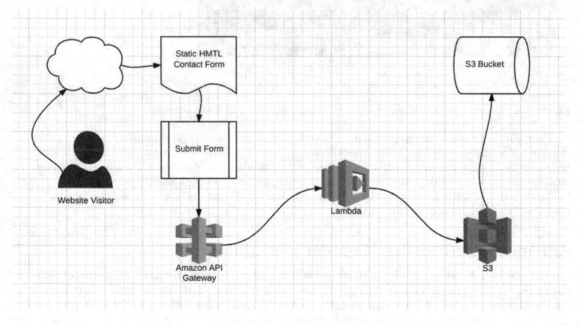

Figure 5-9. *The process flow for your static content contact form*

The beginning of setting up your contact form is to have the HTML code ready on your contact.html page. The following code is the relevant section of code that holds your contact form. You request three simple items from your visitor: name, email address, and a message body.

```
<!-- Contact Form -->
<div>
 <section>
  <header>
   <h2>Request Form</h2>
   <p>You're here to help, drop we a line</p>
  </header>
  <form id="contact-form" action="" method="post">
  <ul>
   <li>
    <label for="contactName">Name:</label><br>
    <input type="text" name="contactName" id="contactName" value="" />
   </li>
   <li>
    <label for="email">Email:</label><br>
    <input type="text" name="contactEmail" id="contactEmail" value="" />
   </li>
   <li>
    <label for="contactMessage">Message:</label><br>
    <textarea name="contactMessage" id="contactMessage" cols="25" rows="3"></textarea>
   </li>
   <li>
    <input type="submit" value="Submit" />
   </li>
  </ul>
  </form>
 </section>
</div>
```

Figure 5-10 shows this code rendered in a web browser. This code is not yet a finished product because, as you may have noticed, in the opening form tag there is a blank action property. This is where you enter the URL to invoke your AWS API.

Figure 5-10. *Web browser rendering of your sample contact form*

Now that you have your HTML code ready, you can log into your AWS account and begin the setup of your contact form process. The setup takes several steps. For reference sake, the following is a high-level list:

1. Create a new S3 bucket to hold the message files that are submitted.

2. Create an IAM Role that your Lambda function will use when processing a message, including a policy for this role so that it has the ability to work with S3.

3. Create a new S3 bucket policy for your message bucket to allow your Lambda IAM User Role permission to save messages to the bucket.

4. Create a Lambda function that uses the IAM role to process messages and save them to your S3 bucket.

5. Create an API Gateway that will be used in your HTML form and will pass your message information to your Lambda function.

6. Add a trigger to your Lambda function set to the new API Gateway you just created.

7. Publish your API Gateway.

8. Test the contact form and verify that a new message arrives in your S3 bucket.

After logging into your AWS Console, head to your S3 service dashboard. Let's create a new bucket to hold your visitor messages. As you'll see in Figure 5-11, I have named mine "nadonhostingcontactform." Creating a new bucket separate from the web content bucket allows you to assign a specific bucket policy that will allow the Lambda function the access it needs to create files in this bucket.

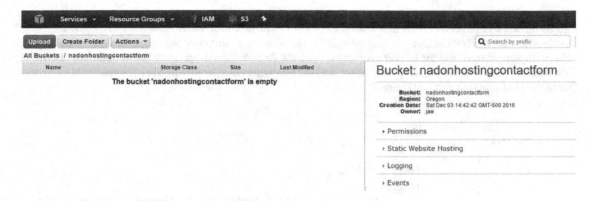

Figure 5-11. *Newly created S3 bucket to hold contact form messages*

Now that you have a bucket in which you can store messages, let's head over to AWS IAM and create a new role that will be used by your Lambda function. Click the Services menu at the top of your console and choose IAM. When the IAM Dashboard loads, click the Roles option in the left-hand navigation and then the Create New Role option to launch the Create Role Wizard.

For this sample, I am creating a new role called "myLamdbaServiceRole." Click the Next Step button and select the AWS Lambda role type, which allows Lambda functions to call other AWS services. In the Attach Policy screen, type S3 in the filter text box, select the checkbox next to AmazonS3FullAccess, and click the Next Step button. After reviewing the details and taking note of your IAM role ARN (you'll use this in the S3 bucket policy), click the Create Role button at the bottom of the screen to create the IAM role. Figure 5-12 shows the Review screen for the role I created.

Figure 5-12. *The Review screen of the Create Role Wizard in AWS IAM*

From here you will head back to S3 to add a bucket policy that allows this new IAM role to access your S3 bucket so that it can create files from your contact form submissions. Browse back to the AWS S3 Dashboard, click the bucket that you created to hold your messages, and click the Properties tab on the top right of the screen to reveal the bucket properties. Click the Permissions drop-down arrow and then choose "Add bucket policy." In the bucket policy editor, add the following code, adjusting the principal ARN value to that of the IAM role that you just created:

```
{
        "Version": "2012-10-17",
        "Statement": [
                {
                        "Effect": "Allow",
                        "Principal": {
                                "AWS": "arn:aws:iam::704427294249:role/myLamdbaServiceRole"
                        },
                        "Action": "s3:*",
                        "Resource": "arn:aws:s3:::nadonhostingcontactform/*"
                }
        ]
}
```

As you can see from the policy above, I am allowing one principal: an AWS account with the Amazon resource name of my newly created IAM role, myLambdaServiceRole. The action I'm allowing is all S3 actions and the resource these actions are allowed on is the new S3 bucket that will hold the website visitor contact form messages. You could be more restrictive, but to keep this process as simple as possible, I'll avoid the additional complexity.

Now that you have a S3 bucket to store the messages and an IAM role to be used by Lambda to store these messages, let's head over to the Lambda service to create your first function.

Click the Services menu and under the heading of Compute, choose Lambda. Click the Get Started Now button at the welcome screen; this will launch you into the New Lambda Function Wizard. If you have already set up functions and worked with Lambda, you may not see the welcome screen. In that case, you will click the Functions option in the left-hand navigation and choose the Create Function button to launch the New Lambda Function Wizard. Figure 5-13 shows the wizard and the first step, which is to choose a blueprint for the function.

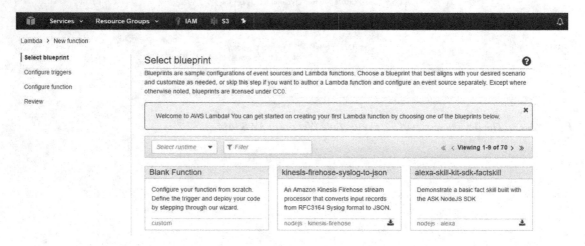

Figure 5-13. *The launch screen of the New Function Wizard in AWS Lambda*

You are going to choose Blank Function for your new function. There are many other premade blueprints available to perform a multitude of tasks and processing. I highly recommend that you spend some time with Lambda after this short sample because having AWS Lambda perform actions across AWS Services is a huge benefit of hosting on this platform.

After selecting the Blank Function blueprint, you can skip the Configure Triggers section for now; you'll come back and do that after you've created an API to be used to trigger this function.

In the Configure Function screen, name your function, give it a description, set the runtime to be used, configure it to use the IAM role that you set up earlier, and enter the code needed to have this function accept input and write to your S3 bucket.

I named my function "processContactFormData" and used the Node.js runtime. My settings are shown in Figure 5-14.

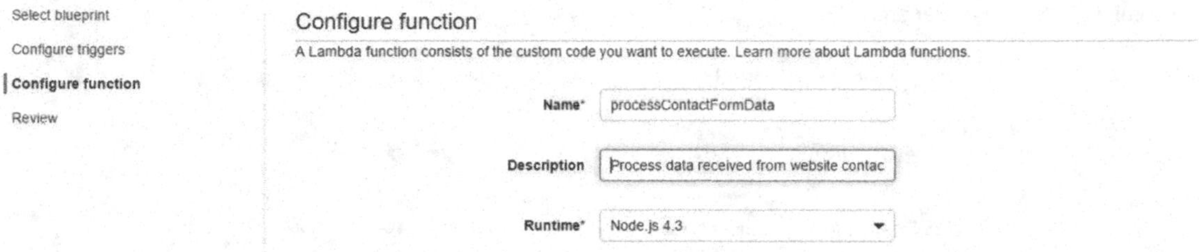

Figure 5-14. *The first section of the Configure Function step in AWS Lambda*

Next, you'll replace the existing code in the wizard with the following code in the Lambda Function Code section of the Configure Function step (remember to adjust this code to point to your S3 bucket because the following code references the one I set up):

```
var AWS = require('aws-sdk');
var s3 = new AWS.S3();

exports.handler = function(event,context) {
    var s3 = new AWS.S3();
    var nowtime = new Date();
    var bodycontent = event.body;

    mykey = nowtime.getTime() + '.txt';
    var param = {Bucket: 'nadonhostingcontactform', Key: mykey, Body: bodycontent};
    var successdata = {filename:mykey};
    s3.upload(param, function(e,data) {
        if (e) {
            console.log(e,e.stack);
        } else {
            console.log(event);
        }
        context.done(null,JSON.stringify(successdata));
    });
}
```

This code is quite simple in nature and it is acceptable for your example. There are improvements that could be made after implementation. This code accepts an event and stores the entire body of that event into a bodycontent variable. It then calls a getTime function and appends the file extension of .txt to that and stores it as the mykey variable. This variable is what will be used as the filename for the object being stored in S3. After this, it calls an S3 Upload function and passes the parameters of the bucket name, object key name, and content, which in turns saves this new object to your S3 bucket with an object name that includes the time of the message and a file extension of .txt.

After adjusting the code in the Function Code section, you will complete the "Lambda function handler and role" section and remaining options for your function. Figure 5-15 shows the values I selected for choosing the IAM role as well as timeout values and additional option configuration for the function.

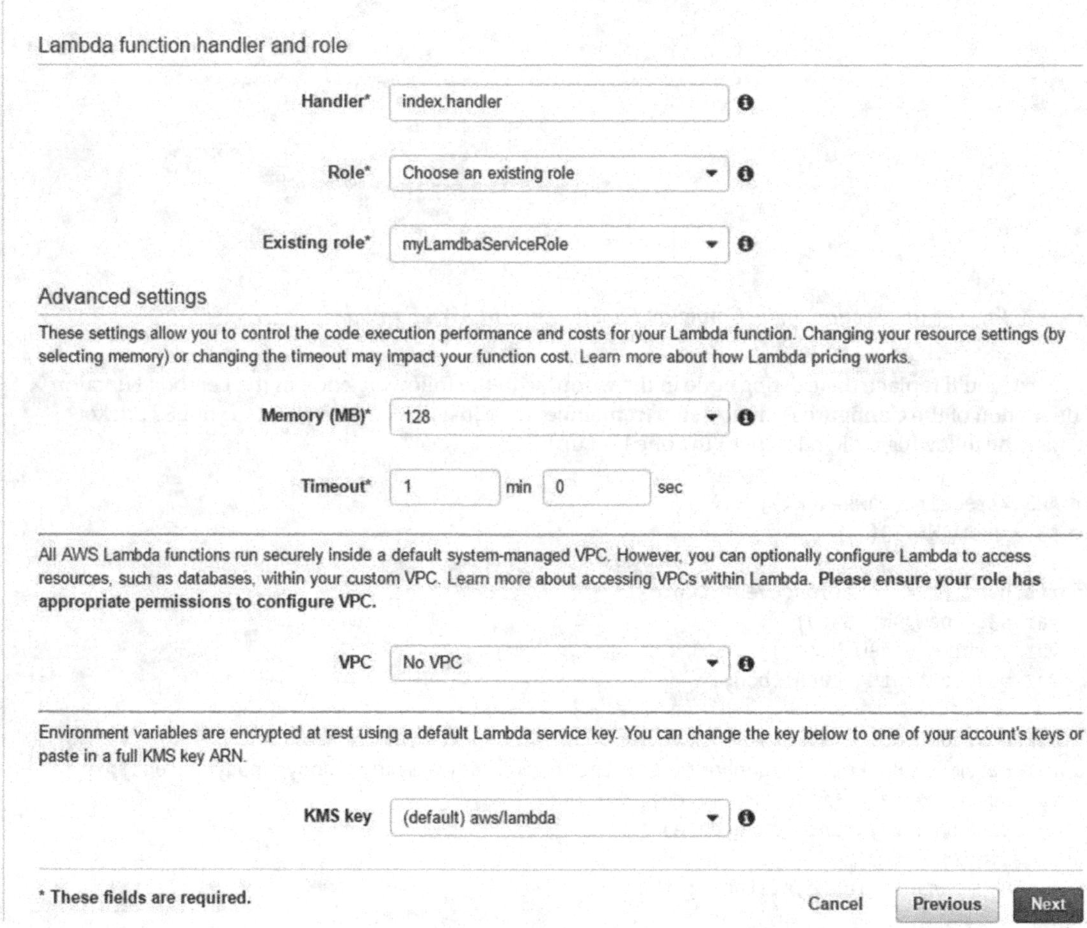

Figure 5-15. *The final sections of the Configure Function step in AWS Lambda*

Once you have filled in the configuration options as shown in Figure 5-15 (adjusting the IAM role to be the one that you created earlier), click the Next button to move to the Review page in the wizard. Once you have reviewed the function configuration, click the "Create function" button to finalize the creation process. You will be returned to the function configuration screen for your new function, similar to what is shown in Figure 5-16.

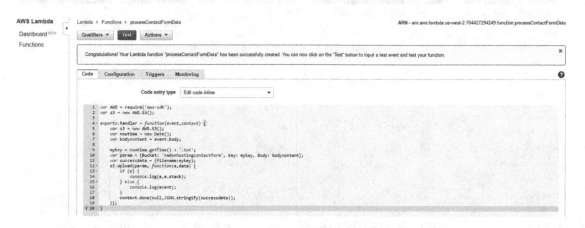

Figure 5-16. *The newly created AWS Lambda function named processContactFormData*

The next step is to create an AWS API Gateway that can be used in the action property of your HTML contact form. To do this, click the Services menu, and under the Application Services heading, choose API Gateway.

Click the Get Started button on the API Gateway Welcome Screen. You may be greeted with a message that says that since this is your first API creation Amazon has selected an example template for you to use. Click OK on that message box and then change the radio button from Example API to New API, as shown in Figure 5-17.

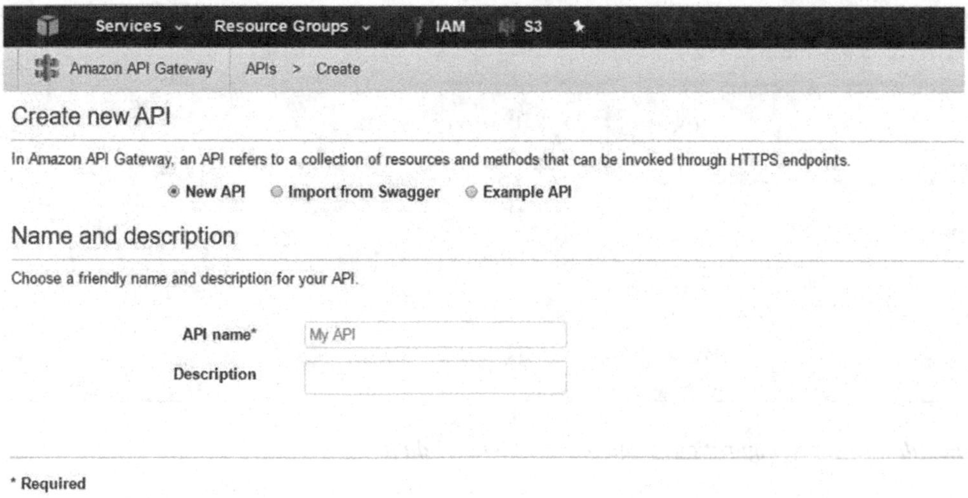

▦ Services ⌄   Resource Groups ⌄   ⫞ IAM   ▦ S3   ⚲

▦ Amazon API Gateway   APIs > Create

Create new API

In Amazon API Gateway, an API refers to a collection of resources and methods that can be invoked through HTTPS endpoints.

        ◉ **New API**　　◯ Import from Swagger　　◯ Example API

Name and description

Choose a friendly name and description for your API.

       API name*   [My API]

       Description   [　　　　　]

---

* Required

Figure 5-17. *The Create New API Wizard in AWS API Gateway*

After selecting the New API radio button, fill in an API name and description. In my case, I chose the name of "myContactForm" and then clicked the Create API button. After the creation of the API you will be returned to a screen similar to Figure 5-18 that shows your new API with the default configuration.

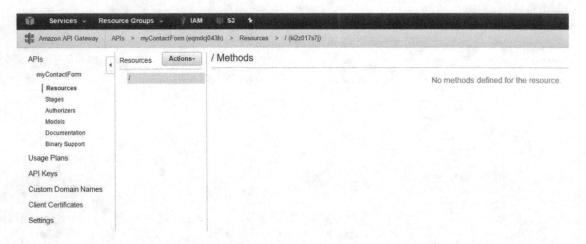

Figure 5-18. *A newly created myContactForm API with default configuration in AWS API Gateway*

The next step is to add a trigger to your Lambda function that uses this newly created API. Click the Services menu, and under the Compute heading, choose Lambda. Under Functions, click your Lambda function; in this example, I called it processContactFormData. This should move you to the function configuration page shown previously in Figure 5-16.

On this page, click the Triggers tab and click the Add Trigger link. This will present a configuration pop-up that asks you to select a trigger type. Click the dashed line box and select API Gateway and then make the necessary adjustments to choose the API that you just created. Also be sure to set the security to Open so that this API can be invoked externally. My settings are shown in Figure 5-19.

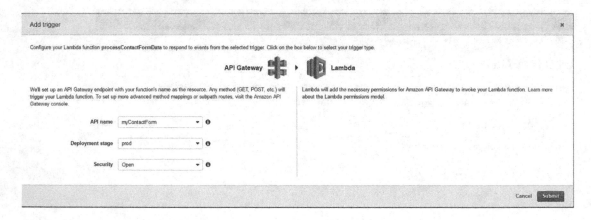

Figure 5-19. *The Add Trigger configuration screen in an AWS Lambda function*

Once you have chosen the API to be used and adjusted the setting to match the screenshot above, click the Submit button. The page will be returned and you will see that you now have that API linked as a trigger for this Lambda function.

The last step of your process is to publish or deploy your API so that it can be used by your contact form. To do this, click the Services menu and under the Application Services heading, choose API Gateway. Click the API Gateway that you created (in my case, it was myContactForm) and you'll now notice that you have an ANY method that is linked to your Lambda function, as shown in Figure 5-20.

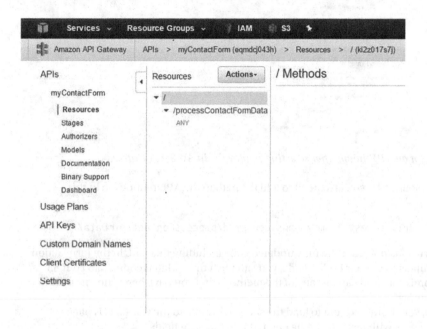

Figure 5-20. *The API Gateway configuration screen with a newly created method to AWS Lambda function*

Click the Actions button at the top of the screen and choose the Deploy API option. This will launch a window asking you to choose a "stage" on which to deploy the API. APIs can support multiple deployment stages so that you can test functionality from various environments. For this example, choose the prod stage and give it a description of Production and then click the Deploy button.

You will be returned to a page similar to the one shown in 5-21, which has a URL at the top of the screen that can be used to invoke your API. This is the URL that you will put in the action property of your Contact Form HTML.

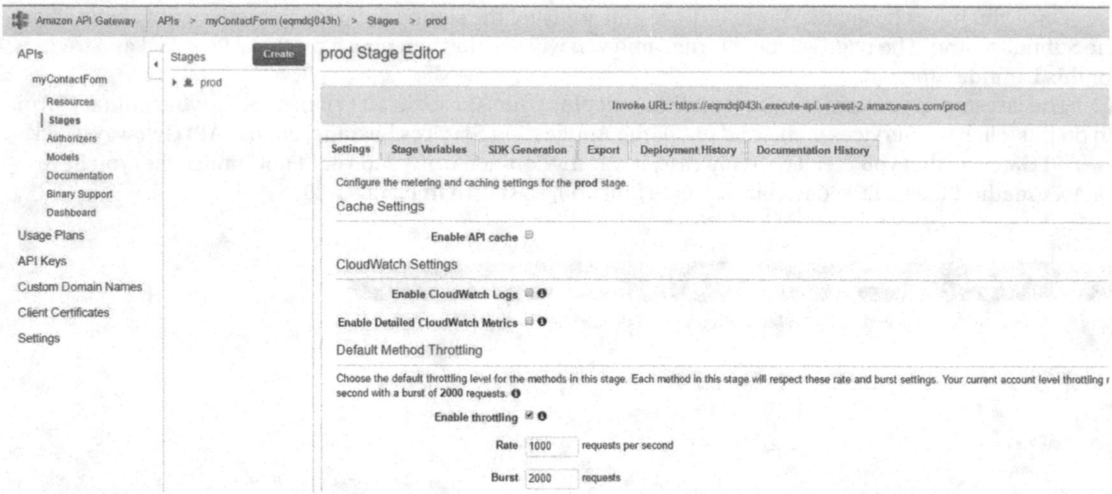

Figure 5-21. *The Invoke URL for an API shown after selecting Deploy the in AWS API Gateway*

To use this Invoke URL in your code, you also need to add the path to the API method, so in this example situation it would be

```
https://eqmdcj043h.execute-api.us-west-2.amazonaws.com/prod/processContactFormData/
```

The sample code given with this book has the fully updated code including this URL in the form action property. Once this has been updated in your HTML code, you can push the updated code up to your S3 bucket and perform a test submission. You can use any of the methods that you have been shown so far to update your code in your S3 bucket.

After updating your code, you should be able to load the site and browse to the Contact Us page. Figure 5-22 shows the updated page with test data being entered into the form fields.

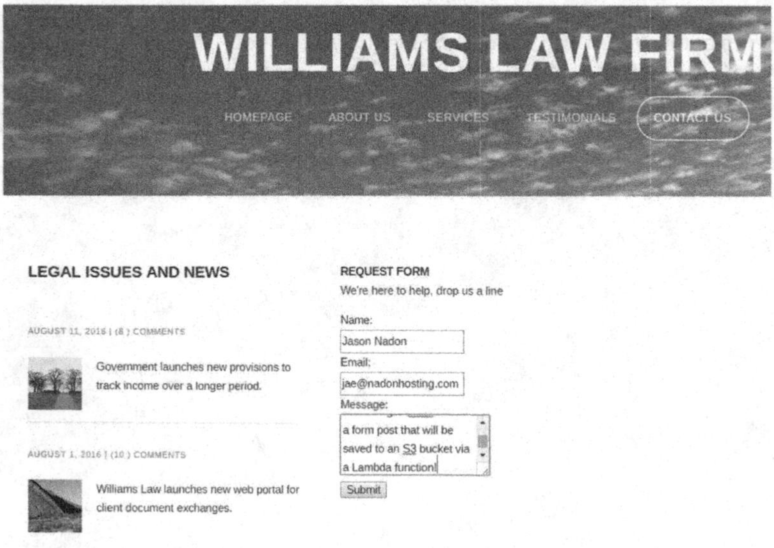

Figure 5-22. *Entering test data into your contact form*

After entering the data, click the Submit button. After the page is submitted, checking your S3 bucket shows a new object named with the format of a timestamp and the file extension of `.txt`, as shown in Figure 5-23.

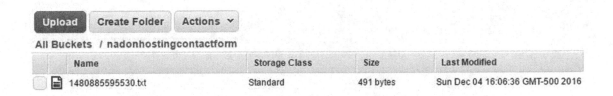

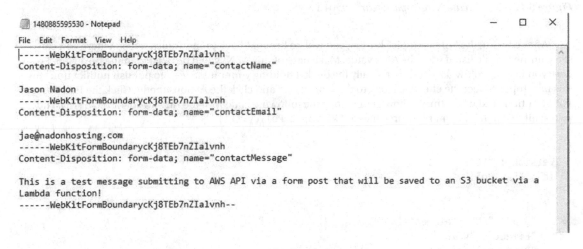

Figure 5-23. *A new file has been added to your S3 bucket after the form submission*

You can inspect this new file by clicking it, choosing Actions, and then choosing Download. Right-click the download link presented and choose "Save File As" to save the file to your local filesystem. When you open the file, you will see a format similar to Figure 5-24 where each section of the form data is listed out.

Figure 5-24. *The contents of the new file that was processed by your Lambda function and saved to S3*

In the above text file you can see contactName, contactEmail, and contactMessage fields; under each is the form data that I submitted in the form.

Getting a Notification of a New Message

It's great that your contact form is now working and visitors to your website can interact with you and leave you a message, but it would not be great to have to check your S3 bucket daily to see if there are new messages. Thankfully the AWS Platform has yet another service that will help you out by letting you know when a new message arrives: Simple Notification Service (SNS). AWS SNS is a notification service that every other service on the AWS Platform can interact with as a way to indicate when an action has occurred. Notifications are sent to topics, and topics can be subscribed to by a variety of methods. To finish off this chapter, I'll walk you through setting up SNS to create a new topic and subscribing to that topic via email so that you'll get an email message when a new message becomes available in your S3 bucket.

The easiest way to set this up is by heading to the SNS dashboard from within the AWS Console. Click the Services menu; under the Messaging heading, choose the SNS link.

From the SNS dashboard, click "Create New Topic" and enter a new topic name, as shown in Figure 5-25.

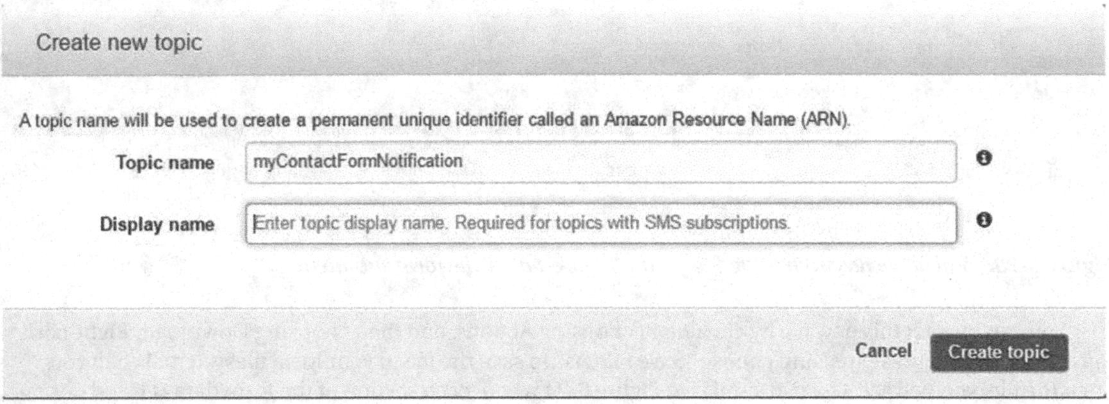

Create new topic

A topic name will be used to create a permanent unique identifier called an Amazon Resource Name (ARN).

Topic name	myContactFormNotification
Display name	Enter topic display name. Required for topics with SMS subscriptions.

Cancel   Create topic

Figure 5-25. *The Create New Topic wizard in AWS SNS*

After clicking the "Create topic" button, you will be brought back to the Topics screen where you can see your new topic listed with the ARN value. Make note of this ARN; it will be needed in the next step. From here you need to allow S3—and specifically the bucket holding your messages—to publish notifications to this new topic. Select the checkbox next to the topic name and click the Actions menu. Click the Edit Topic Policy option, and when the window opens, copy the following code into the Advanced view tab (this code is also available in the chapter resource files as SNS_Topic_Policy.txt):

```
{
  "Version": "2008-10-17",
  "Id": "SNS-Policy",
  "Statement": [
    {
      "Sid": "SNS-Statement-ID",
      "Effect": "Allow",
      "Principal": {
        "Service": "s3.amazonaws.com"
      },
      "Action": "SNS:Publish",
      "Resource": "arn:aws:sns:us-west-2:704427294249:myContactFormNotification",
      "Condition": {
        "ArnLike": {
          "aws:SourceArn": "arn:aws:s3:*:*:nadonhostingcontactform"
        }
      }
    }
  ]
}
```

You will need to update this code in two spots. The first is the Resource property where you should have the ARN of your SNS topic that you just created. The second is the aws:SourceArn property where you should have the name of the S3 bucket that you created to hold your messages. Once you've adjusted the code accordingly, click the Update Policy button.

From here, you'll head to the S3 bucket that you created to hold these messages. Click the Services menu and click the S3 service link. From the dashboard, select the bucket you created to hold your messages and then choose to make the properties of the bucket visible by clicking the Properties tab near the top right-hand corner of the screen. Expand the Events section and fill out details as shown in Figure 5-26, giving the configured event a name, selecting when the event should be triggered, and choosing to publish the event notification to SNS and the topic you created above.

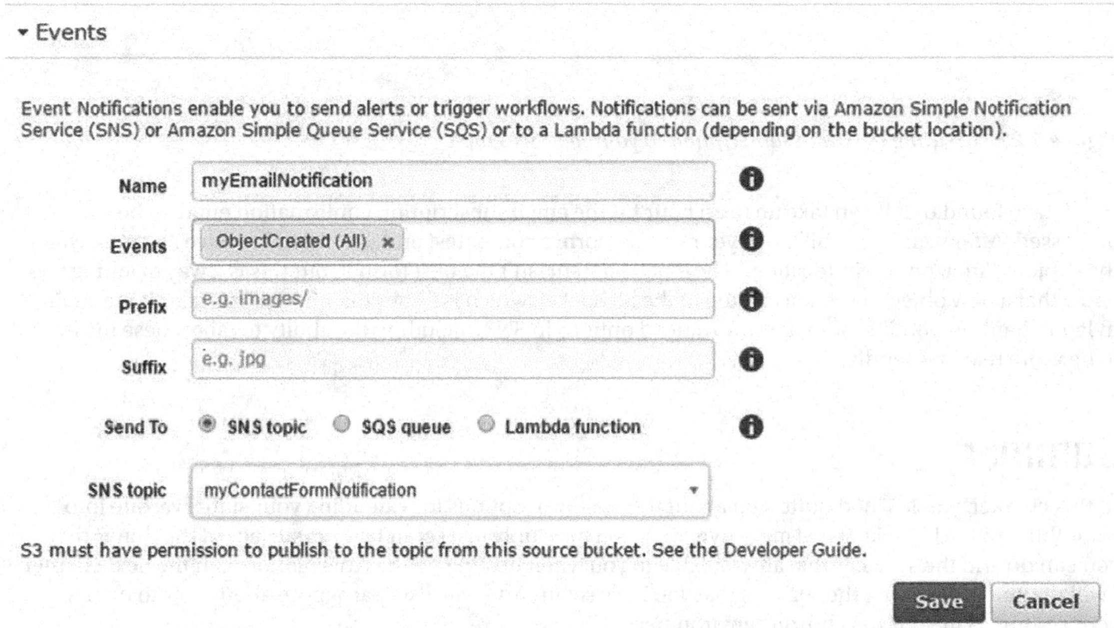

Figure 5-26. *Enabling events to publish notifications to your new SNS topic*

After entering the information the above event configuration form, click the Save button to create the event notification.

Your last step is to head back to SNS and subscribe to your new topic. From the SNS Dashboard, click Topics and select the checkbox next to the name of the topic you recently created. Click the Actions menu and choose "Subscribe to topic." Configure the subscription option to use email as the notification method and enter an email address where you would like to receive email notifications. Click the Save Subscription button. A confirmation email will be sent to the email address that you enter in this configuration; you will need to confirm that you want to receive email before you will be able to test your contact form again to see if you receive a notification email. Figure 5-27 shows the configuration options I used for my topic.

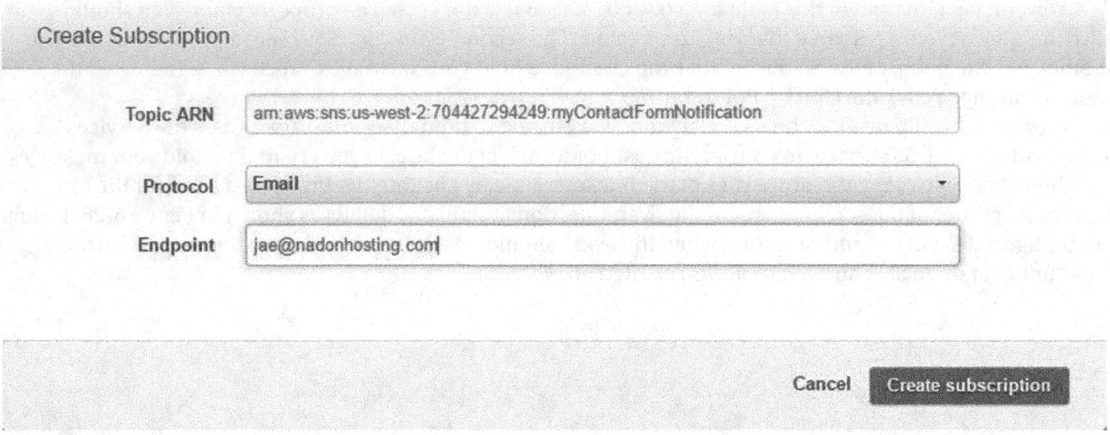

Figure 5-27. *Creating an email subscription to your new SNS topic*

I have found that it can take up to an hour for the email subscription confirmation email to be processed. After waiting a while, give your contact form another test and you should receive an email with the subject "Amazon S3 Notification." The email content isn't the best format, but this is a way of letting you know that a new object has been created in the S3 bucket, which is better than having to check it manually. In later chapters, you'll explore more advanced options in SNS, including the ability to tailor these messages to be more reader-friendly.

Summary

In this chapter, you learned quite a bit about the variety of options for extending your static website into something that will make it feel more dynamic. You have only just scratched the surface of the things that you can do and the services that are available to you when hosting on the AWS platform. In the next chapter, I will discuss monitoring the services that you have set up. You will also learn more about how to manage your resources in your new hosting environment.

CHAPTER 6

■ ■ ■

Logging and Monitoring

In the last chapter, you learned about options to help you extend the static content of your site to bring in dynamic content using HTML tags and JavaScript as well as how you can use AWS platform services such as the AWS API Gateway to process data for you without the need for server infrastructure. With you relying heavily on the AWS platform and services for the hosting of your website content (S3), domain name (Route53), access control (IAM), and other AWS services (API Gateway and Lambda), I think it's now time that I spend a chapter talking about how you can monitor these services so that you can be alerted when changes occur or if the services stop working as expected. In this chapter, I will introduce logging for the services that you have already set up and the AWS monitoring service, CloudWatch. The foundation that you build in this chapter will lend itself to future services that are used within the AWS platform because CloudWatch is something that can be used with all AWS services.

Introducing CloudWatch

AWS CloudWatch is a management service that allows you to monitor the resources you have in AWS for health and performance. CloudWatch gathers data points at set intervals; they are referred to as metrics. The metrics gathered depend on the service and resource being monitored by CloudWatch. Some CloudWatch metrics are configured by default for the majority of the AWS services and can be fine-tuned and adjusted to give you a way to gather additional information about your resources. Many default metrics are collected at 5-minute intervals and are not billed at an additional rate. Some resources allow for the metrics to be collected at lower intervals, such as 1-minute intervals; however, this usually has to be enabled and is charged to the resource's AWS account. There is also a way to create and send custom metrics that you define to CloudWatch for reporting purposes. I will talk about creating custom CloudWatch metrics in the second section of this book when you will work with the deployment and hosting of a CMS. With the services that you have been introduced to so far, there is some limited CloudWatch integration, so I will just give a couple examples that can be built upon in later chapters. A quick example of CloudWatch metrics can be found in Figure 6-1, which is from the Dashboard view of the API Gateway Service that you set up in the previous chapter.

© Jason Nadon 2017

J. Nadon, *Website Hosting and Migration with Amazon Web Services*, DOI 10.1007/978-1-4842-2589-9_6

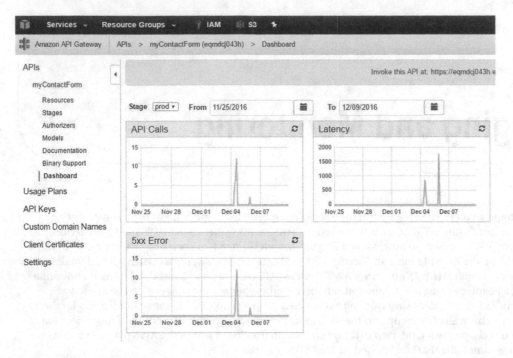

Figure 6-1. *The API Gateway Service Dashboard view shows CloudWatch metrics that are gathered by default for this service*

AWS Service Logging and Monitoring

Now that you have started to use the AWS platform and various services, I believe it is important to cover how to enable logging and monitoring of those services. There are those who feel that turning on logging is not a good idea because of the AWS "pay as you go" pricing model, and it's true; if you enable logging for everything and configure monitoring at the lowest intervals, using these services will end up costing you more. The opposite opinion is that enabling basic logging and basic monitoring will not increase your cost significantly but will give you visibility into AWS service performance and health and will allow you to plan for the future. In this section, I'll talk a bit about the logging and monitoring options for each service and the best practices to enable for each service.

S3 Logging and Monitoring

AWS S3 is the service that you have most utilized to this point in the book. You have set up your static HTML content in S3 and enabled static website hosting on your bucket. You have also created a new bucket to hold your HTML form submissions and configured an event to let you know when a new object is created in this bucket. Outside of this, you have not explored many of the logging or monitoring options for S3.

As noted, sometimes CloudWatch dashboards are built right into the service being monitored. You'll see evidence of this in other AWS services such as Elastic Compute Cloud (EC2). As you look at what is available in S3, there aren't any CloudWatch metrics available from within the S3 dashboard but there are metrics available from within the CloudWatch dashboard. To access the CloudWatch central management screen where you can view metrics across all services, log into the AWS Console and click the Services menu in the top left-hand corner of the screen. Under the Management Tools heading, click the CloudWatch option.

After clicking CloudWatch, you will be brought to the default screen for management and interaction with CloudWatch metrics that are being gathered for services that you use on the AWS platform. From here, you can click the Browse Metrics button and you will be presented with a summary of services that you're using across your account, which is based on your previous work in this chapter. It is important to note that CloudWatch is region-specific, so you will see metrics for the resources used in the specific region that is currently selected in the AWS Console. In Figure 6-2, note that you have CloudWatch metrics available for Route 53 and S3.

Figure 6-2. *The CloudWatch Browse Metrics view shows available CloudWatch metrics grouped by AWS service, which can be drilled into for real-time reporting*

From this screen you can select a service and see what metrics are available for further analysis. The top of the screen has a graph area, which is where the selected metrics will display over a selected time frame. By default, the graph view is over a 3-hour period.

S3 is listed under the AWS namespaces section with two available metrics that can be viewed or graphed. Click the S3 box to see what metrics are available to you. When you click the S3 link, you'll see four storage metrics available. Clicking the Storage Metrics link shows the metrics that are related to the S3 buckets you have set up.

In Figure 6-3 you can see the available metrics for two of your S3 buckets. The metrics are related to bucket size and object count. Although these may not seem like very valuable metrics, they can be because you will be billed based on the amount of storage used in S3. As you add objects to your S3 buckets and more visitors use your contact form, your bucket size will grow and you will be charged accordingly. You haven't done so yet, but when you enable logging on AWS services, the log data is stored in S3, so that means you'll have another set of metrics to view.

	BucketName (4) ▲	StorageType	Metric Name
☐	nadonhostingcontactform	StandardStorage	BucketSizeBytes
☐	nadonhostingcontactform	AllStorageTypes	NumberOfObjects
☐	www.nadonhosting.com	AllStorageTypes	NumberOfObjects
☐	www.nadonhosting.com	StandardStorage	BucketSizeBytes

Figure 6-3. *Storage metrics available to you in CloudWatch for your S3 buckets*

CloudWatch is valuable to you because it gives you a way to see the metric value when you click it. Let's click one of the metrics available to you. Figure 6-4 shows the metric level detail for the BucketSizeBytes metric on the nadonhostingcontactform S3 bucket. Adjust the data range for the graph by selecting the Custom button and choosing a two-week period.

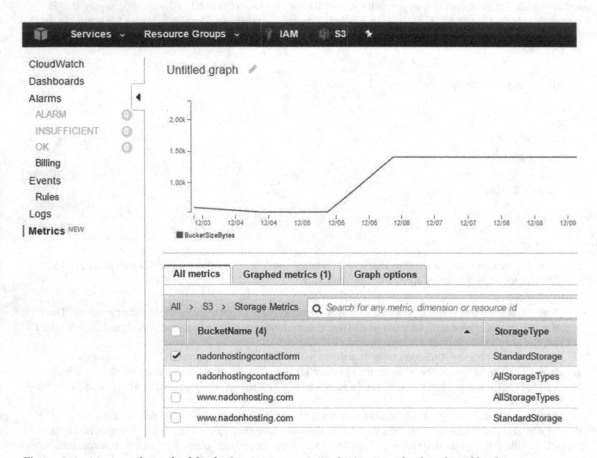

Figure 6-4. *A two-week graph of the the S3 storage metric BucketSizeBytes for the selected bucket*

From this view, you can see that you haven't used much storage at all in the Contact Form bucket. If this is a metric that interests you, you can track this metric in an easier way by adding it to a custom dashboard. CloudWatch dashboards are a collection of selected metrics in graph format that can be easily viewed from the Dashboards menu. To add this metric graph to a dashboard, let's first name this graph. Click the edit icon next to the Untitled graph text. You can see this in Figure 6-4. This will allow you to edit the name of the graphed metric. Name it "S3 Bucket Size - Contact Form." Once you have named the graph, you can add it to a dashboard for future viewing by clicking the Actions button and choosing "Add to dashboard," as shown in Figure 6-5.

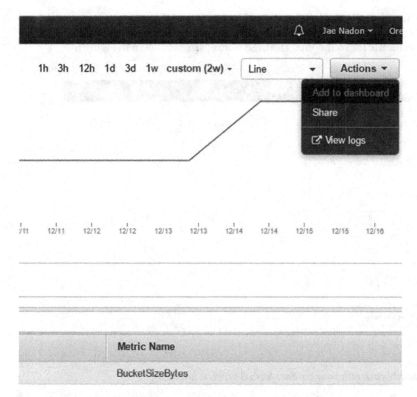

Figure 6-5. *The newly named graph with "Add to dashboard" selected*

When you click the link to add the graph to the dashboard, you're presented with a dialog box that asks you to give a name to the new dashboard. Name this new dashboard "S3StorageMetrics," as shown in Figure 6-6.

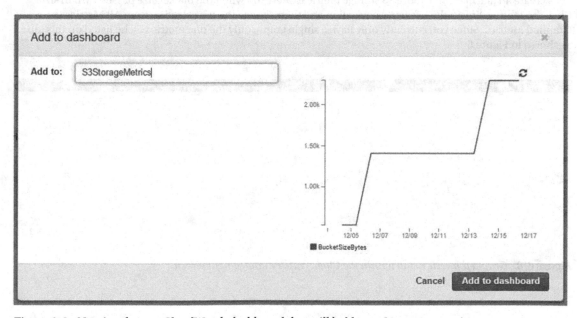

Figure 6-6. *Naming the new CloudWatch dashboard that will hold your S3 storage metric*

After you have selected a name, click the "Add to dashboard" button to add the metric to a new dashboard. After the screen refreshes, you will now see the new dashboard screen for the S3StorageMetrics dashboard that has the one graph metric for your contact form S3 bucket size, as shown in Figure 6-7.

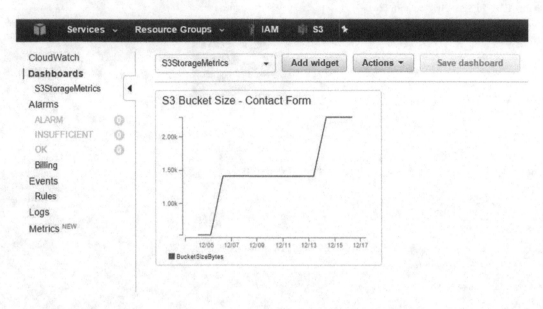

Figure 6-7. *New CloudWatch dashboard with your contact form S3 metric graph*

CloudWatch helps you with graphing and viewing given metrics, but the real power of CloudWatch comes in the ability to monitor and alert you of thresholds that have been passed. In CloudWatch terms, these are called alarms and they can be set on any given metric gathered and evaluated by CloudWatch. Let's create an alarm for the above S3 storage metric to alert you when the bucket size passes 1MB in size. Click the Metrics link in the left-hand navigation and then change the tab selection from All Metrics to Graphed Metrics. Since you currently only have a single graph, only the one metric will be listed on this tab, as shown in Figure 6-8.

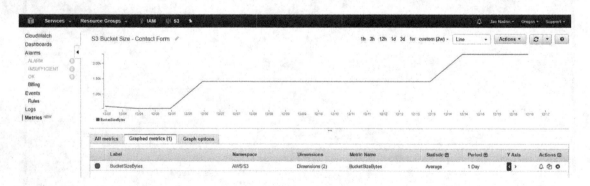

Figure 6-8. *Graphed metric detail within the CloudWatch management screen*

With your metric selected in the bottom half of the screen, you can see the options that you can edit to change the view in the graph above it. To the far left, you have options under the Actions heading, shown up close in Figure 6-9.

Figure 6-9. Close view of the Actions options. Icons shown are for Create Alarm, Duplicate, and Remove

The icons listed in the Actions section per metric allow you to create an alarm, duplicate it, or remove the metric. If you click the icon shaped like a bell, this will start the Create Alarm Wizard within the context of this specific metric. If you start from this point, you skip the first step of the wizard, which is to select which metric you want to create an alarm for, and move directly to Step 2 of the wizard where you define the threshold and additional information shown in Figure 6-10.

Create Alarm ✕

1. Select Metric   **2. Define Alarm**

Alarm Threshold

Provide the details and threshold for your alarm. Use the graph on the right to help set the appropriate threshold

Name: [   ]

Description: [   ]

Whenever: BucketSizeBytes

is: [>= ▾] [0]

for: [1] consecutive period(s)

Actions

Define what actions are taken when your alarm changes state.

Notification	Delete
Whenever this alarm: [State is ALARM ▾]	
Send notification to: [Select a notification list ▾] New list Enter list ❶	

[+ Notification] [+ AutoScaling Action] [+ EC2 Action]

Alarm Preview

This alarm will trigger when the blue line goes up to or above the red line for a duration of 1 day

BucketSizeBytes >= 0

2,500
2,000
1,500
1,000
500
0
    12/12   12/14   12/16
    00:00   00:00   00:00

Namespace: AWS/S3

BucketName: [nadonhostingcontactform]

StorageType: [StandardStorage]

Metric Name: [BucketSizeBytes]

Period: [1 Day ▾]

Statistic: ● Standard ○ Custom

[Average ▾]

Cancel [Previous] [Next] [**Create Alarm**]

Figure 6-10. The Create Alarm Wizard on Step 2

Within this step of the wizard you can name your alarm, set the threshold for the alarm, and select how and who you want to notify when the alarm is triggered. For this example, under the Alarm Threshold section, since you want to be notified when the S3 bucket passes 1MB in size, set the threshold under "Whenever: BucketSizeBytes" is ">=" 1024 bytes "for 1 consecutive period."

Under the Actions section, for the notification, create a new list and then enter your email address. As part of this process, you will also need to specify a name for the list. After you click the Create Alarm button, you will be required to confirm your email address subscription for this specific alarm. There is another option here to send to an SNS topic. If you choose this option, you may see the one that you set up earlier in this section of the book available as a selection option. Another option is to set up a new SNS topic related to CloudWatch alarms and to send all alarm notifications to this topic. This way you can centrally manage who subscribes to that topic and receives the alarm notifications.

Now you can click the Alarms link in the left-hand navigation to see the status of the alarms that you've set up. In this example, you set the threshold to 1024 bytes, which if you remember from earlier was actually under the current value for the S3 bucket. This will immediately set the alarm into a state of "Alarm." If you want to modify the settings of an alarm, including the threshold value, you can select that alarm from the main Alarms screen and then click the Modify button to enter the editing mode. If you update the value to 2500 bytes, it will clear the alarm and move it into the OK state. Now when the S3 bucket grows past 2500 bytes in size, you will receive an email notification that your threshold has been crossed and that this monitor has moved into the state of "Alarm."

Now that you've seen what metrics are being collected by CloudWatch in regard to the AWS S3 service and you've learned how you can use CloudWatch to monitor these metrics, let's take a look at what options are available for logging in S3.

Logging options for S3 as well as most services in AWS are available via the AWS Management Console screen for the service. To access S3 logging options, let's log into the AWS Console and then click the Services menu and choose the S3 service. It is worth noting that there are multiple types of logs within the AWS platform. The ones that you are going to focus on in this chapter are specific to the service and requests. From the S3 central management site you will see the list of your S3 buckets. Select one bucket and then choose the Properties tab. Within the Properties tab, expand the Logging option, as shown in Figure 6-11.

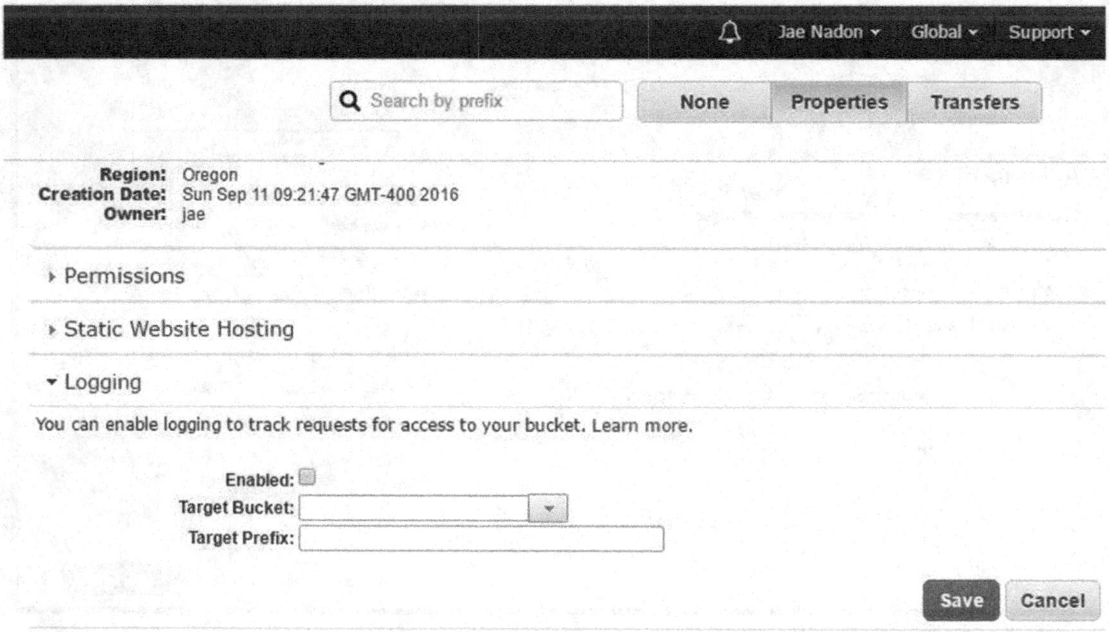

Figure 6-11. Logging options for a specific bucket are viewed from within the Properties screen

Logging within S3 is enabled on a per bucket basis. To enable logging for a specific bucket, click the Enable button and then choose the bucket where you would like to store the log data. A best practice is to create a separate bucket to hold your service logs. The reason for this is when you enable logging and choose a bucket to store the logs, log delivery permissions are added to that bucket and it would add complexity to buckets like your website static content bucket. For this example, create a new bucket first called nadonhosting-logs and then enabled logging on the www.nadonhosting.com bucket to use this new S3 bucket for logs. Enter the prefix of website-logs/ so that it will be easy to identify the logs coming from static website content object access. It is worth noting that AWS offers best effort delivery on logging, which means that you should not rely on getting logs in real time. Logs are delivered within a few hours of setting logging up for your service. If near real-time communication or notification is needed, look to configure events within the S3 bucket properties. More information on this topic can be found at http://docs.aws.amazon.com/AmazonS3/latest/dev/NotificationHowTo.html.

The possible log data collected for S3 object access can include the following for each log entry;

1. Bucket Owner

2. Bucket Name

3. Time

4. Remote IP

5. Requestor

6. Request ID

7. Operation

8. Key

9. Request URI

10. HTTP Status

11. Error Code

12. Bytes Sent

13. Object Size

14. Total Time

15. Turn-Around Time

16. Referrer

17. User-Agent

18. Version ID

More details about specifics for each of these entries can be found at https://docs.aws.amazon.com/AmazonS3/latest/dev/LogFormat.html. Figure 6-12 shows the log data stored in the new logging bucket.

```
www.nadonhosting.com [18/Dec/2016:15:18:22 +0000] 24.57.80.57 8f391d7ef70d42261d27d10450ff86345c81fc·
www.nadonhosting.com [18/Dec/2016:15:18:22 +0000] 24.57.80.57 8f391d7ef70d42261d27d10450ff86345c81fc·
www.nadonhosting.com [18/Dec/2016:15:27:18 +0000] 24.57.80.57 8f391d7ef70d42261d27d10450ff86345c81fc·
www.nadonhosting.com [18/Dec/2016:15:27:18 +0000] 24.57.80.57 8f391d7ef70d42261d27d10450ff86345c81fc·
www.nadonhosting.com [18/Dec/2016:15:27:18 +0000] 24.57.80.57 8f391d7ef70d42261d27d10450ff86345c81fc·
```

Figure 6-12. *Log data file detail for a specific bucket viewed in a text editor*

Lambda Logging and Monitoring

Similar to S3, the Lambda service has the ability to have logging and monitoring enabled. As with the S3 service, I'll start with CloudWatch monitoring and move into discussing logging options afterward. On the dashboard of the Lambda service, accessed from the AWS Console, you'll see CloudWatch graphs that show some statistics regarding all of your Lambda functions within the selected region. Figure 6-13 shows the default dashboard with four Lambda metrics in CloudWatch graphs.

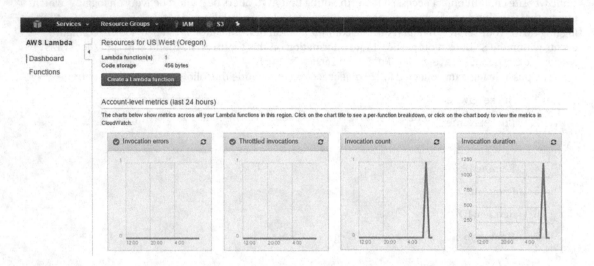

Figure 6-13. *Dashboard showing CloudWatch graphs of Lambda function metrics across a given region*

You can also access function-specific logs by clicking the name of the function under the Functions menu and then clicking the Monitoring tab. The other way for you to explore available CloudWatch metrics, as discussed earlier in the chapter, is to access the CloudWatch central management screen from the AWS Console, which is available under Services, Management Tools. From this page, click the Metrics link in the left-hand navigation to access all of the AWS services that have available CloudWatch metrics. Figure 6-14 shows the same metrics available in Figure 6-13 but from the perspective of the CloudWatch service.

	FunctionName (4)	▲	Resource	Metric Name
☐	processContactFormData		processContactFormData	Duration
☐	processContactFormData		processContactFormData	Throttles
☐	processContactFormData		processContactFormData	Invocations
☐	processContactFormData		processContactFormData	Errors

Figure 6-14. *Lambda function metrics available through the CloudWatch metrics interface*

From here you can view detailed information about a given metric, which you could add to a new dashboard for easier access. Another option is to create a dashboard that has a view of all the metrics that you feel are critically important and have this as an AWS Service Overview Dashboard. You learned the steps to do this earlier in the chapter, so I won't reiterate them here.

In terms of logging for Lambda, log data is sent to CloudWatch via the configuration of the Lambda function. In the Lambda Function example earlier in this section, you did not implement any custom logging in your function. If you want log data to be collected by CloudWatch, you need to add a log stream within CloudWatch. The easiest method for creating a log stream specific to your Lambda function is to head back to the Lambda service from the AWS Console. Click the Functions option and then click the name of the function for which you want to create a log stream. Click the Monitoring tab, and then click the "View Logs in CloudWatch" link in the upper right-hand corner of the screen. This will launch the CloudWatch Log Groups page within the context of searching for a log stream for this specific Lambda function. Since there isn't one currently, none will be found. Click the "Create Log Stream" button to create a stream specific for this Lambda function. This will present a dialog box as shown in Figure 6-15, with the log group prefilled; you will need to enter a name for the log stream.

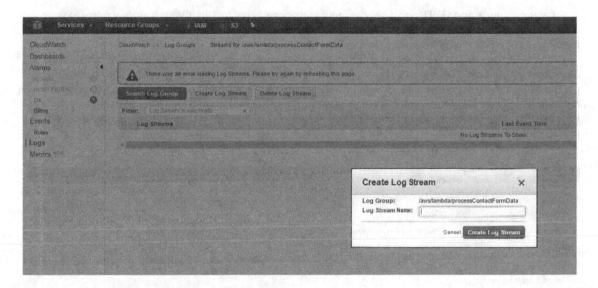

Figure 6-15. *Creating a CloudWatch log stream for a Lambda function*

After the log stream has been set up you will have the ability to send log data to CloudWatch from your Lambda function.

API Gateway Logging and Monitoring

The API Gateway Service has similar CloudWatch graphs available from the service dashboard as the Lambda service. You saw an example of this in Figure 6-1. A variety of additional metrics can be found from within the CloudWatch central management screen. Figure 6-16 shows the API Gateway CloudWatch metrics available for your implementation of your Contact Form API.

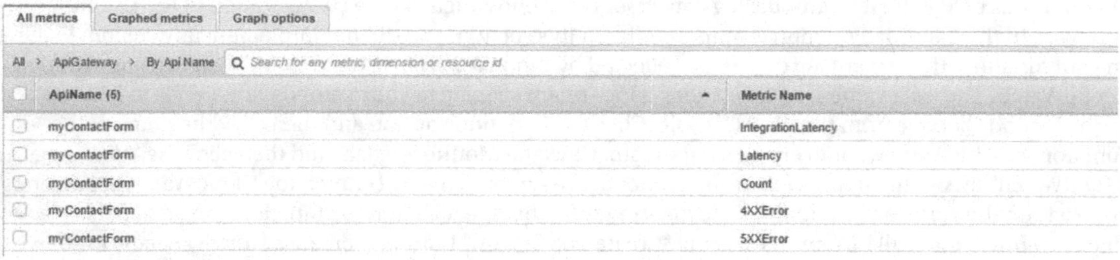

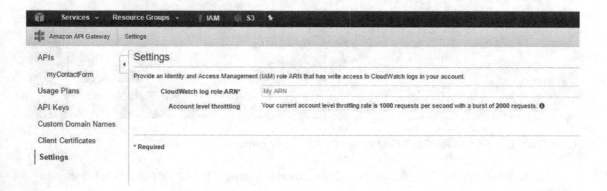

Figure 6-16. *CloudWatch metrics available for your implementation of the API Gateway Contact Form*

Latency, count, and HTTP errors are the main metrics gathered by CloudWatch as they relate to your API Gateway implementation. As you add features, methods, and additional complexity to a given API, more metrics will become available to be tracked in CloudWatch.

In terms of logging, you can set up your API Gateway to send logs to CloudWatch similar to what was described for the Lambda service. To do so, you need to access the API Gateway from the AWS Console. On the API Gateway overview screen, click the Settings link in the left-hand navigation. This will present a screen like Figure 6-17 where you can set up an IAM role to be used to send logs from API Gateway to CloudWatch. This can be an existing role that has proper permissions, or you may choose to set up a new role for this purpose.

Figure 6-17. *CloudWatch integration from the Settings screen of the API Gateway service*

Route 53 Logging and Monitoring

The last service that you want some monitoring visibility into is your DNS service, Route53. You set up your domain to use this service, and you can set up health checks to verify that your domain name and the service behind the domain name are responding as expected. Health checks are set up from within the Route53 management console and send information to CloudWatch.

To create a new health check, you first need to log into the AWS Console and then browse to your Route53 service page by clicking the Services menu or the shortcut to the service that you created earlier. From the Route53 service page, you can click the "Create health check" button under the Availability Monitoring section, or click the "Health Checks" link in the left-hand navigation and then click the "Create health check" button. Both methods will start the Route53 Create Health Check Wizard. In the first step of the wizard you define a name for the health check and what you want to monitor; the choices are monitoring an endpoint (such as a domain name or IP), the status of another health check, or the state of a CloudWatch alarm. Let's focus on the first type of monitor as this type will enable you to check the status of your domain name and its response. Figure 6-18 shows the first half of the configuration discussed above, as well as the endpoint configuration, which I'll discuss below.

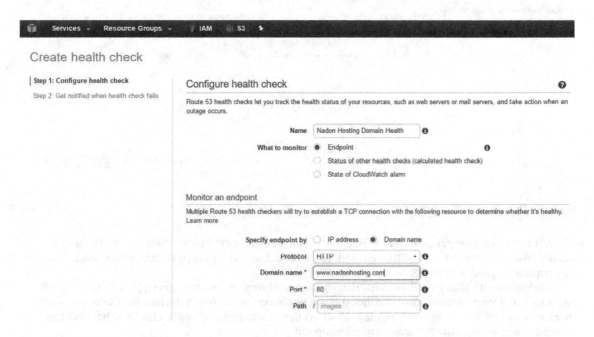

Figure 6-18. The Route53 Create Health Check Wizard with the configuration of the first health check

Under the "Monitor and endpoint" section of your configuration, you can chose to monitor a domain name rather than an IP, so add the www.nadonhosting.com domain name into the domain name field and chose port 80 as the port to monitor. You could, of course, change these options if you were serving your website content via some method other than the static website hosted S3 bucket that you are using, such as an EC2 instance or multiple instances behind a load balancer, but for your implementation this configuration should suffice.

In the "Advanced configuration" section you can also enable additional configuration items such as the interval at which to check the domain name, the failure threshold, whether you want to search for a string on the page returned (this could be helpful when pulling dynamic content from another source as a way of alerting you that the third party source did not deliver the content you were expecting), additional CloudWatch graphing options, and the AWS regions where you want to perform the health checks. In general, you can leave these options at the default settings.

The bottom of the page notes that this is a "Basic" health check type and there is a link to the pricing document. Health checks are included for AWS hosted/registered domains, but if you're reaching outside of the AWS platform to check an external service there is a fee associated with each health check. I recommend reviewing the pricing document and making sure that you understand the pricing before moving to the next step.

The second step of the wizard asks if you want to create a CloudWatch alarm and notification to alert you when the domain has moved into an unhealthy state. Figure 6-19 shows configuration options that I chose: I set up a new SNS topic and to send an email to my email address. Note that since this will be a new SNS topic you'll need to confirm that you want to subscribe to it before you will receive any email messages from this topic.

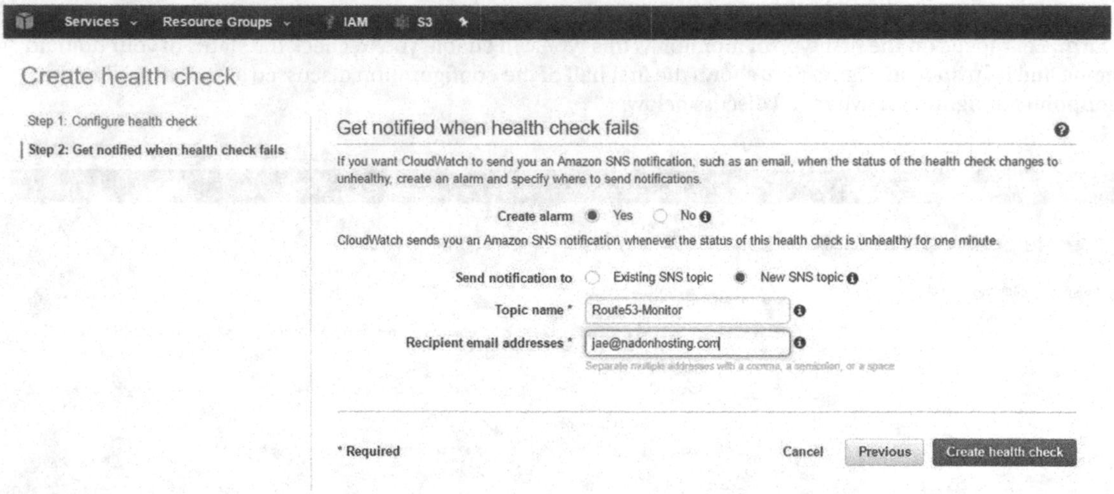

Figure 6-19. *Notification options*

After reviewing information and clicking the "Create health check" button, the new health check will be created, a new SNS topic will be created, and an email will be sent to your address to confirm your subscription request to that SNS topic.

Clicking Health Checks in the left-hand navigation will bring up your configured health check. It will take a moment for data to be populated, but you will be able to cycle through the tabs for a selected health check to see information collected. Figure 6-20 shows the various regional health checkers that AWS has requesting a response from the domain name endpoint.

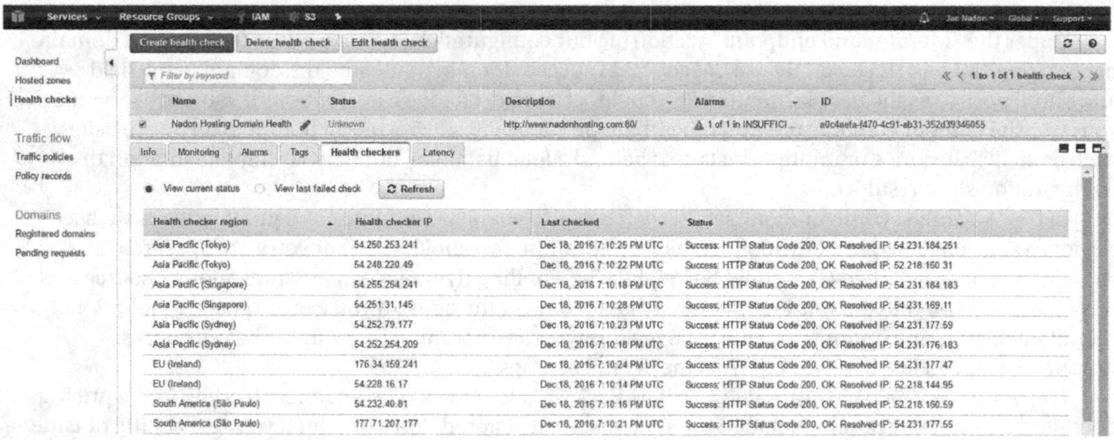

Figure 6-20. *The Route53 Health Check configuration with the Health checkers tab's data/responses displayed*

After a few moments data will start to be collected and the status of the health check should move from "Unknown" to "OK." Figure 6-21 shows the Monitoring tab of the newly created health check showing each of the 30-second intervals as well as the updated status of the domain name monitor.

Figure 6-21. *The Route53 Health Check configuration with Monitoring tab displayed and updated domain health status of "OK"*

In regard to logging, Route53 does have integration with CloudTrail for security and auditing logging (as do all AWS services), but this is outside the scope of this chapter. Don't worry; I'll be covering CloudTrail in great detail in future chapters.

External Analytics and Monitoring

In the previous section, you explored logging and monitoring across several of the services that you are currently using in the AWS platform. This section will talk about other sources that you can use to gather data about the usage and health of your static content website.

Google Analytics for Web Statistics

In addition to being able to see data about who is accessing your static website content through AWS S3, you may want to view additional information in an easy-to-read format. Google Analytics is a powerful platform for gathering statistical information about your website use and visitor information. There are entire books dedicated to Google Analytics, but I want to focus in on a use case for the static website you've set up. This will be a very basic implementation and is in no way an exhaustive introduction to the product. For that, I recommend visiting www.google.com/analytics/analytics/features/ after performing the basic setup below.

In your setup of Google Analytics, you'll be focused on these steps:

1. Set up a Google account (skip this if you already have a Gmail account).

2. Sign up for a free Google Analytics account.

3. Set up tracking code for a static website.

4. Add tracking code to pages for which you would like information tracked using Google Analytics.

To set up a new Google account if you don't already have one, visit `https://accounts.google.com/SignUp`. The next step is to sign into your Google account and then visit this link and click the Sign Up button for a free Google Analytics account: `https://analytics.google.com/analytics/web/provision/`.

Under the New Account screen, choose the Website option and fill in the relevant details. Figure 6-22 shows the configuration I used for my sample static website.

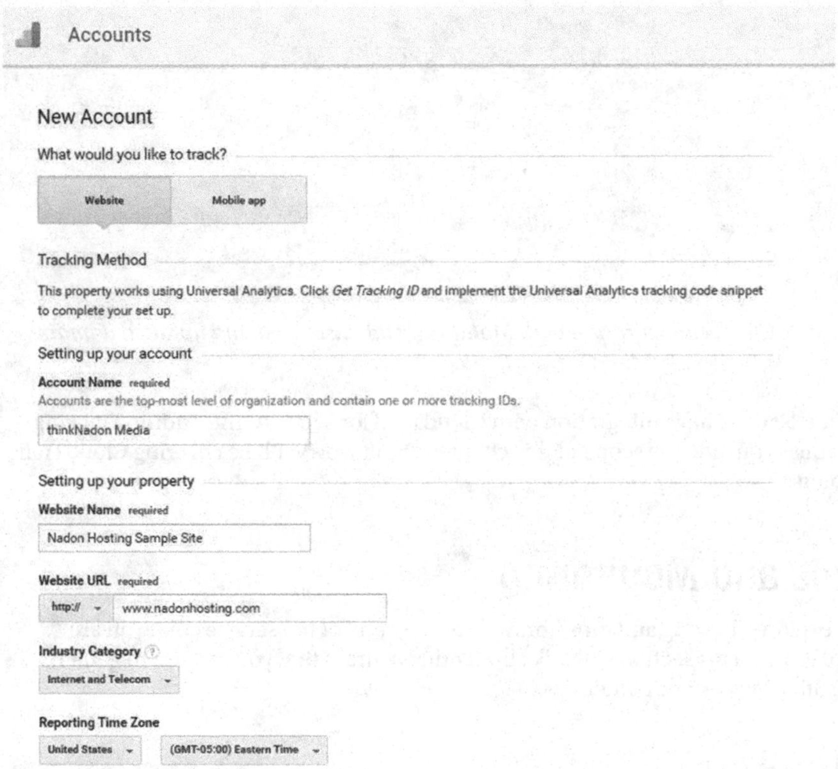

Figure 6-22. *Google Analytics new account setup screen*

Once you have entered the information needed, click the Get Tracking ID button. You will be prompted to accept the Google Terms of Use Agreement. Then you will be brought to a screen where you can select the JavaScript code (located under the Website Tracking section) that you can add to the pages that you want to track with Google Analytics. You'll want to add this script between the HTML <head> tags alongside the other script elements.

Once you update your HTML code on the pages that you would like tracked, you will need to upload the new version of these files to AWS S3. You're a pro at this by now, so I will skip the details for this step.

After you have updated your static content files with the Google Analytics tracking code, the first visit will start being tracked in Google Analytics. Figure 6-23 shows the start of data being collected for the sample static website.

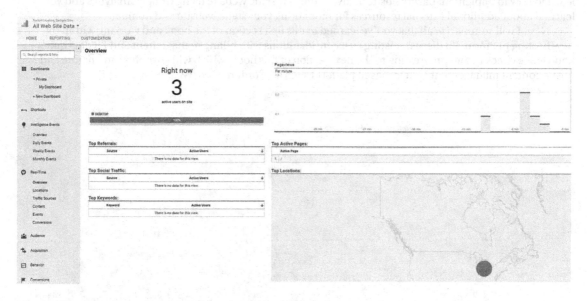

Figure 6-23. *Google Analytics real-time view with new data starting to flow in based on the tracking code added to the static HTML pages*

You now have configured Google Analytics and will be able to get a view of how many visitors come to your website, the pages, geographical and other data about the visitor, and much, much more. Using Google Analytics is a great option to give you a quick way to see how your static website is being used, but the tool is much more powerful than this and can be used to measure marketing campaign effectiveness and visitor preferences and actions in more complex implementations.

Domain Monitoring

Earlier in the chapter, I discussed Route53 monitoring and logging. While this is a great option within the AWS platform, here are some other low-cost and easy-to-implement options.

SiteUptime is a service that will monitor the domain and other services. It has a free monitoring level that will monitor your domain name from eight locations. I have used this service in the past and found that is a great option for basic site/domain monitoring. You can find out more about the product at www.siteuptime.com/compare.php. You can also view an online demo of the product at www.siteuptime.com/users/demo_login.php.

Summary

This chapter covered the basics of logging and monitoring the services that you are currently using within the AWS platform. You learned how to view CloudWatch metrics, set up dashboards for easier viewing, and set up CloudWatch alarms to notify you when services are performing at lower levels than specified. You learned how to implement basic website analytics on your static website using Google Analytics and you learned about additional external resources for monitoring your static website and domain.

Next, I will summarize all that you've learned in this first section of the book and working within this new hosting platform. I'll discuss hosting cost considerations with billing management and I'll do a quick knowledge check before progressing to the next section of this book, which will cover how to migrate and host a content management system-based platform such as WordPress on AWS.

Part 1: Hosting a Static Website in Amazon Web Services Wrap-Up

You covered a lot of ground in the first section of this book, which has been focused on hosting a static content website in Amazon Web Services. You explored AWS and the management console. You set up and managed users, groups, and policies. You explored services like S3 in good detail to give you a solid base to build from and get the most out of AWS as your new hosting platform. You also looked at ways that you can leverage other services that AWS offers to extend the reach and efficiency of your static website, including showing how you can collect data from visitors without even needing a web server! Before you move into the second section of this book, which will focus on how to migrate and host a content management type website on AWS, let's take a moment to reflect on a couple items that I think are important to discuss.

Each summary section of this book has a knowledge check where I summarize the services you've used and give links to additional resources so you can learn more about these services and features. In addition, I will talk about cost considerations for the example site in each section.

Knowledge Check

HTML Static Content: I discussed this early in the book: what we refer to when we talk about static content is a collection of files that produce content that doesn't dynamically change when rendered by a browser. I showed how using scripting languages such as JavaScript can allow you to interact with your website visitors, but the processing of those more dynamic features are actually occurring on the client side of the session and are not being invoked or served by a web server.

AWS IAM (Identity and Access Management): You learned about the Amazon Web Services Free Tier and how you can take advantage of its services at a significantly reduced cost for the first year. As part of this, you signed up with what is referred to as a root account and learned how IAM can help you manage access by creating users, groups, and assigning permissions through policies applied to those users and groups.

AWS S3 (Simple Storage Service): I discussed S3 in detail and how files are organized into buckets and folders. You learned that S3 is an object-based system and, although you can interact with it in a way that is similar to a file system, each item in S3 is an object that has its own properties and can be managed independently. S3 offers storage that is extremely highly available and fault tolerant.

AWS CLI (Command Line Interface): You learned how to install the AWS command line interface and issue commands to perform tasks using your access keys. Using the CLI can be extremely efficient for performing tasks without needing to log into the AWS Console, such as syncing files between a local system and AWS S3.

AWS S3 Static Website Hosting: You learned how to enable website hosting on an S3 bucket and deliver static content such as HTML, CSS, JavaScript, and image files in a browser.

AWS Route53: You learned how to set up a domain name in Route53, Amazon Web Services' highly available DNS service. You learned how to transfer a domain to AWS and how to add DNS entries pointed to your S3 hosted content so that your website content is available to visitors typing in your domain name. Route53 has an SLA of 100%, meaning that it will always be available to serve your DNS requests.

Embedded Content: You learned methods for embedding other content from external sources on your website, including sources such as Facebook and Google Maps.

AWS Lambda: An AWS Compute service that offers users resources to be used without the need for dedicated server infrastructure. You used this service to receive and process form data from API Gateway.

AWS API Gateway: An application program interface that enables you to expose methods to be used to exchange data across the Internet.

AWS CloudWatch: An enterprise monitoring service that is integrated into all AWS services.

Web Analytics: Data collected and reported in an easy-to-consume view. You learned how to set up and use Google Analytics on your static website content.

Cost Considerations

When evaluating a move to a new web hosting company or platform, one of the main considerations is cost. There are many low-cost options available to those looking to host content similar to what has been discussed in this scenario. Most value web hosts also offer some of the services covered in this section, such as domain registration and renewal, DNS services, and more. What I will offer up as a selling point for the AWS platform is the rate at which new services and offerings are released, which is faster than any technology company of this size. Amazon also gives those hosting with them an excellent break at the free-tier level to try all of their services at very little cost. Many of these services may be considered overkill for hosting a static website and simple HTML content, but the cost, high availability, and fault tolerance of the storage that your web files will be hosted on should be an attractive feature when shopping around for a host.

Billing Management

I have not yet discussed AWS billing management, so now is a good time to touch on it briefly. After you log into your account in the AWS Console, you can access the Billing Management screen by clicking your account name as shown in Figure 6-24 and choosing the My Billing Dashboard link.

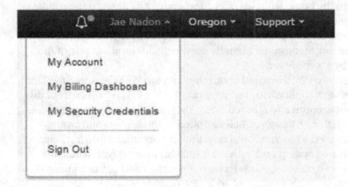

Figure 6-24. *Accessing billing management from within the AWS Console*

Once you access the billing dashboard you will see summary information about your account and the current billing cycle. This view will show you the current invoice amount as well as a predicted invoice total based on service usage to this point in the given billing cycle. An example is shown in Figure 6-25.

Figure 6-25. *Monthly spend summary screen from within the billing dashboard*

You can see that I've already spent $2.42 on the services I'm using with the AWS platform; by the end of the month, the forecasted bill is estimated at $3.29 based on my current usage patterns. You can also see that my previous month billing was $2.01. From within the billing dashboard you can also see all of the account features in the left-hand navigation. You can use Bills and Payment History to view your current and past invoices. You can set CloudWatch alarms to alert you when your spending surpasses a threshold that you can set up under the Budgets link. You have a lot of flexibility and options to manage all the features of your account billing.

For the scenario discussed in this first section, you are using quite a few services. The Bills link in the left-hand navigation will give you a breakdown of your billing by service, as shown in Figure 6-26.

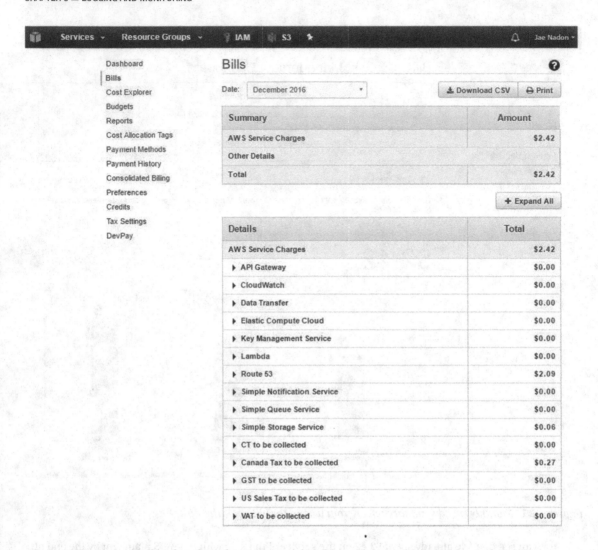

Figure 6-26. *Current bill broken down by services used in the current monthly invoice period*

As you see, the majority of my fees are coming in because I'm using the Route53 DNS service. Amazon charges a premium for this but remember that it has a 100% SLA. If you don't want to spend the extra money, you can register the domain through a value registrar such as GoDaddy and then point the domain at the S3 endpoint DNS name. This model offers little in terms of redundancy or flexibility, though. Having hosted for years at value hosting services, I honestly believe that $3-$5 per month in hosting fees for what you have in terms of available services and features on the AWS platform is well worth it.

PART II

■ ■ ■

Hosting a Platform/CMS Website in Amazon Web Services

CHAPTER 7

■ ■ ■

Platform/CMS Website Scenario

Welcome to Part Two of web hosting and migration using Amazon Web Services. In this chapter, you will explore your second web hosting scenario: the Platform/CMS model. A content management system (CMS) is a platform that is made up of files and data sources, and has user and content management capabilities as it relates to web content. The most popular implementation for a CMS-type website is a weblog (most commonly referred to as a *blog*) where content can be entered via a web UI and that content can be managed via the CMS management interface. Although a blog is a frequent purpose for the deployment of a CMS-type website, other uses are small businesses, special interests, or even corporate web content. At the time of writing this book, three very popular versions of CMS platforms are WordPress, Drupal, and Joomla. This section of the book will give you a good foundation of how to use AWS platform services to be able to host any of these CMS web applications. To do this, I will dedicate the next chapter to discussing the structure of a CMS web application and how you can use AWS to host your site. I will spend some time discussing migration options for those who may have a current blog or website that uses one of the above platforms but want to move it to AWS from their current hosting provider. I will introduce new AWS services and use a few that you're already familiar with from earlier chapters.

Website Content Overview

This hosting scenario will consist of a CMS platform website, which has the function of being set up to host web content related to a (mock) challenge to promote an active lifestyle and healthy living. The main content of the site is the blog content that will be authored by multiple administrators. Visitors will consume that blog content; they can also sign up to join the challenge. Your goals are to set up the CMS platform site on AWS in an easily repeatable fashion, get the main structure of the site administration set up, and post your first message to your visitors. The main areas that you'll focus on for this website scenario are as follows:

- **Home:** The home page will be the landing page for the website. This page will hold basic information for the challenge site, a call to action to sign up for the challenge, and your most recent blog content.

- **Administration:** This section will be secured by the CMS web application and will help you set up your website. Your focus here will be to have a properly configured web server and database to be able to install your CMS platform so that you can access this area and create users as well as manage your content.

- **About:** You'll set up a page that has content linked off the home page that explains more about the challenge and the origin of the idea.

- **Contact:** You'll set up a contact page that has contact details for your Challenge Leaders.

Website Asset Overview

In your example, you will be deploying the WordPress CMS to AWS to host your site. Where possible, I will give examples of migrating content from existing hosting providers and ways to move data between existing CMS sites and the newly deployed site. Figure 7-1 shows the file structure of a WordPress CMS website.

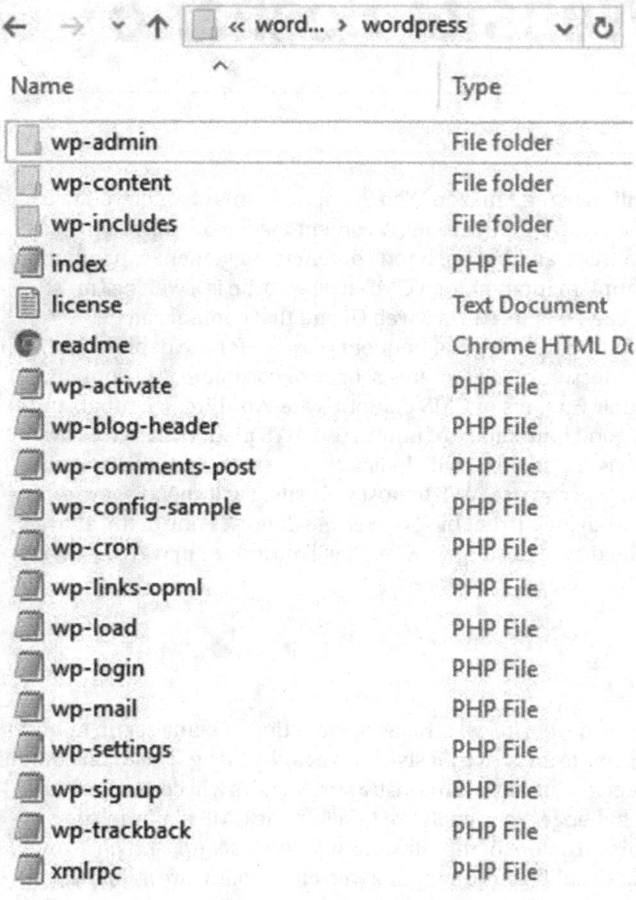

Name	Type
wp-admin	File folder
wp-content	File folder
wp-includes	File folder
index	PHP File
license	Text Document
readme	Chrome HTML Dc
wp-activate	PHP File
wp-blog-header	PHP File
wp-comments-post	PHP File
wp-config-sample	PHP File
wp-cron	PHP File
wp-links-opml	PHP File
wp-load	PHP File
wp-login	PHP File
wp-mail	PHP File
wp-settings	PHP File
wp-signup	PHP File
wp-trackback	PHP File
xmlrpc	PHP File

Figure 7-1. *The directory listing with file structure for your Wordpress CMS website scenario*

As you can see in Figure 7-1, the structure of the website is broken down into folders for the Administration section (`wp-admin`) and main content (`wp-content`). Note that the majority of the files are of type PHP. PHP is a *server-side processing language* that can be embedded into HTML or on its own. For PHP code to be processed the web server must be able to interpret it, which requires web server modules to handle such tasks. Installing a web server and the needed PHP interpreter modules will be part of your installation tasks for getting your CMS up and running. In addition to these requirements, CMS sites also load their web content dynamically (at runtime) from a data source such as a database. You will need to set this up as well; for this need you'll turn to the AWS RDS (Relational Database Service) for assistance. I'll get into detail about the requirements for most CMS-style systems in the next chapter, so I won't go too deep right now.

AWS Services Introduced/Used

The following are the AWS services used in this scenario. Some you have used already; some are new.

- **AWS S3**: Amazon Web Services Simple Storage Service will play another large role in your website hosting implementation. You'll use it to host static files, as you did in the first section of the book, but this time you won't enable the website hosting option on your buckets because they will be read from your web server instead.

- **AWS EC2**: Amazon Web Services EC2 (Elastic Cloud Compute) Service will be used to create a virtual server that will host your web server instance. You will learn how to launch an instance and how you can choose settings such as operating system and size of server. You will see how you can pass along additional parameters at launch time that will install software for you and get the web server up and running as quickly as possible. Within EC2 I will also discuss concepts such as security groups, elastic IP addressing, and elastic block storage.

- **AWS RDS**: Amazon Web Services Relational Database Services is a fully managed service that enables you to leverage AWS infrastructure to host your database services and workloads. In your example, RDS will be used as your primary data source for your CMS application. This will hold data content that relates to website users and post data and other web content such as uploaded images. RDS is not a requirement; you could load your own database server on the same EC2 virtual server instance that your web server application will be running on, but introducing RDS and separating the database server from the web server will give you a better foundation for what will commonly be used in larger scale website implementations. The "fully managed" aspect and benefits of using AWS RDS also include the ability to move many of the administrative overhead tasks such as patching the database server and automatic backups to AWS rather than having you responsible for these tasks.

Summary

This chapter presented the second hosting scenario, the Platform/CMS website. There is a lot of information to cover and I'm ready to get started. Are you? Good; let's begin!

Architecture of a CMS Website

The last chapter introduced the concept of a CMS-based website and how they are used across the Internet today. I discussed that you're going to be using the WordPress CMS in this hosting scenario and deploying it to the AWS platform. In this chapter, I'll talk about the structure and requirements for hosting your CMS. I'll take a look at the architecture and similarities of three major CMS applications. I will walk through, in more detail, the example web scenario and the assets that you will need to set up to be hosted in AWS. Finally, I'll talk about data export and migration options for moving an existing CMS website from a hosting provider to AWS.

CMS Structure Overview and Requirements

Although there are many different CMS applications available, they do have similar structure and make-up in that there will be a collection of static files and application files, and most will require some data source, usually in the form of a database. The three web applications that you'll focus on are WordPress, Drupal, and Joomla. Figure 8-1 shows the file structure comparison across these three CMS platforms.

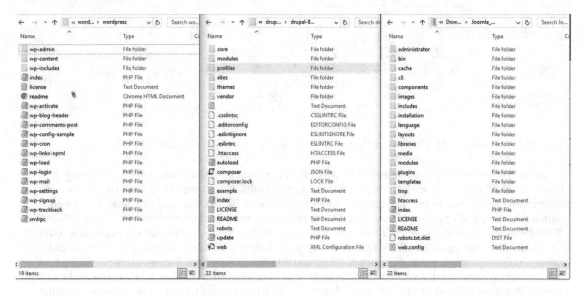

Figure 8-1. A directory listing comparison showing the file structure of WordPress, Drupal, and Joomla

You can see that each of the platforms is made up a collection of files. What you won't see in the file structure is the database; each of these platforms requires the connection to a database to complete the installation. What you do notice is file folders to hold various items such as content, themes, templates, sites, modules, plug-ins, and more. These are common shared features of a CMS. Since the data content is stored in a database and the static files are stored in the file system, it is easy to adjust website attributes such as the template that is used or header images. Each page is dynamically created at runtime by combining static components such as design elements and data components such as post or page content to bring the page to the visitor when they view it via their browser. The main engine that handles the work necessary to construct and display the page is the web server and the application modules/interpreter loaded on the web server. This is why we refer to a CMS as being a "dynamic" website; the content viewed in the browser is assembled and processed at runtime by the web server and the client browser. This differs from static content, which has all processing done via the client browser.

As mentioned, each of these systems requires a data source such as a database to hold application data and the application configuration. The database is a collection of tables and records and data held in each of those records. Figure 8-2 shows the database table structure for a Joomla CMS compared to the table structure for a WordPress CMS as seen from within MySQL Workbench.

Figure 8-2. *Database table structure comparison between Joomla and WordPress CMS*

You will notice similar data tables in the two CMS application data structures shown in Figure 8-2. It is worth noting that these are just example comparisons of table structures of two CMS sites that are very different from each other in terms of features that have been enabled. As your website usage grows and features, plug-ins, and applications are added on to your CMS, additional data tables will be created and will hold configuration and application data for those features/modules. The WordPress example is a simple structure shown after basic installation has been completed. The basic data structure has tables to hold application configuration, posts, comments, users, and additional metadata. I won't dig in very deep on the database configuration at this point other than to say that both examples are MySQL databases and that you can host MySQL databases using AWS RDS. I'll get into much more detail on database server and hosting options in AWS in chapters to come, but for now you just want to understand that there is a requirement for CMS application and content data and that it is stored in structures as shown above.

In addition to the database components, the CMS systems will have a mix of static files and application files. Examples of static files are assets such as images, CSS files, JavaScript files, and HTML files. Application files are things such as PHP files, which are the pages that contain content that will be interpreted and run by the web server.

Architecture Considerations

As I've discussed, the main considerations that you need to think about when choosing a hosting platform for a CMS website are the following:

1. **Static Files**: No specific requirement other than the ability to store these files.

2. **Application Files**: You require a web server and runtime interpreter to be able to dynamically generate the web pages and to handle application functions.

3. **Data Source**: You require a database to store data related to your CMS, including application configuration details and content-related data.

There is more than one way to approach hosting your CMS website. You could architect your site so that all the considerations noted above are loaded on the same web server. This means that that one resource is responsible for running the web server application and application interpreter, would act as a database server hosting the database requirement, and would act as a storage solution to hold the relevant static and application files. For a simple CMS implementation on a website that is either a development site or a low traffic website, this option is perfectly acceptable and simple to set up. An example of this design is shown in Figure 8-3.

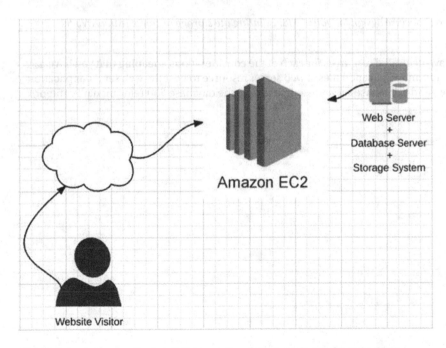

Figure 8-3. *An example of an "all-in-one" architecture design for your CMS*

As your use case moves more towards a production website, especially one that may need to service an unknown amount of website visitors, your architecture design should evolve into a design that isolates the considerations above in a way that offers ease of management and minimizes risk of disruption by adding layers of abstraction. A second option is to separate your static and application files away and not host them on the web server/database server, as shown in Figure 8-4.

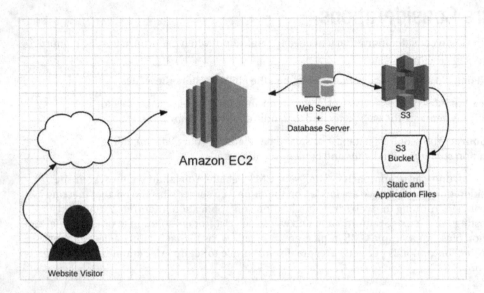

Figure 8-4. *An alternate architecture design for your CMS, isolating the storage resource using AWS S3*

A third option is to have dedicated resources for each of the considerations, meaning that you have a storage resource for the static and application files, a web server resource to host the web server application and application interpreter, and a database server resource to host the database and relevant data content, as shown in Figure 8-5.

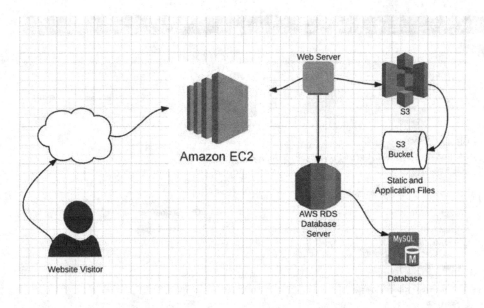

Figure 8-5. *An alternate architecture design for your CMS, isolating the storage resource using AWS S3 and database resources using AWS RDS*

The decision about which design to implement is dependent upon your use case. In this case, you have no idea how busy the website will be in terms of traffic. The first two options may be the most cost effective, but the last option will be the best in terms of scalability if site usage is high. Using AWS "fully managed" services such as AWS RDS for your data layer also allows for storage to scale behind the scenes without your manual intervention. If you used a single EC2 server instance as the resource for all of your CMS considerations, it would mean that you need to allocate more storage if your databases grow to a size where more space is needed. RDS database storage will grow as needed and you will just be charged for what you use.

Before I spend too much time talking about AWS RDS, it is probably best to start with an introduction to the AWS EC2 (Elastic Cloud Compute) service you'll use to stand up your web server.

Introduction to EC2

No matter which architectural design you choose, each choice needs an introduction to AWS EC2 because they all use it as the resource that serves your web server component. Although I will be using a much more efficient method of setting up the example CMS website in later chapters, for this chapter I want to cover the basics of EC2 for those who haven't had a chance to work with it previously. You will focus on launching a web server instance using the AWS Console and you'll learn the commands to do the same work using the AWS CLI.

EC2 is an AWS service that offers virtual server instances to be created as compute resources for your applications. The EC2 service is actually a collection of resources related to the compute instances that you can create, things such as networking resources, storage, and security. In this chapter, you'll focus on the creation of a new instance of a web server with the goal of creating the virtual server instance, installing the web server application, and testing it to see that it correctly serves up the default test page.

The first way that you'll create your web server is to launch it through the AWS Console. After logging into your account, click the Services menu and choose EC2. This will bring you to the EC2 Dashboard shown in Figure 8-6.

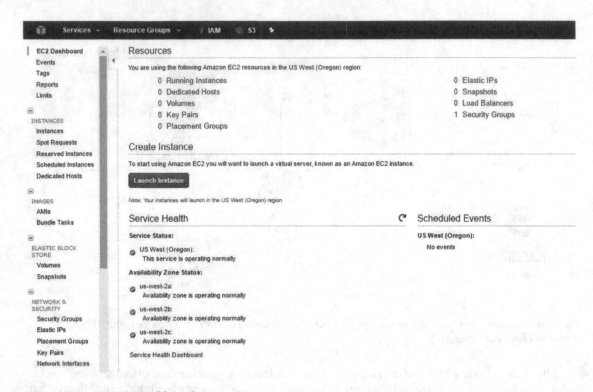

Figure 8-6. *AWS EC2 Dashboard view*

Under the Resources section, you can see that you currently have no instances running. Actually the only thing that you have defined is a single security group. Security groups define inbound and outbound network configurations and are applied to resources in AWS to control access to those resources. As you create your new web server, you will create a new security group for use with your web servers; more on that in a bit.

To launch a new web server, click the Launch Instance button. This will start the EC2 Launch Instance Wizard. The high-level overview of launching an instance is listed in the following steps:

1. Choose an AMI (Amazon Machine Image) to be used as the base template for your web server. For this example, choose the first Amazon Linux AMI by clicking the Select button to the right of the description of the AMI.

2. Choose an instance type. Instance types can be described as the type of virtual server that you would like to process your compute needs. Attributes of instance types are based on the amount of processing resources and optimization. Available instance types range from the very smallest (T2.micro) to multi-processor virtual servers that can handle the largest compute processing. For this example, T2.micro should be selected by default. To move to the next step, click the "Next: Configure Instance Details" option.

3. Configure Instance: This section allows you to add any configuration details to your instance to be evaluated at launch. You'll leave all fields at their default value with exception of the UserData field, which can be found by expanding the Advanced Details section. In the UserData section, enter the text included in this chapter's sample files. The file is called UserData.txt. This file is a bash script

that will be evaluated at launch. The script updates the server, installs the Apache Web Server and PHP applications, adjusts the web server configuration, and creates a sample PHP file to display server information, which will act as a test to confirm that the server is up and interpreting PHP code properly. Once you have copied the text from the UserData.txt file into the text field on the wizard, click the "Next: Add Storage" button.

4. Configure Storage: In this section you can add a storage-related configuration for your instance. For this example, you will leave all the settings at their default, which will add an 8GB SSD storage drive to your instance as the root storage device. Click the "Next: Add Tags" button.

5. Configure Tags: In this section you can optionally add tag information to your instance. This can be helpful when organizing and reporting on many instances. For this example, let's add the value of Web Server under the only tag currently defined, which is the Name tag. Click the "Next: Configure Security Group" button.

6. Configure Security Group: In this section of the wizard, you can apply an existing security group or create a new one to be applied to your instance. Let's leave the option defaulted to create a new security group. Name the security group "Web Server Security Group" and leave the description in place. You should notice that by default the security group created will have port 22, which is the SSH management port (the way you can connect to the server to log in and manage it directly), open to the world. You could limit this to a subset of IP ranges, or only "your own IP" to minimize the security risk of anyone else being able to log in. For this example, since you just want to stand up a web server and don't actually have a current need to log into it for management, let's remove the port 22 entry and add one for port 80 (HTTP). Remove the first rule by clicking the X to the far right of the port 22 rule. Then click the Add Rule button. In the Type drop-down, select HTTP. In the Source drop-down, choose the Anywhere option. This means that anyone will be able to access this server via port 80/standard HTTP calls. Click the "Review and Launch" button.

7. Review and Launch: Review the configuration information you entered in the wizard and then click the Launch button to start the creation of your instance. When prompted about a Key Pair, choose the drop-down and select "Proceed without a key pair" option, select the acknowledge checkbox, and click the Launch Instances button.

After you have completed these steps, your web server instance will begin to launch in the background. You can check on the status of the launch by browsing back to the EC2 Dashboard via Services ➤ EC2. Once here, click the Instances link in the left-hand navigation to see a list of your instances. You should see something similar to what is displayed in Figure 8-7.

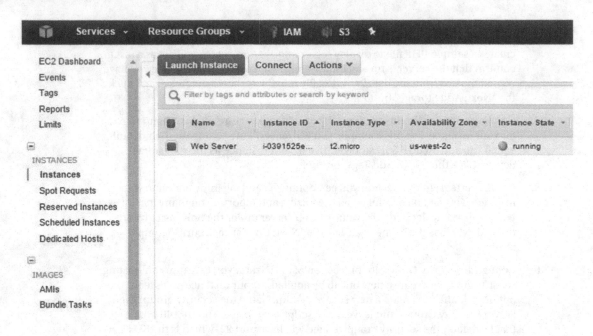

Figure 8-7. *AWS EC2 instances view with your newly launched web server instance*

Near the middle bottom of the screen you should see text for "Public DNS," which is the DNS name that can be used in a web browser to access your new instance. Place the code below in a web browser address bar and substitute the section `<public.dns.amazonaws.com>` with the value of your instance's public DNS. From Figure 8-7, the address I will use is `http://ec2-35-163-74-240.us-west-2.compute.amazonaws.com/phpinfo.php`:

`http://<public.dns.amazonaws.com>/phpinfo.php`

If all is successful, you should be greeted by a page similar to Figure 8-8.

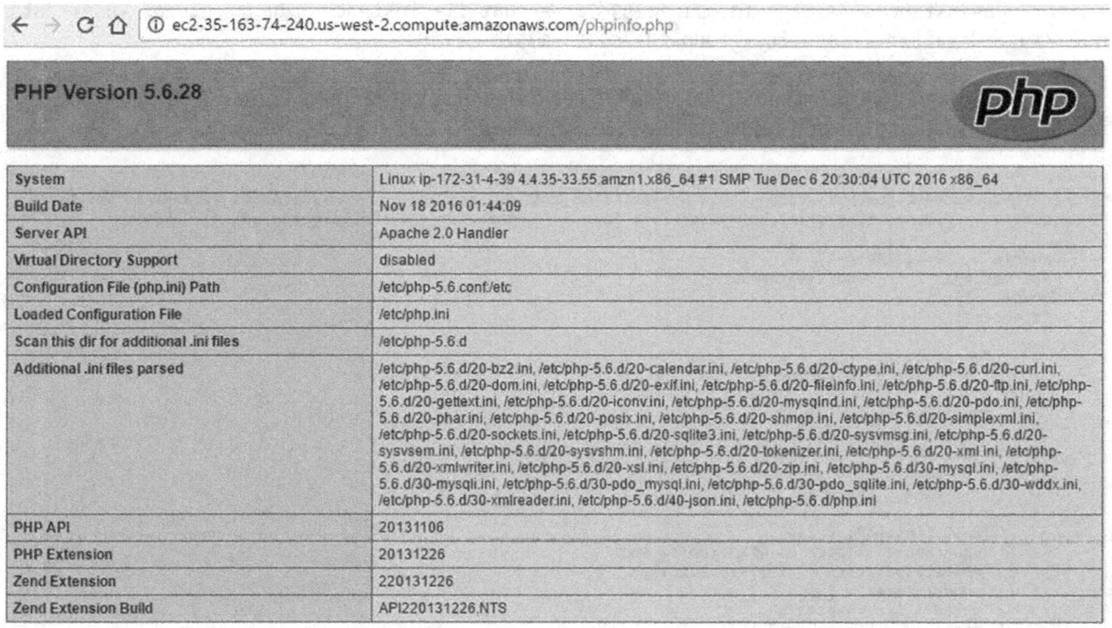

Figure 8-8. *Accessing your new web server instance via the public DNS name and PHP Server Information page*

As you can see, not only do you have a web server responding to your request, but the page verifies that this web server can interpret PHP code, which means that the Apache Web Server and PHP were loaded on the server as specified in the User Data configuration during your instance launch! Although the options that you chose through this setup don't allow you to easily manage this server instance, it does show how easy it is to launch a web server instance and to specify launch configuration to load applications and perform tasks at time of launch.

Let's get rid of this instance from your account by heading back to the Instances window in the EC2 service. Select the single instance that you just created and click the Actions button. From this menu, choose Instance State and click the Terminate option. This will let you know that you're about to terminate the instance and remove the attached storage. Confirm that this is what you want to do and click the "Yes, Terminate" button.

Launching an EC2 Instance with AWS CLI

The true power and flexibility of AWS as a platform is that anything that can be done using the AWS Console can be done using the command line interface. Your CLI should still be configured up to your AWS account from the S3 sync example that you performed in the first section of this book. To launch an EC2 instance, open a command prompt window and browse to the directory where you have the userdata.txt file used in the above example. Enter the code below to launch an EC2 instance in your account. The code below calls to the AWS CLI; tells it to use the EC2 service; runs the run-instances command; passes the AMI ID of the Amazon Linux AMI at the time of the writing of this book; creates one instance; uses the instance type of t2.micro; passes the userdata.txt file which loads the Apache Web Server and PHP modules; and applies the ID of the Web Server Security Group that you created earlier. Note that you will need to adjust the security group ID to match the one in your account since the one in the command below is specific to my account and security group that was created earlier. To obtain your security group ID, browse to the EC2 Dashboard in the AWS Console and under the Network and Security link in the navigation pane, click the Security Groups option. From within this view, click the name "Web Server Security Group" and you will find the security group ID in the Description pane. It will be formatted similar to "sg-12345678".

```
aws ec2 run-instances --image-id ami-1e299d7e --count 1 --instance-type t2.micro --user-data
file://userdata.txt --security-group-ids sg-5381752b
```

Once the above code is executed, you should receive metadata information about the new instance back in the command prompt window, as shown in Figure 8-9.

```
C:\Users\thinkNadon\Documents\Writing\2016\Apress\Nadon_Ch08_Figures>aws ec2 run-instances --image-id ami-1e299d
7e --count 1 --instance-type t2.micro --user-data file://userdata.txt --security-group-ids sg-5381752b
{
    "OwnerId": "704427294249",
    "ReservationId": "r-003dd5a451e641a67",
    "Groups": [],
    "Instances": [
        {
            "Monitoring": {
                "State": "disabled"
            },
            "PublicDnsName": "",
            "RootDeviceType": "ebs",
            "State": {
                "Code": 0,
                "Name": "pending"
            },
            "EbsOptimized": false,
            "LaunchTime": "2017-03-07T01:09:54.000Z",
            "PrivateIpAddress": "172.31.23.221",
            "ProductCodes": [],
            "VpcId": "vpc-9e9b8dfa",
            "StateTransitionReason": "",
            "InstanceId": "i-0cf9e06d00de539e5",
            "ImageId": "ami-1e299d7e",
            "PrivateDnsName": "ip-172-31-23-221.us-west-2.compute.internal",
            "SecurityGroups": [
                {
                    "GroupName": "Web Server Security Group",
                    "GroupId": "sg-5381752b"
                }
            ],
            "ClientToken": "",
            "SubnetId": "subnet-86576ee2",
            "InstanceType": "t2.micro",
            "NetworkInterfaces": [
```

Figure 8-9. *Metadata is returned from the AWS CLI command, showing information about your newly launched instance*

You can now go back into the console to grab the Public DNS name for this newly created instance. Or you can use the CLI to get information about your instances by using the following command:

```
aws ec2 describe-instances
```

If you place the Public DNS in a web browser and add the PHP page name as you did in the section above, you should be presented with the PHP Server Information page, only this time you didn't have to walk through the graphical wizard.

The benefit in doing something like this is that the commands used are easily adapted to include full virtual server instance configuration and can then be saved for safe storage just in case you ever need to recreate the instance quickly in the future.

A couple things about the command you used above. First, the term "AMI ID" may not be something that you are familiar with, and as I mentioned, the ID associated with the Amazon Linux AMI will change as that server image is updated or patched. An AMI is an Amazon Machine Image, and you can think of each of them as a unique server templates to be used to launch the instances you request. AMIs are used to launch new instances, and you can also create your own custom AMI from an existing running AWS EC2 instance, allowing you to "clone" an existing server and its configuration much easier than if it were a physical server located in a data center. Each AMI has an identifier, the AMI ID, which is used to reference it.

"Spring Challenge" WordPress Site

Now that you know a bit about how you can stand up a web server to be used in AWS EC2, let's introduce the sample site that will be used in the rest of this web hosting scenario. You have set up a site on `http://wordpress.com`, which is the commercial site for WordPress. The company offers free and premium hosting of the WordPress CMS platform sites on their own infrastructure. In this case, WordPress itself will host all static/application files and databases, and act as a web server host for your site.

I've opted for the "free" site option to use an example of a site that is hosted external to AWS, but one that you'll migrated over to being hosted on WordPress using AWS Platform resources. Figure 8-10 shows the home page of the WordPress site that I have set up.

Figure 8-10. *The sample site used in the CMS example: a site hosted at wordpress.com for your "Spring Challenge" website*

This website is a simple WordPress site with a home page, about page, contact page, and blog. Figure 8-11 shows you logged into the administration part of the WordPress CMS for your sample site.

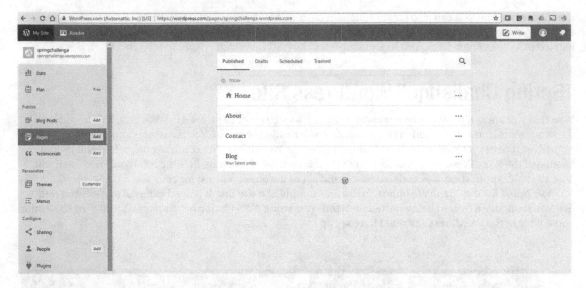

Figure 8-11. *The WordPress Administrative Interface for your sample site*

This website will be the one that migrates to AWS. In the next section, I'll talk about possible migration paths for moving CMS websites to new hosting providers and I'll provide an export file of this sample site that can be used for the rest of this section. You may want to set up your own wordpress.com site or maybe you already have one that you're looking to migrate. I will include the steps necessary to get the export file in the next section.

Migration Paths for CMS Sites

As I've discussed in this chapter, the components and considerations when hosting a CMS website break down into the static files, application files, and related database content. This means that if you're interested in performing a migration of your CMS site from one hosting provider to another, you need to find a way to move these things to your new provider.

In the best case scenario, you have access to all of the files and database at your current host, but there will be times when you don't have access. If you do have access to the files, you can copy them locally using an FTP program. If you have access to the database server, you can likely perform a database backup and possibly restore this database at your new hosting provider.

In this example, you have a hosted version of a WordPress site at wordpress.com. In this case, you have no access to the file system and no access to the database server. I consider this one of the most limiting in terms of options, but this makes it a good example because the methods used here will be able to be used by anyone hosting a WordPress site, regardless of whether they have access to the file system files and database.

For your example site, you'll go ahead and log into your account at wordpress.com and you'll access the WordPress Administration interface for your WordPress site. Once logged in, you'll click the Settings option in the left-hand navigation. If you have a self-hosted WordPress site or a WordPress site hosted at another provider such as GoDaddy, the steps will be the same. The Administrative interface will be available at your WordPress URL with "/wp-admin" added on to the URL. You will need to know your administrative account and password to log in.

Once on the Settings screen in the WordPress Administrative interface, you should see an option for Export, as shown in the top navigation bar in Figure 8-12.

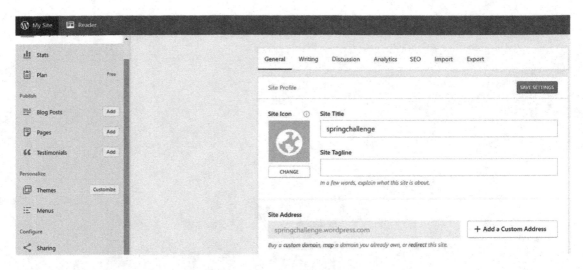

Figure 8-12. *The Wordpress Administrative Interface showing the Settings screen*

Click the Export menu option. From here you can choose which data you want to export. In this example, I'm going to leave the default settings alone and just click the Export All button. When completed, you'll see a message that a download link has been sent to your email account. Log into your email and click the link in the email to download the export file. The file will be in zip compressed format and will contain an XML file with your post data. It is worth noting that images and other assets attached to your post will need to be downloaded from the existing site and uploaded to the new one separately. I've attached this sample file in this chapter's folder under the name sampleXMLexport.xml.

Joomla doesn't have an export option within the interface like WordPress does, but the methods to migrate to a Joomla site are similar in that you move the static and application files and database via methods that are available to you. Here is a link to the Joomla documentation site for the migration steps: https://docs.joomla.org/Copying_a_Joomla_website.

Drupal has a module called Node Export that can be loaded to allow for migration between Drupal sites. Methods discussed earlier will also work, including a full backup and restore of the database file and copying over the existing static and application file system to the new provider.

Summary

This chapter talked about the components of a CMS website and considerations encountered when choosing to migrate or host such a website. I gave a quick introduction to AWS EC2 and how to launch a virtual server instance via the AWS Console as well as via the command line interface. You previewed the wordpress.com hosted site that you'll be working to migrate to AWS. Finally, you learned about migration options for these CMS platforms. In the next chapter, you're going to focus on the storage resources that you'll use for your website's static and application files.

CHAPTER 9

■ ■ ■

Static and Dynamic Storage Options in AWS

The last chapter focused on the architecture and components of a CMS website. I discussed that one of the main components that you need to plan for is static content and application file storage. In this chapter, you'll go over your options for using AWS S3 for storing your static and dynamic files. You'll also learn about EC2 EBS (Elastic Block Storage) and how it can be attached to your virtual server instance but can persist even if the virtual service instance goes away. Having data on EC2 EBS storage enables some storage and server management, such as being able to move storage between virtual server instances and creating snapshot backups of your website data.

Static Hosting in S3, Revisited

As you likely remember from the first web hosting scenario, AWS S3 is an object-based storage system that is a low cost, unlimited storage, and high availability solution for storing your files. In the first scenario, I showed how you can use S3 to host your static HTML, CSS, and JavaScript files that make up your web content. You created S3 buckets, attached policies to control permissions to your bucket and objects within them, and walked through the setup of S3's static website hosting option for S3 buckets.

Now that you're looking at your second hosting scenario, the CMS website, you may be wondering how this service can fit in to this scenario. Of course, you could still use it to host your static content such as images, but a core component of a CMS website is the ability for users to upload content. This uploaded content needs a place to be stored and retrieved, and using S3 is a great option for such content.

The benefits in putting this type of content in S3 are multi-fold. First, S3 is highly available storage and uses a more robust infrastructure than hosting your data anywhere else. Second, using a storage source that is detached from the CMS installation means that it will offer greater portability. If, for some reason, you need to change where your CMS website is hosted, you could set it up and point it to the same storage which is resting securely in S3. A third benefit is that you can leverage another AWS service, CloudFront, to act as your content distribution network to deliver your content globally in a low-latency fashion. CloudFront copies the S3 content you choose to AWS Edge locations; when visitors request content from your website, it will deliver that content via the closest Edge location to them, thereby giving that visitor the best possible experience in terms of content latency and network delivery. Although CloudFront and its features are outside the scope of this chapter, I will cover the setup in detail later in the book.

There are multiple ways to set up your CMS to use S3 as a storage source. The first is to manually edit configuration files. Using this option, you can create an S3 bucket to hold your content, copy the content manually to S3, make the content public, and update the configuration in your CMS to point to your S3 bucket for chosen storage options. An easier method exists for some CMS platforms. WordPress, for

© Jason Nadon 2017
J. Nadon, *Website Hosting and Migration with Amazon Web Services*, DOI 10.1007/978-1-4842-2589-9_9

example, has an Amazon Web Services plug-in available at `https://wordpress.org/plugins/amazon-web-services/` that will allow you to enter bucket details and security credentials and will update the WordPress configuration files to use that S3 bucket for any future upload content.

Joomla CMS has several extensions available that deliver similar results. One of the popular choices created by developer JoomlArt is JA Amazon S3, which is available at `https://extensions.joomla.org/extension/ja-amazon-s3`. This extension allows for multiple accounts and is quite useful when you're hosting multiple Joomla websites off the same servers.

Drupal CMS has similar extensions that allow users to extend the platform to use S3 as a file system for additional storage. For more information about one of the extensions, go to `www.drupal.org/project/s3fs`.

Dynamic Hosting in AWS

As discussed, separation of CMS content from the web application has benefits in terms of portability and redundancy. When you refer to dynamic file hosting, what you're talking about is the application files that are used by the web server software. You may remember from the previous chapter that your CMS components include the web server which interprets the PHP code at runtime and the PHP code itself can be referred to as the dynamic/application files. They can be located on the same storage as the web server, or can be detached from that file system by being located on an external system. You could use S3 for this, but I suggest another method: using AWS EC2's volume storage system EBS to host your dynamic/application files. In the solution files that you will share in later chapters, you will use EBS to host the CMS application files separate from your web server, which will use your virtual server instance ephemeral storage. Ephemeral storage is local file system storage that is attached to your virtual server instance at launch. You may remember that in the last chapter when you created a new instance it was created with an 8GB storage volume. This volume was ephemeral in nature, which means that when the server instance is terminated, the storage volume and the data on it are destroyed. Using an EBS storage volume allows you the opportunity to load data on this volume that can persist, even if the virtual server instance is lost/terminated. This can enabled you to rebuild or upgrade your web server without having to reload CMS specific files and data. You can also easily copy this volume storage to a second copy that allows you to upgrade your CMS separately and then cutover to the new version when ready.

Amazon EBS Volume Storage

EBS can be used as volume storage and can be attached to any virtual server instance. Although you'll handle this in a much easier fashion in your sample stack creation script later in this section, it is worth going over the basics of how a volume is created and attached to an instance.

Amazon EBS Volumes are located under EC2. You can access or create volumes by logging into the AWS Console and clicking the Services menu and then choosing EC2. From the EC2 Dashboard, click the Volumes link in the left-hand navigation under the Elastic Block Store section.

Click the Create Volume button to launch the EBS Create Volume Wizard. The options that you can select in this one-screen wizard are shown in Figure 9-1.

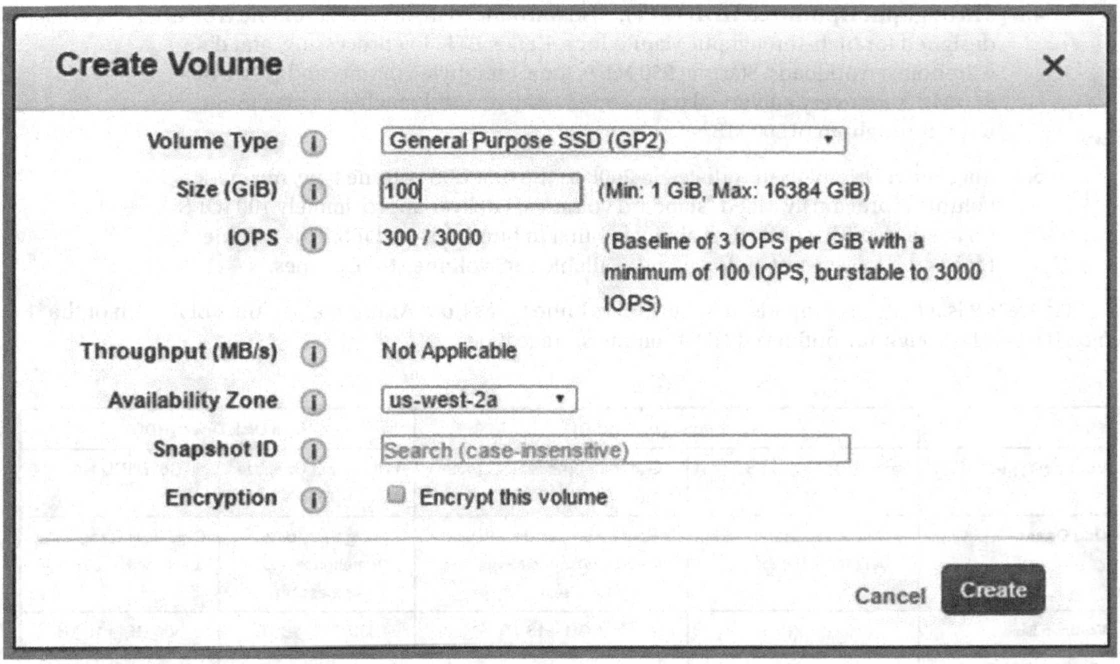

Figure 9-1. *The EC2 EBS Create Volume Wizard*

The options available to you in this screen are to choose the type of volume, size, speed/throughput (if applicable based on type chosen), location, snapshot information, and encryption configuration. Let's discuss these options in a bit more detail.

The types of volumes supported in EBS are described in the following list:

1. **General Purpose SSD (GP2):** General purpose volumes provide the ability to burst to 3000 IOPS per volume, independent of volume size, to meet the performance needs of most applications and also deliver a consistent baseline of 3 IOPS/GiB. This is the default selection and, in most cases, the best choice for applications like CMS platforms.

2. **Provisioned IOPS SSD (IO1):** Provisioned IOPS volumes can deliver up to 20000 IOPS and are best for EBS-optimized instances. This option is best when you have selected an EBS-optimized virtual server instance. In the last chapter, you selected a t2.micro, which is not an EBS-optimized instance type. More information on EBS-optimized instances can be found at http://docs.aws.amazon.com/AWSEC2/latest/UserGuide/EBSOptimized.html#ebs-optimization-support.

3. **Cold HDD (SC1):** A fairly new, price conscious volume option, introduced early in 2016. Designed for workloads similar to those for a throughput-optimized HDD that is accessed less frequently. Starts at 80 MB/s for a 1 terabyte volume, and grows by 80 MB/s for every additional provisioned terabyte until reaching a maximum burst throughput of 250 MB/s.

4. **Throughput Optimized HDD (ST1)**: Also introduced in 2016, this volume type is designed for high-throughput MapReduce, Kafka, ETL, log processing, and data warehouse workloads. Starts at 250 MB/s for a 1 terabyte volume, and grows by 250 MB/s for every additional provisioned terabyte until reaching a maximum burst throughput of 500 MB/s.

5. **Magnetic**: Originally introduced in 2008 as the first EBS volume type, magnetic volumes (previously called "standard volumes") deliver approximately 100 IOPS on average, with a best effort ability to burst to hundreds of IOPS. This volume type is the lowest cost option of the available EBS volume storage types.

Figure 9-2 is a feature comparison of the EBS volume types from Amazon at the time of launch of the cold HDD and throughput-optimized HDD volume storage types.

	Solid State Drive (SSD)		Hard Disk Drive (HDD)	
Volume Type	Provisioned IOPS SSD (io1)	General Purpose SSD (gp2)	Throughput Optimized HDD (st1)	Cold HDD (sc1)
Use Cases	I/O intensive NoSQL and relational databases	Boot volumes, low-latency interactive applications, dev, test	Big data, data warehouses, log processing	Colder data requiring fewer scans per day
Volume Size	4 GB – 16 TB	1 GB – 16 TB	500 GB – 16 TB	500 GB – 16 TB
Max IOPS/Volume	20,000 (16 KB I/O size)	10,000 (16 KB I/O size)	500 (1 MB I/O size)	250 (1 MB I/O size)
Max IOPS/Instance (using multiple volumes)	48,000	48,000	48,000	48,000
Max Throughput/Volume	320 MB/s	160 MB/s	500 MB/s	250 MB/s
Max Throughput/Instance	800 MB/s	800 MB/s	800 MB/s	800 MB/s
Price	$0.125/GB-month + $.065/provisioned IOPS/month	$0.100/GB-month	$.045/GB-month	$.025/GB-month
Dominant Performance Attribute	IOPS	IOPS	MB/s	MB/s

Figure 9-2. *AWS EBS volume storage type comparison chart from AWS documentation, available at* https://aws.amazon.com/blogs/aws/amazon-ebs-update-new-cold-storage-and-throughput-options/

In the example for this volume creation, choose "Magnetic" as your volume type with a size of 10GB. Choosing this volume types makes the IOPS and throughput options "Not Applicable" because this is not configurable for this type of volume.

Leave the location of the volume set to the default availability zone. It is important to note that volumes are created in availability zones within a region and are limited to use in the region scope. That means a volume created in the US-West-2 region cannot be accessed from the US-East-1 region.

Snapshot IDs allow you to select from stored volume snapshots stored (and publically available/or within your account) and use one as an "image" for the volume to be created from. An example when you might have a need for this is if you had an existing volume that needed to be grown in size. Taking a snapshot of that EBS volume and then creating a new larger volume that is based on the snapshot of your previous volume will copy all of the information that is in the snapshot to the new volume. This can be quite handy and is something that takes a large amount of time to accomplish outside of the AWS platform! Figure 9-3 shows the snapshots available to my account at the time of writing. For this example, however, let's not choose a snapshot to be used as an image.

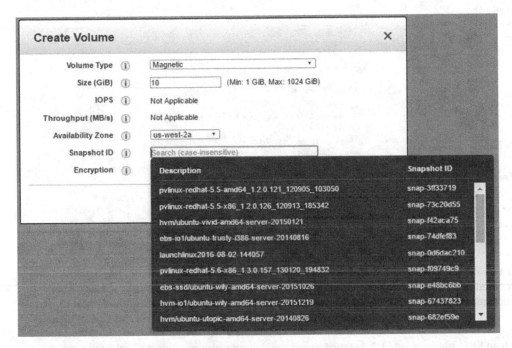

Figure 9-3. *AWS EBS volume storage snapshots available to my account that could be used as an image upon which to base a new volume*

The last option for you to select in the New Volume Creation Wizard is whether you want to encrypt the volume or not. Volumes that are created from encrypted snapshots are automatically encrypted, and volumes that are created from unencrypted snapshots are automatically unencrypted. If no snapshot is selected, you can choose to encrypt the volume. Encryption offers a way to encrypt the data stored on the volumes using AWS Key Management Service. When encryption is used, data stored on the volume, data moving between the instance, and the volume and snapshots are encrypted. Since this is just an example, let's not enable encryption, but for your CMS platform implementation I do suggest using encryption wherever possible as an additional security measure and way to protect against data theft.

Now that all options have been chosen, click the Create button to start the volume creation. Within a few moments you'll see your new volume being created and within a minute or two the state should be updated to "Available," as shown in Figure 9-4.

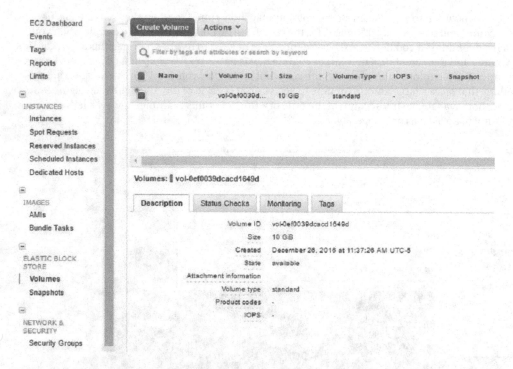

Figure 9-4. *Your newly created EBS volume is now listed as "Available" under the EC2 Volumes screen*

With the volume now being in an available state, you can attach it to a virtual server instance. By using the script provided in the last chapter, you can easily launch a new instance to attach this volume. After running the command using the AWS CLI, you can check in EC2 under the Instances menu option to see your new virtual instance starting up. Once it has moved into the "Running" state, you can attach the new volume.

To attach an EBS volume to an EC2 instance, select the Volumes menu option and select the volume you would like to work with by clicking on the Volume ID. Click the Actions button near the top of the screen and choose Attach Volume. This will bring up the screen shown in Figure 9-5 where you can select the instance that you want to attach the volume to and then press the Attach button.

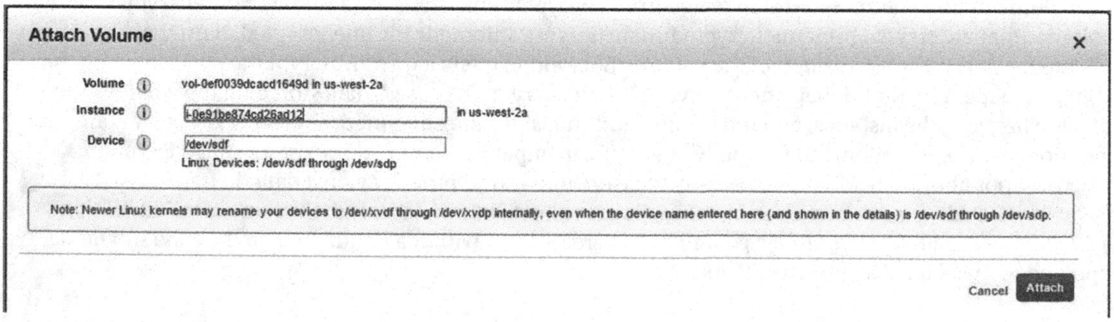

Figure 9-5. *Choose a virtual server instance and attach your volume*

The attach process will usually take less than a minute; once it has been attached you will see that the status is "OK" and the relevant attachment information on the Volumes information screen. This volume is now attached to this instance and available for data storage use.

From the Volumes screen you will also notice that there are tabs that hold additional information about your volumes, including the Monitoring tab which has quite a few CloudWatch metrics to give you a good indication of how your volume is performing. As with all CloudWatch metrics, you have the ability to set up alerting if there are specific metrics that you would like to monitor closely and be alerted if thresholds that you define are surpassed. Figure 9-6 shows the standard monitoring metrics included for EBS volumes.

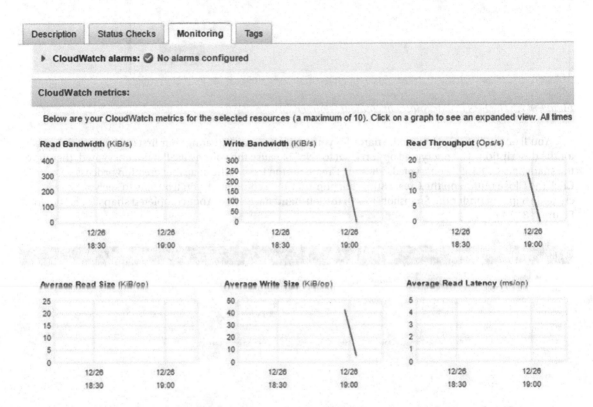

Figure 9-6. *The EBS Volume Monitoring tab showing default CloudWatch metrics being gathered*

The last action that you'll take on this newly created volume is to take a backup of the volume, which is known as a snapshot. From the Volumes screen, select the volume that you just created by clicking the Volume ID. Click the Actions button near the top of the screen and select Create Snapshot to launch the Snapshot configuration screen shown in Figure 9-7.

Create Snapshot   ✕

Volume	ⓘ	vol-0ef0039dcacd1649d
Name	ⓘ	
Description	ⓘ	
Encrypted	ⓘ	No

Cancel   Create

Figure 9-7. *The EBS Create Snapshot configuration screen*

You'll enter TestSnapshot for the name for your snapshot and "Creating your first backup of a volume" for the description. The encrypted option is set to "No" because the volume itself it not encrypted, therefore the snapshots will not be encrypted. Click the Create button to start the snapshot creation process. Click the Close button on the Create Snapshot pop-up. Once completed, you'll be able to see your newly created snapshot under the Snapshots link in the left-hand navigation. Your completed snapshot is shown in Figure 9-8.

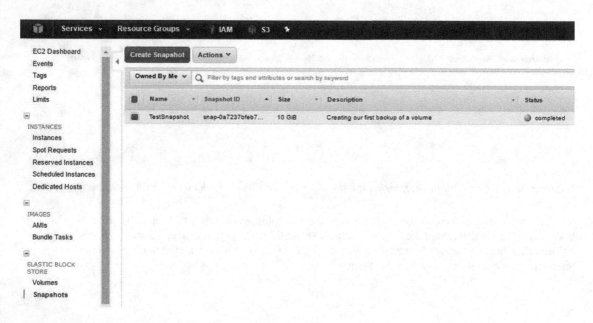

Figure 9-8. *The EBS Snapshots screen with your newly created volume snapshot selected*

Summary

This chapter discussed options for storage when dealing with your CMS platform scenario. AWS has many options when it comes to storage and the management of your data. You added a new tool to your arsenal in the form of EC2's EBS volumes. AWS also has data lifecycle management options for data stored in S3 that you'll explore further in your third hosting scenario. Now that I have talked about storage for the first two components of your CMS website scenario (static and application files), in the next chapter I'll address the database solution that you'll use for your scenario: AWS RDS.

CHAPTER 10

■ ■ ■

Database Services in AWS

In the last chapter, I gave an overview of storage options available for static and application data files for the CMS website. I revisited AWS S3, introduced EC2 EBS volume options, and discussed how detached storage can simplify the management of your CMS, improve performance, and make your website more fault tolerant. Isolating services using the AWS platform also places the responsibility for availability of the core services such as compute and storage into the hands of Amazon, who has mastered the challenge of scaling architecture and service availability. In this chapter, I am going to talk about database services available in AWS. I'll introduce AWS RDS, discuss database types that can be hosted on RDS, walk through the manual and scripted setup of RDS services, and introduce remote management tools that may help with the administration of your RDS data source.

AWS Relational Database Service

Amazon Web Services offers several services for your data requirements. One of the most popular options is a fully managed relational database management system (RDBMS) that allows you to use AWS to host several different types of relational databases. Relational databases allow for the organization of a collection of data in a hierarchy that consists of databases, tables, records, and cells that contain data that can easily and efficiently be accessed, searched, and indexed.

AWS also offers data services that are outside of the RDBMS architecture, like DynamoDB (a No-SQL based system), RedShift (a data warehousing system), and ElastiCache (an in-memory caching system) to help optimize and organize any data that you may need to manage.

AWS RDS is similar to other AWS services in that it is easy to get started with; since it is a fully managed service, there is not a lot of work to be done to keep it up and running after configuration. This allows you to focus on the management of the data within the database rather than the management of the database service and server. Amazon has designed this service with scalability and availability in mind and although I'll be covering simple, single availability-zone installations in this chapter, I'll look at the highly available fault-tolerant and recovery benefits in later chapters in the book.

Database Hosting Using RDS

AWS RDS can be accessed by logging into the AWS Console, clicking the Services menu, and under the Database section, choosing RDS. As you've done with other services, you can also add this service to the quick start menu at the top of the browser as a way to quickly access this service in future visits.

© Jason Nadon 2017

J. Nadon, *Website Hosting and Migration with Amazon Web Services*, DOI 10.1007/978-1-4842-2589-9_10

If this is the first time that you have accessed RDS, you'll be greeted with the service welcome page that has overview information about the service and several calls to action to get started using the service and creating your first database.

Before you get start creating your first database, let's discuss the different types of databases that can be hosted on AWS RDS.

1. **Amazon Aurora**: A MySQL-compatible, AWS-optimized database service developed and supported by Amazon AWS.

2. **MySQL**: A very popular open source database format. RDS offers a hosted version of the MySQL Community Edition server.

3. **MariaDB**: A popular, MySQL-compatible, open source database format. RDS offers a hosted version of the MariaDB Community Edition server.

4. **PostgreSQL**: A popular, scalable, open source database. Designed for high volume workloads.

5. **Oracle**: Designed for large, mission-critical applications. Many complex software applications rely on Oracle Database Services as their data provider. AWS RDS supports multiple versions of Oracle Server, including Enterprise Edition, Standard Edition, Standard Edition One, and Standard Edition Two.

6. **Microsoft SQL Server (MSSQL)**: Designed for medium and large mission-critical applications. Many software applications rely on Microsoft SQL Server Database Services as their data provider, especially Microsoft products such as SharePoint. AWS RDS supports multiple versions of SQL Server, including SQL Server Express, Web Server Edition, Standard Edition, and Enterprise Edition.

For your CMS website, MySQL or Amazon Aurora are the most likely choices, mainly because all of the CMS applications that you're utilizing (WordPress, Drupal, and Joomla) support MySQL as the source of their data. Amazon Aurora is optimized for the AWS platform, but it also ineligible for the AWS free tier use, so for your example and for a test implementation, I recommend using MySQL as the database engine.

Database Creation Using the AWS Console

From the AWS RDS welcome screen, click the Get Started button. If the welcome screen hasn't been displayed in your account, you can click the Instances link in the left-hand navigation and then choose the Launch DB Instance button to start the New Database Instance Wizard.

In the first step of the wizard, you'll be asked to select your database engine, as shown in Figure 10-1. For this example, select MySQL as your database engine by clicking the MySQL tab and then clicking the Select button to move to the second step of the wizard.

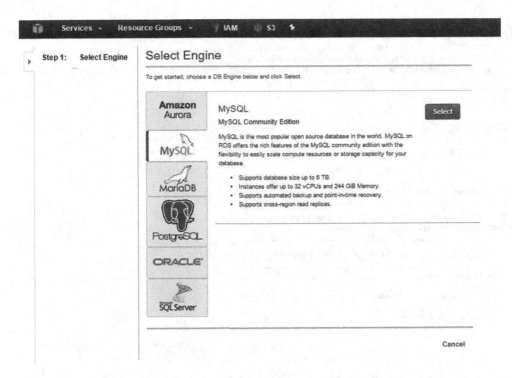

Figure 10-1. *The first step of the Launch DB Instance wizard, showing the selection of a database engine*

In the second step of the wizard, you will be asked whether your MySQL implementation is going to be used for production or for dev/test use. Let's choose the radio button for dev/test because you want to set up a basic instance that will allow you to see the features of RDS, but this implementation won't be used for your production website. Once you have selected the radio button under Dev/Test for MySQL, click the Next button to move on to the next step.

In the third step of the process you'll specify your database instance configuration. In this case, you're talking about an "instance" as a "server instance," so you'll need to choose what size of server to run and how much space to allocate to the instance. Since you want to stay within the parameters of the AWS free tier pricing, check the checkbox labeled "only show options eligible for RDS free tier."

Fill in the remaining fields as shown in Figure 10-2, replacing the DB instance identifier with one of your own and choosing an administrative username and password. One completed, click the Next Step button to move to the final step of the wizard.

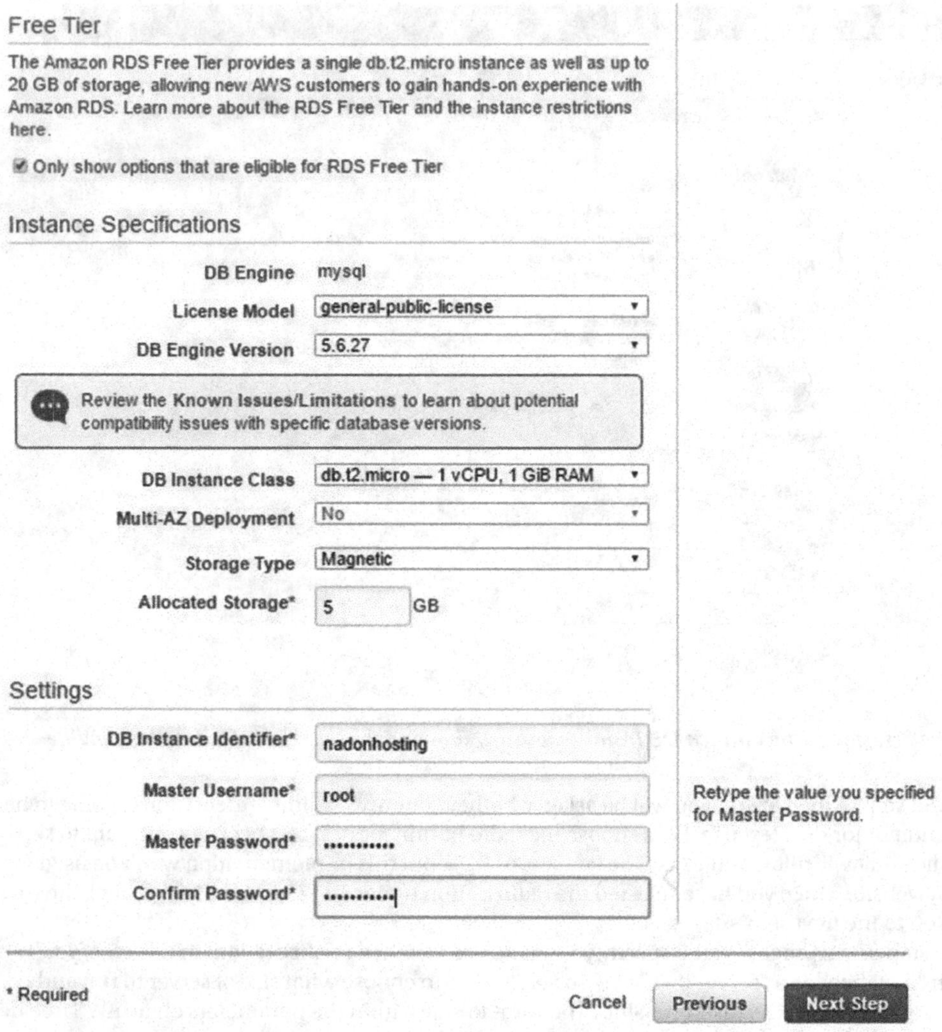

Free Tier

The Amazon RDS Free Tier provides a single db.t2.micro instance as well as up to 20 GB of storage, allowing new AWS customers to gain hands-on experience with Amazon RDS. Learn more about the RDS Free Tier and the instance restrictions here.

☑ Only show options that are eligible for RDS Free Tier

Instance Specifications

DB Engine	mysql
License Model	general-public-license ▾
DB Engine Version	5.6.27 ▾

💬 Review the Known Issues/Limitations to learn about potential compatibility issues with specific database versions.

DB Instance Class	db.t2.micro — 1 vCPU, 1 GiB RAM ▾
Multi-AZ Deployment	No ▾
Storage Type	Magnetic ▾
Allocated Storage*	5 GB

Settings

DB Instance Identifier*	nadonhosting	
Master Username*	root	Retype the value you specified for Master Password.
Master Password*	●●●●●●●●●●●	
Confirm Password*	●●●●●●●●●●●	

* Required   Cancel   [Previous]   [Next Step]

Figure 10-2. The third step of the Launch DB Instance wizard, showing the database instance configuration details

In the final step, you will specify advanced configuration details for your database instance. You will specify which network (VPC) to install the instance into (in your case, you'll leave this set to the default) and the security group to be used (leave this set to create a new group as part of the instance creation and leave the publically accessible option set to "Yes" so that you can manage your instance from client tools on your local computer). You will leave the database name blank so that no database is set up at the time of instance creation.

Now you can configure one of the benefits of AWS RDS: automatic backups. You can select a retention period and maintenance window of when to perform the backups. You can enable enhanced monitoring if desired, and lastly you can have AWS RDS perform upgrades to your version of MySQL if preferred. Select the options shown in Figure 10-3 and click the Launch DB Instance button to start the creation process.

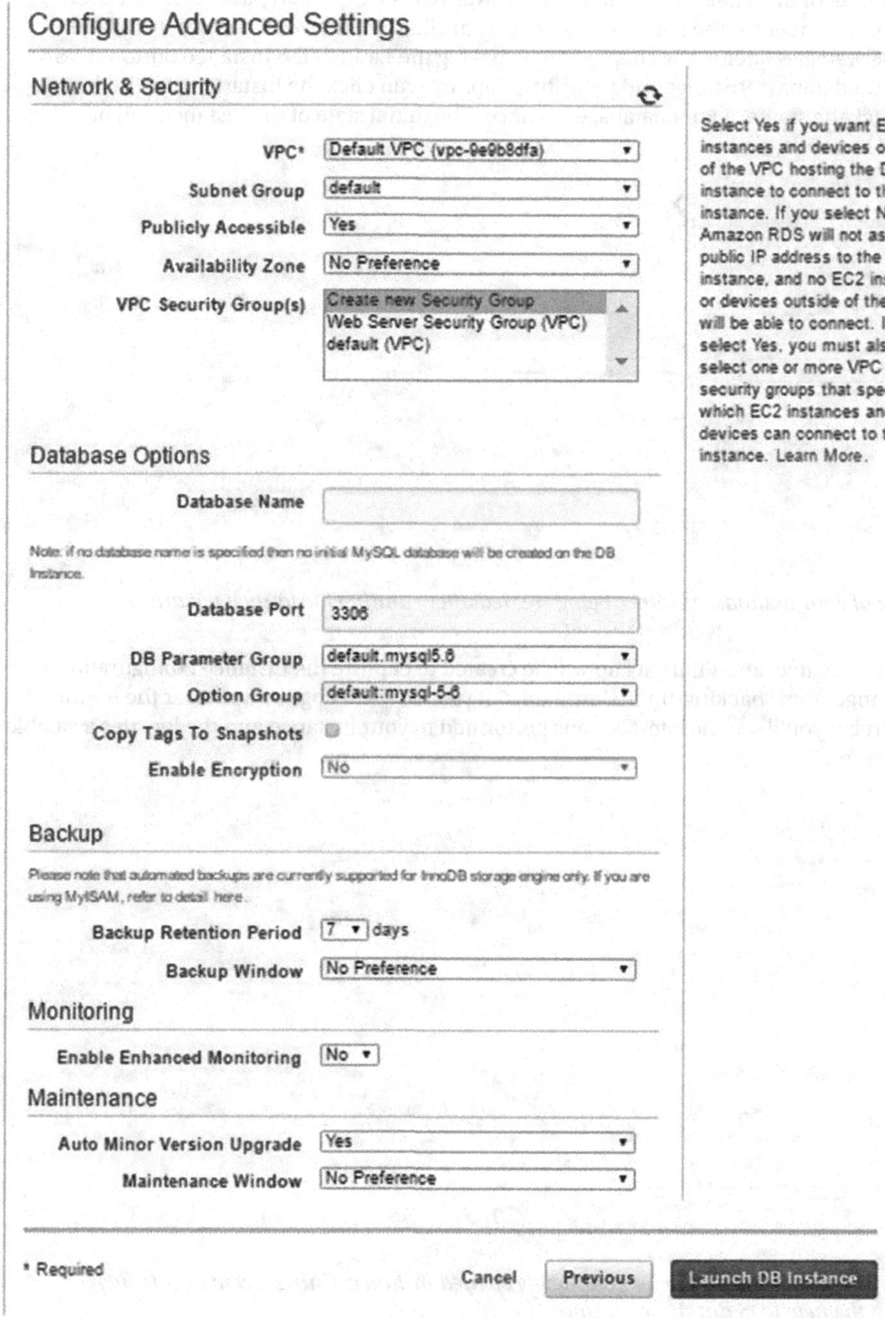

Configure Advanced Settings

Network & Security

VPC*	Default VPC (vpc-9e9b8dfa) ▼
Subnet Group	default ▼
Publicly Accessible	Yes ▼
Availability Zone	No Preference ▼
VPC Security Group(s)	Create new Security Group ▲ Web Server Security Group (VPC) default (VPC) ▼

Select Yes if you want EC2 instances and devices outside of the VPC hosting the DB instance to connect to the DB instance. If you select No, Amazon RDS will not assign a public IP address to the DB instance, and no EC2 instance or devices outside of the VPC will be able to connect. If you select Yes, you must also select one or more VPC security groups that specify which EC2 instances and devices can connect to the DB instance. Learn More.

Database Options

Database Name	

Note: if no database name is specified then no initial MySQL database will be created on the DB Instance.

Database Port	3306
DB Parameter Group	default.mysql5.6 ▼
Option Group	default:mysql-5-6 ▼
Copy Tags To Snapshots	☐
Enable Encryption	No ▼

Backup

Please note that automated backups are currently supported for InnoDB storage engine only. If you are using MyISAM, refer to detail here.

Backup Retention Period	7 ▼ days
Backup Window	No Preference ▼

Monitoring

Enable Enhanced Monitoring	No ▼

Maintenance

Auto Minor Version Upgrade	Yes ▼
Maintenance Window	No Preference ▼

* Required   Cancel   Previous   **Launch DB Instance**

Figure 10-3. *The final step of the Launch DB Instance Wizard, showing the advanced database instance configuration details*

It is good to make note of the database instance administrative username and password because you'll need to use them to connect to the database instance from client tools as well as from installation programs for your CMS websites later in the chapter. After clicking the Launch DB Instance button AWS will create your new RDS database instance and security group. You can click the Instances link in the left-hand navigation to check the status of your database instance. The initial state of the instance will be set to "creating," as shown in Figure 10-4.

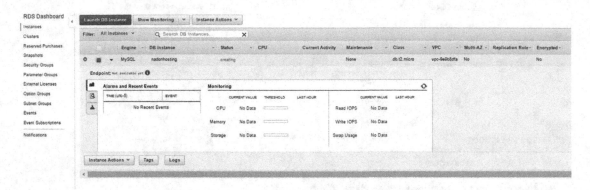

Figure 10-4. *The view of your database instance being created after running the launch wizard*

After the instance is created, an initial backup will be created to capture the instance configuration and then the status will change from "backing-up" to "available." If you click the Logs button near the bottom of the instance details screen, you'll see the latest actions performed to your instance and the log files available to you, as shown in Figure 10-5.

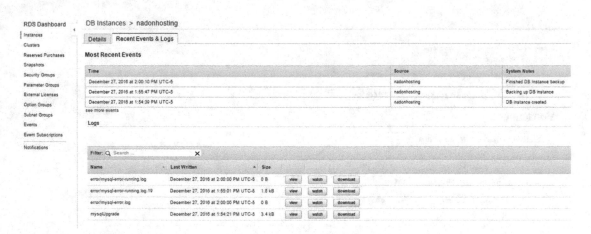

Figure 10-5. *Logging information is shown for your newly created instance, listing recent events such as the creation and backup of the new RDS database instance*

By choosing the Details tab on the page shown above (also available from the Instances ➤ Instance Actions ➤ See Details link) you can see your full database instance detail information including the endpoint location for your instance. Take note of this value, shown highlighted in Figure 10-6, because you'll need it later in the chapter for connecting to the system. The endpoint value is your connection point for your database instance; you can also refer to it as your database server.

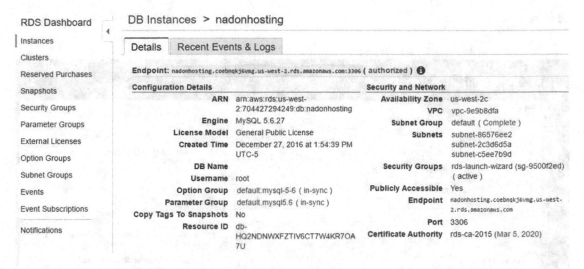

Figure 10-6. *The Details screen with the database instance endpoint value highlighted*

Database Instance Creation Using the AWS CLI

As with most things in AWS, the steps you just performed to create the above RDS database instances can also be completed by using the AWS command line interface. The following command will create the same instance as you did above using the console. I've included a template file that can be used in the chapter source resources, saved as AWS_RDS_CLI_Launch.txt. Simply substitute your own values to create the RDS instance using the CLI.

```
aws rds create-db-instance \
    --db-instance-identifier nadonhosting \
    --db-instance-class db.t2.micro \
    --engine MySQL \
    --allocated-storage 5 \
    --master-username root \
    --master-user-password myrootpassword \
    --backup-retention-period 7
```

Connecting to RDS Remotely for Database Management

Now that you have configured an AWS RDS database instance, you can use client tools to connect to the instance and manage your data. Since you have used MySQL as the database engine type for your RDS instance, you'll use MySQL Workbench to connect to the RDS endpoint. MySQL Workbench is available from http://dev.mysql.com/downloads/workbench/.

After you have downloaded and launched the MySQL Workbench application, the first thing that you'll need to do is configure a connection to the RDS database instance. Once you launch the application, you should be presented with the home screen. From the home screen, click the plus sign next to MySQL Connections to start the Setup New Connection Wizard, as shown in Figure 10-7.

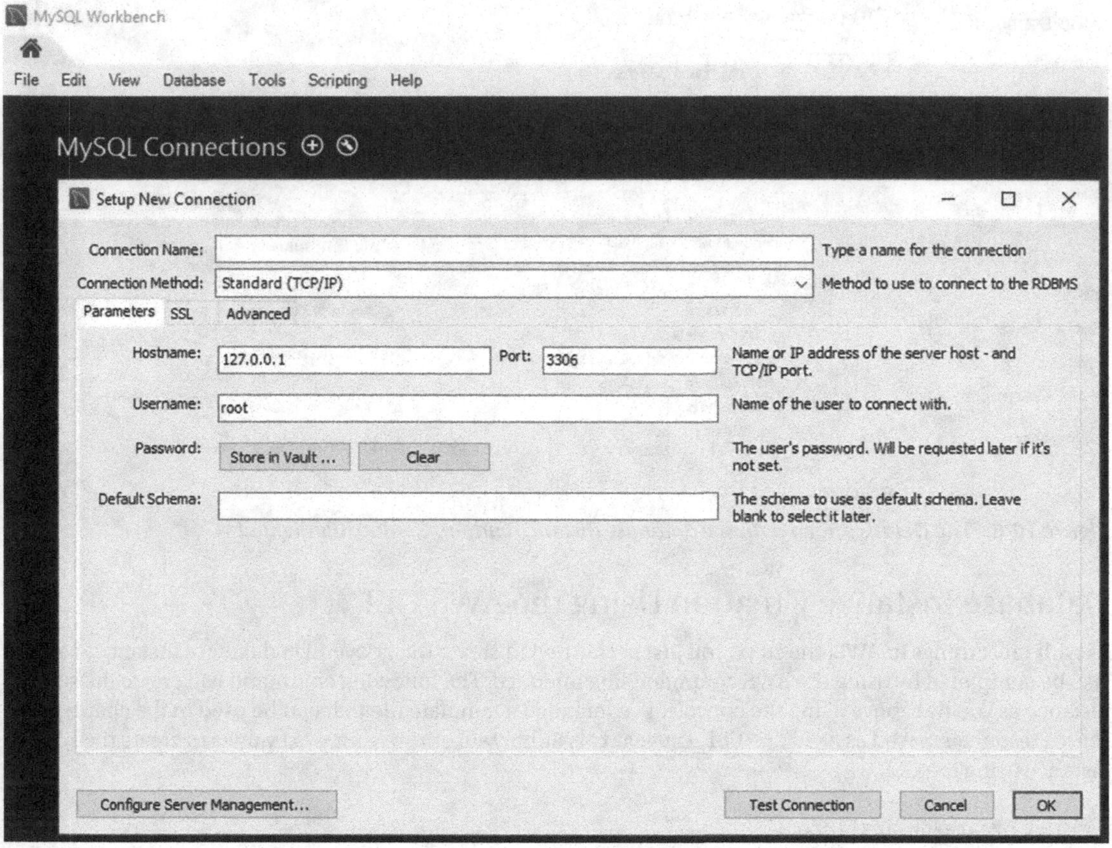

Figure 10-7. MySQL Workbench New Connection Setup Wizard

From the New Connection screen, choose a connection name and enter the AWS RDS endpoint value (for the example I created above, the value I would enter in here is `nadonhosting.coebnqkj6vmg.us-west-2.rds.amazonaws.com`). Leave the port set to 3306. The RDS database instance creation created a security group for you and allows connections over this port. You'll also need to enter your administrative username that you set up in the AWS RDS Database Instance Creation Wizard. Once you have this information, click the Test Connection button and you should be prompted to enter in your administrative password for the database instance. Once entered, a test connection is established and you should receive confirmation of connecting to the database instance, as shown in Figure 10-8.

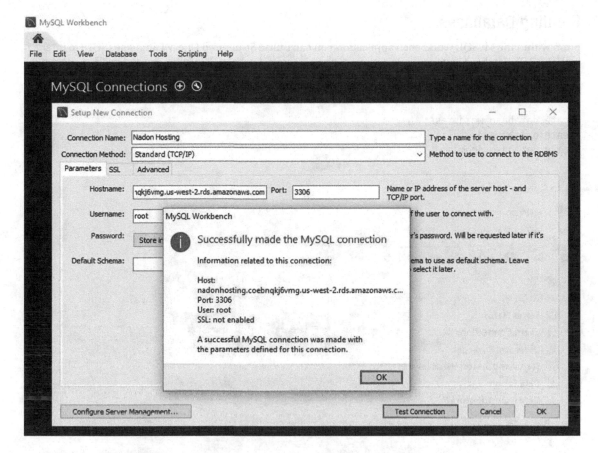

Figure 10-8. *MySQL Workbench New Connection Setup Wizard showing a successful test connection to your AWS RDS database instance*

If you do not receive a message that tells you that you've successfully connected to the RDS instance, you may need to double-check the settings on your RDS security group to verify that connections are allowed from your IP address. By default, the RDS security group that is created is locked down and you'll need to add your IP address to be able to connect with MySQL Workbench from your local computer to manage the instance.

Click the OK button after the successful connection test to save the new connection to your MySQL Workbench. Double-click the new connection to launch a session connection to the RDS database instance. You can now manage all aspects of data that will be loaded on this RDS database instance. MySQL Workbench has administrative tools that allow for direct querying of the server and databases on the instance. You should notice that there are two databases that currently exist on your RDS instance, innodb and sys, which are databases used by the MySQL server application hosted in RDS.

Creating Databases

From within the MySQL Workbench application you can utilize Structured Query Language (SQL) to interact with the RDS database instance to do actions such as create a database. The following code will create three databases on your instance, one for each of the CMS website platforms. The new databases are shown in Figure 10-9.

```
create database wordpress;
create database drupal;
create database joomla;
```

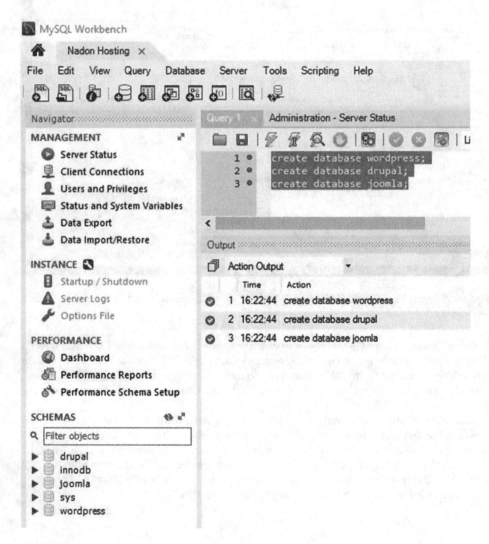

Figure 10-9. *MySQL Workbench Query screen with the SQL statement to create three new databases and the result of executing this statement, showing the new databases created on your AWS RDS instance*

Although this is a simple example, using SQL queries you can interact and manage most every aspect of data on your RDS database instance. You can create users, assign privileges, create tables, and import and export data using the tools available in MySQL Workbench. You'll revisit this tool before the end of this chapter to learn how to view and export CMS data that is created from an installation of the platform. This process can be used to take a backup of your data and migrate it to a new instance, if needed.

Using RDS as a Standalone Data Source

Using tools such as MySQL Workbench you can see that the AWS RDS service can be used as an independent data storage solution. Once an RDS database instance has been initiated, it can be used and managed by you in any means you require. You may even choose to use this as your database platform of choice for web applications hosted externally from the AWS platform. Although unconventional, you could host a blog or CMS website at one hosting provider and still point to AWS for your database instance and data.

Web Server/CMS Installation

In this section, I'll walk you through the installation of each of the CMS platforms I've been discussing in this web hosting scenario. Using the AWS CLI, you will launch an EC2 virtual server instance, install the Apache Web Server application with PHP modules loaded, install MySQL DB server on the same host (although you'll use the AWS RDS instance that you set up above), download a copy of the CMS platform to be deployed, unzip the archive, and prep the CMS for you to walk through the installation. You will use a web browser to point to the freshly launched AWS EC2 web servers and will browse to the installation wizards for each platform. During the installation steps for each CMS, you will provide setup information manually and will point the web server to your AWS RDS database instance for the data source to be used to complete the setup. At the end of each section you will have a generic, running version of each CMS platform. Before this can work, however, you'll need to open up traffic to be allowed from the web server security group inbound on the RDS security group. While you're making this edit, you'll also add port 22 for management via SSH from just your IP address (the most secure).

Complete the following steps to add the web server security group to the existing RDS security group that was created for you as part of the AWS RDS database instance creation:

1. Click the Services menu from within the AWS Console and click EC2.

2. Click the Security Groups link in the left-hand navigation.

3. Click the rds-launch-wizard group name to select that security group.

4. Click the Inbound tab in the Security Group properties section near the bottom of the screen.

5. Click the Edit button.

6. Click the Add Rule button.

7. Choose MySQL/Aurora in the type drop-down.

8. Choose Custom under the Source column.

9. In the text box next to the Source column, type "Web Server Security Group" and select the group to add the Security Group ID to the text box.

10.   Click the Add Rule button.

11.   Choose SSH in the type drop-down.

12.   Choose My IP under the Source column.

13.   Click the Save button.

Joomla Install Using the AWS CLI and User Data File

I have included a file with this chapter called UserData_Joomla.txt. The contents of the file are as follows:

```
#!/bin/bash
yum update -y
yum install -y httpd24 php56 mysql55-server php56-mysqlnd
service httpd start
chkconfig httpd on
groupadd www
usermod -a -G www ec2-user
chown -R root:www /var/www
chmod 2775 /var/www
mkdir /var/www/html/joomla
wget https://github.com/joomla/joomla-cms/releases/download/3.6.5/Joomla_3.6.5-Stable-Full_
Package.tar.gz
tar -xvzf Joomla_3.6.5-Stable-Full_Package.tar.gz -C /var/www/html/joomla
find /var/www -type d -exec chmod 2775 {} +
find /var/www -type f -exec chmod 0664 {} +
echo "<?php phpinfo(); ?>" > /var/www/html/phpinfo.php
cp /var/www/html/joomla/installation/configuration.php-dist > /var/www/html/joomla/
configuration.php
find /var/www/html/joomla/installation -type d -exec chmod 2775 {} +
find /var/www/html/joomla/configuration.php -type f -exec chmod 0666 {} +
```

This code will look familiar to what you used earlier in this section of the book; however, this script has the addition of MySQL as well as downloading and extracting the Joomla CMS. For Joomla, you also need to create a configuration.php file and set the permissions on it. From the workstation configured with the AWS CLI, the command you'll enter follows, which is a modified version of the AWS EC2_CLI_Launch.txt file that was provided in Chapter 8:

```
aws ec2 run-instances --image-id ami-1e299d7e --count 1 --instance-type t2.micro --user-data
file://userdata_Joomla.txt --security-group-ids sg-5381752b --key-name nadonhosting
```

This code will launch a new EC2 virtual instance using the UserData file that is specific for the Joomla CMS. After running the command above to launch the instance, wait a couple of minutes to allow the instance to spin up, load software, and pass health checks. After a few minutes, browse to the following URL replacing the bold text with your EC2 virtual instance DNS name):

http://**ec2-35-166-130-167.us-west-2.compute.amazonaws.com**/joomla/

Opening the above page in a browser should present you with the screen shown in Figure 10-10.

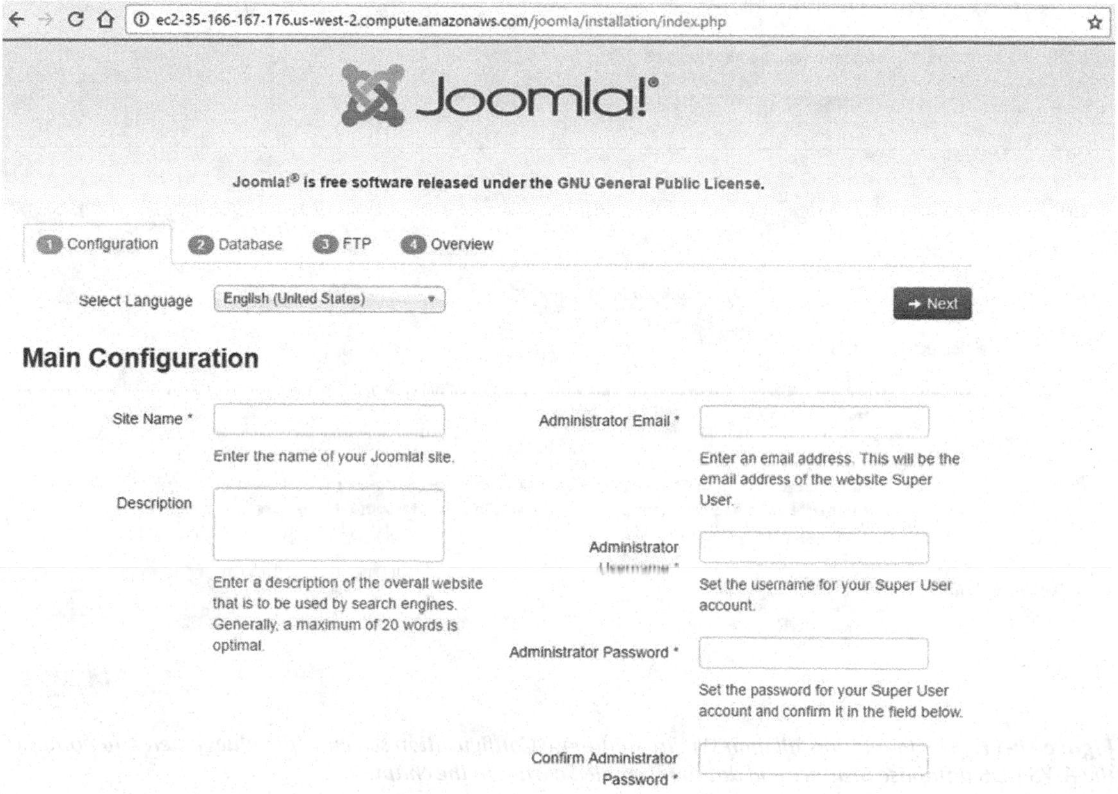

Figure 10-10. *The Joomla Installation Wizard running on an AWS EC2 virtual server instance that was started using the sample User Data file for Joomla CMS*

Fill in relevant details about your site on the first page, including the creation of an administrative user that will be associated with the Joomla CMS. Please take note of this information because you'll need it to log into the site later. Click the Next button to move onto the Database Configuration page. This is where you will enter your AWS RDS-relevant information including endpoint, username, password, and database to be used (see Figure 10-11). It is worth noting that for a production-level setup, it is best practice to create a specific user that can be used to connect to the database instance that is *not* the MySQL root user account. I've used it here for ease of configuration.

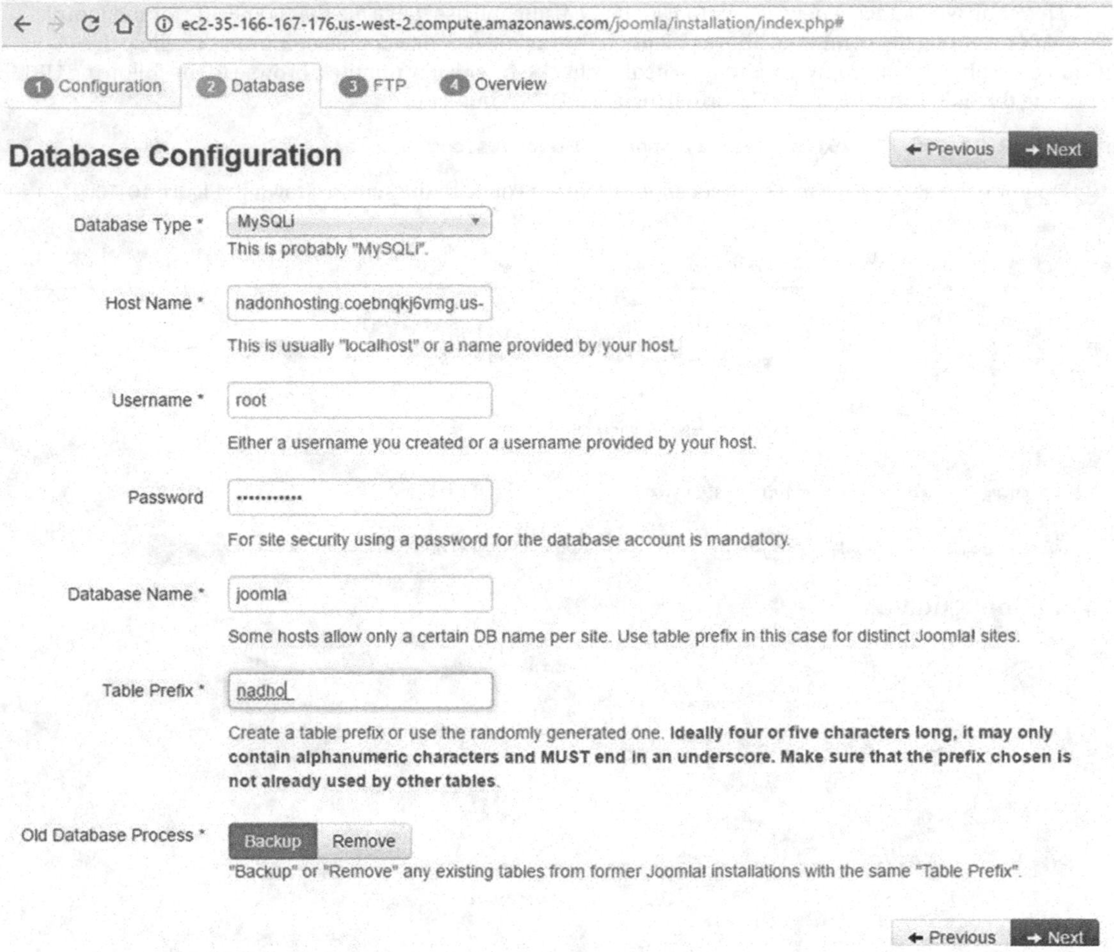

Figure 10-11. *The Joomla Installation Wizard Database Configuration screen with values entered to point to the AWS RDS database instance and database created earlier in the chapter*

In the third step of the process, Joomla asks if you want to set up FTP for your site. Leave it set on the default, which is to *not* set it up for this example. In the last step of the process, the configuration data should be reviewed and should look similar to the screen displayed in Figure 10-12. Note that you've chosen to install sample data with the installation.

Figure 10-12. *The final step before the installation proceeds. You have selected to install sample data with your installation*

In addition to the sample data being installed, you have also selected the option to send summary information to your administrative email address at the end of the installation. After clicking the Install button, you will see the CMS installation progress through to the end and a success screen. Note that Joomla requires you to remove the installation directory before using the site, so you'll have to use a client application to connect to the server to manage it. As shown in previous chapters, you can use the key pair that you called to in the CLI launch statement and the PuTTy client application to connect to this newly launched instance. Once connected, issue the following command to rename the installation directory, which will then allow you to get to your newly created Joomla site:

```
sudo mv /var/www/html/joomla/installation/ /var/www/html/joomla/installation_old/
```

You can verify your installation by looking into the tables under the joomla database that you created in MySQL Workbench. Figure 10-13 shows that new tables exist under the joomla database that you created earlier and that they were created by the installation process.

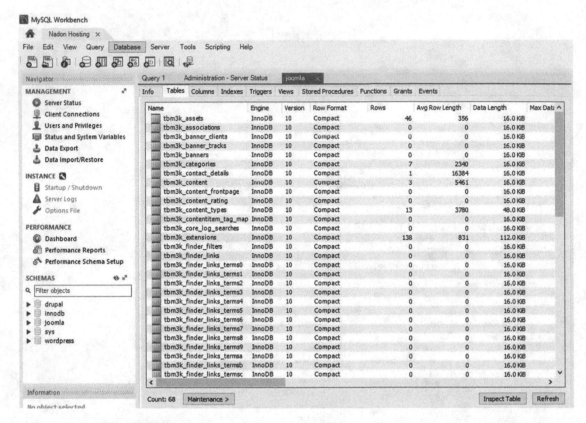

Figure 10-13. *Post Joomla installation you can see the new table structure created under the joomla database that you created earlier in the chapter*

Drupal Install Using the AWS CLI and User Data File

I have included a file with this chapter called `UserData_Drupal.txt`. The contents of the file are as follows:

```
#!/bin/bash
yum update -y
yum install -y httpd24 php70 php70-mysqlnd php70-mbstring php70-gd mysql55-server
service httpd start
chkconfig httpd on
groupadd www
usermod -a -G www ec2-user
chown -R root:www /var/www
chmod 2775 /var/www
wget https://ftp.drupal.org/files/projects/drupal-7.53.tar.gz
tar -xvzf drupal-7.53.tar.gz -C /var/www/html
find /var/www -type d -exec chmod 2775 {} +
find /var/www -type f -exec chmod 0664 {} +
echo "<?php phpinfo(); ?>" > /var/www/html/phpinfo.php
chown -R root:www /var/www/html/drupal-7.53
chmod 2775 /var/www/html/drupal-7.53/sites/default
mkdir /var/www/html/drupal-7.53/sites/default/files
```

```
find /var/www/html/drupal-7.53 -type d -exec chmod 2775 {} +
find /var/www/html/drupal-7.53/sites/default/files -type d -exec chmod 2776 {} +
find /var/www/html/drupal-7.53 -type f -exec chmod 0664 {} +
cp /var/www/html/drupal-7.53/sites/default/default.settings.php > /var/www/html/drupal-7.53/
sites/default/settings.php
find /var/www/html/drupal-7.53/sites/default/settings.php -type f -exec chmod 0776 {} +
```

This code will look familiar to what you used earlier; however, this script has the addition of MySQL as well as downloading and extracting the Drupal CMS. From the workstation configured with the AWS CLI, the command you'll enter follows, and it is a modified version of the AWS EC2_CLI_Launch.txt file that was provided in Chapter 8:

```
aws ec2 run-instances --image-id ami-1e299d7e --count 1 --instance-type t2.micro --user-data
file://userdata_Drupal.txt --security-group-ids sg-5381752b --key-name nadonhosting
```

This code will launch a new EC2 virtual instance using the UserData file that is specific for the Drupal CMS. After running the command above to launch the instance, wait a couple of minutes to allow the instance to spin up, load software, and pass health checks. After a few minutes, browse to the following URL, replacing the bold text with your EC2 virtual instance DNS name:

http://**ec2-35-166-130-167.us-west-2.compute.amazonaws.com**/drupal-7.53/

Opening the above page in a browser should present you with the screen shown in Figure 10-14.

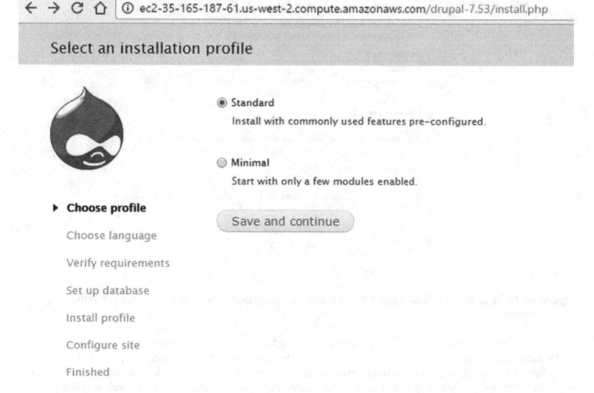

Figure 10-14. *The Drupal Installation Wizard running on an AWS EC2 virtual server instance that was started using the sample User Data file for Drupal CMS*

In the first step, you'll progress with a Standard installation and click the "Save and continue" button. In the second step, you'll choose your language. The third step in the process will verify server requirements to move forward with the installation of Drupal and, if passed, will arrive at the Database Configuration screen showed in Figure 10-15.

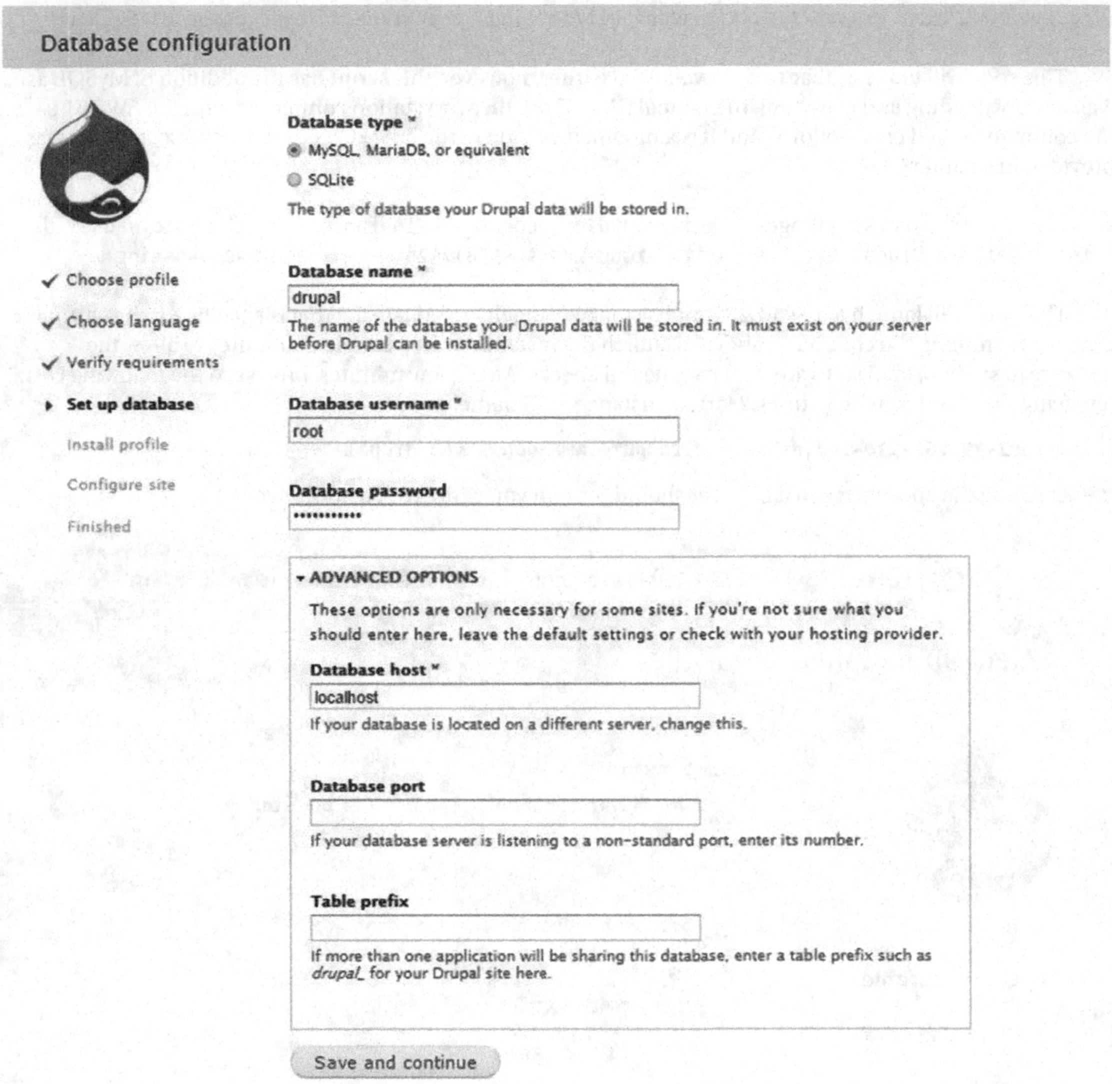

Database configuration

Database type ˮ
- ⦿ MySQL, MariaDB, or equivalent
- ◯ SQLite

The type of database your Drupal data will be stored in.

✓ Choose profile

✓ Choose language

✓ Verify requirements

▸ **Set up database**

Install profile

Configure site

Finished

Database name ˮ

```
drupal
```

The name of the database your Drupal data will be stored in. It must exist on your server before Drupal can be installed.

Database username ˮ

```
root
```

Database password

```
••••••••••
```

▾ ADVANCED OPTIONS

These options are only necessary for some sites. If you're not sure what you should enter here, leave the default settings or check with your hosting provider.

Database host ˮ

```
localhost
```

If your database is located on a different server, change this.

Database port

```

```

If your database server is listening to a non-standard port, enter its number.

Table prefix

```

```

If more than one application will be sharing this database, enter a table prefix such as *drupal_* for your Drupal site here.

(Save and continue)

Figure 10-15. *The Drupal Installation Wizard Database Configuration screen, which is step 4 of the Drupal install*

On the Database Configuration screen, you will choose MySQL as the database type and enter in the name of the database where you would like the data stored. You will then fill in the username and password for your RDS database instance and click the Advanced Options link to expand additional fields where you can enter in the RDS database instance endpoint in the Database Host field, enter the database port of 3306, and add table prefix if you'd prefer to have one. Click the "Save and continue" button to proceed with the installation of Drupal.

When the installation completes, you will move to the next step of the process, which will have you fill in site configuration details such as the administrative account, email address, and site name. The installation also reminds you now that the settings.php file has been updated by the installation process you should adjust it so that it is no longer "writable." To do this, log into the EC2 virtual instance using PuTTy and the key pair that you specified in the CLI launch script and run the following command after the setup is complete:

```
sudo chmod 664 /var/www/html/drupal-7.53/sites/default/settings.php
```

Once you have filled in the site configuration details, click the "Save and Continue" button and proceed to the final page in the wizard, as shown in Figure 10-16, which informs you that the installation process is complete and offers a link to view your new site.

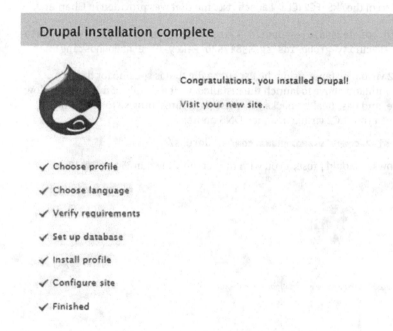

Figure 10-16. *The completed Drupal Installation Wizard*

WordPress Install Using the AWS CLI and User Data File

I have included a file with this chapter called UserData_Wordpress.txt. The contents of the file are as follows:

```
#!/bin/bash
yum update -y
yum install -y httpd24 php56 mysql55-server php56-mysqlnd
service httpd start
chkconfig httpd on
groupadd www
usermod -a -G www ec2-user
chown -R root:www /var/www
chmod 2775 /var/www
```

```
wget https://wordpress.org/latest.tar.gz
tar -xvzf latest.tar.gz -C /var/www/html
find /var/www -type d -exec chmod 2775 {} +
find /var/www -type f -exec chmod 0664 {} +
chown -R root:www /var/www/html/wordpress
chmod 2775 /var/www/html/wordpress
find /var/www/html/wordpress -type d -exec chmod 2777 {} +
find /var/www/html/wordpress -type f -exec chmod 0666 {} +
echo "<?php phpinfo(); ?>" > /var/www/html/phpinfo.php
```

This code will look familiar; however, this script has the addition of MySQL as well as downloading and extracting the WordPress CMS. From the workstation configured with the AWS CLI, you'll enter the following command, which is a modified version of the AWS EC2_CLI_Launch.txt file that was provided in Chapter 8.

```
aws ec2 run-instances --image-id ami-1e299d7e --count 1 --instance-type t2.micro --user-data
file://userdata_Wordpress.txt --security-group-ids sg-5381752b --key-name nadonhosting
```

This code will launch a new EC2 virtual instance using the UserData file that is specific for the WordPress CMS. After running the command above to launch the instance, wait a couple of minutes to allow the instance to spin up, load software, and pass health checks. After a few minutes, browse to the following URL, replacing the bold text below with your EC2 virtual instance DNS name:

http://**ec2-35-166-130-167.us-west-2.compute.amazonaws.com**/wordpress/

Opening the above page in a browser should present you with the screen shown in Figure 10-17.

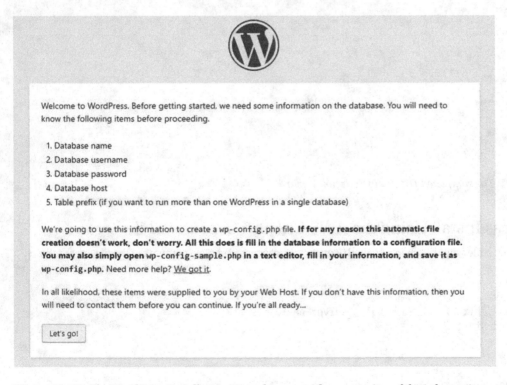

Figure 10-17. *The WordPress Installation Wizard screen with an overview of the information needed to progress through the installation*

Click the "Let's go!" button to begin the installation wizard. You will enter a database name, the RDS database instance username and password, and the RDS database instance endpoint and table prefix, if desired, as shown in Figure 10-18.

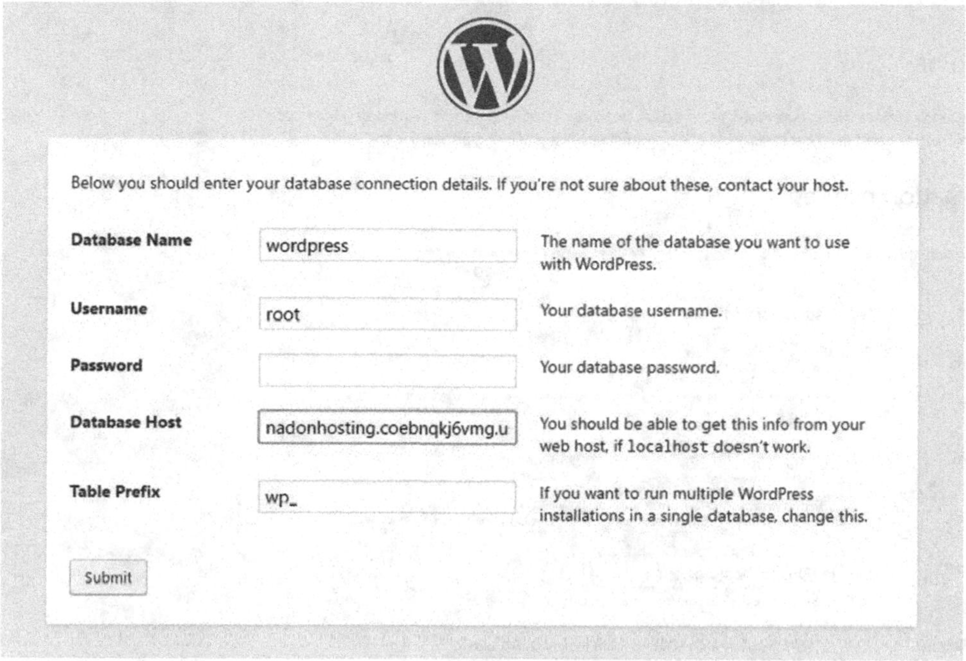

Figure 10-18. *The WordPress Installation Wizard Database Configuration screen*

After you have filled in the needed information, click the Submit button to move on to the next step of the process.

The installation program will test the connection to the database endpoint and, if successful, will let you know that it's ready to start the installation. Click the button presented and the next step will collect site configuration details such as site title, administrator username and password to be created, email address, and other options, as shown in Figure 10-19.

Figure 10-19. *Filling in the required informtion*

Once you have entered in the information requested, click the Install WordPress button to start the installation of the WordPress CMS on the server and the setup of the database in the RDS database instance.

When the installation completes, you will be returned to the Administrative Sign-In page. You can now log in with the administrative username and password that you specified in the site configuration step above. This will then allow you to access the WordPress CMS administration so that you can complete the rest of the site setup.

Exporting/Importing Data Using MySQL Workbench

Before I end this chapter, I want to show you how to use a client-side tool such as MySQL Workbench to back up the data that is stored in AWS RDS because there isn't a native way to move the data from AWS in an exportable format. As you learned earlier, it is as simple as setting up a new connection to connect your RDS database instance endpoint with this client software and then you can browse through databases that are set up on RDS.

In Figure 10-20, you can see that I've logged into my RDS instance with the MySQL Workbench client and browsed to the recently installed Drupal CMS database.

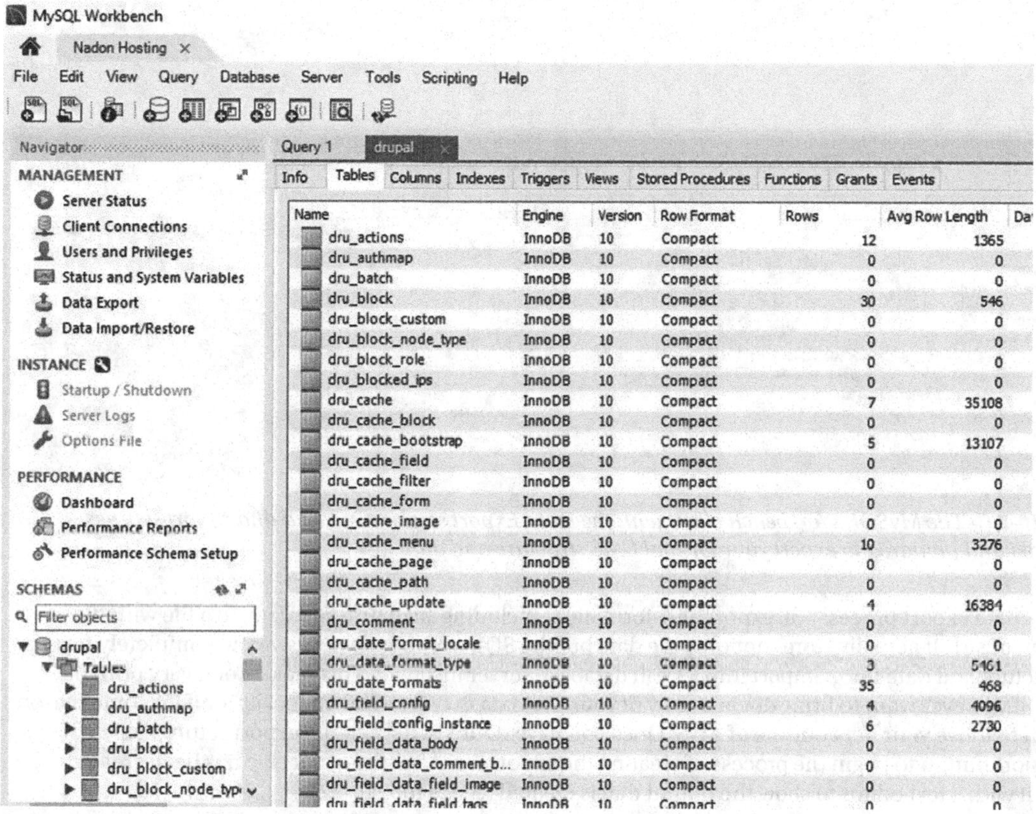

Figure 10-20. *The MySQL Workbench client with the recently installed Drupal CMS database open to table view*

With this view open, you can click the Server menu item and choose Data Export. When the Data Export screen opens, you will be presented with a screen that lists all of your databases on the RDS database instance. On this screen, you can select the database that you would like to export (you do have the ability to select multiple, but my suggestion is to keep each database exported as its own file) and ensure that the drop-down box that describes what you would like to export is set to "Dump Structure and Data" so that all tables and the data included within them will be exported. You also have the ability to include database objects such as stored procedures, functions, database triggers, and events. My suggestion is to export as much of the data as possible. Your settings are shown in Figure 10-21.

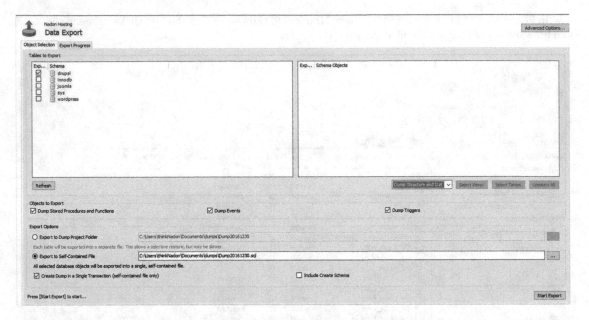

Figure 10-21. *The MySQL Workbench client with the Data Export screen displayed and export settings configured and prepared to export your Drupal CMS structure and data*

This data export process will export all information, including structure and data, to a file with the extension of sql. It actually stores not only the data but the SQL commands necessary to completely recreate this structure and data upon import into a fresh database server instance. This makes for a very portable solution if you ever want to bring down a copy of your live data to be worked on locally, or if for some reason you want to move your data outside of AWS. Once you have double-checked the export settings, click the Start Export button to begin the process of creating the export file. After the export file has been created, opened it with a text editor to show the output that is created (see Figure 10-22).

```
 1  ⊟-- MySQL dump 10.13  Distrib 5.6.24, for Win64 (x86_64)
 2  |  --
 3  |  -- Host: nadonhosting.coebnqkj6vmg.us-west-2.rds.amazonaws.com     Database: drupal
 4  |  -- -----------------------------------------------------
 5  L-- Server version    5.6.27-log
 6
 7     /*!40101 SET @OLD_CHARACTER_SET_CLIENT=@@CHARACTER_SET_CLIENT */;
 8     /*!40101 SET @OLD_CHARACTER_SET_RESULTS=@@CHARACTER_SET_RESULTS */;
 9     /*!40101 SET @OLD_COLLATION_CONNECTION=@@COLLATION_CONNECTION */;
10     /*!40101 SET NAMES utf8 */;
11     /*!40103 SET @OLD_TIME_ZONE=@@TIME_ZONE */;
12     /*!40103 SET TIME_ZONE='+00:00' */;
13     /*!40014 SET @OLD_UNIQUE_CHECKS=@@UNIQUE_CHECKS, UNIQUE_CHECKS=0 */;
14     /*!40014 SET @OLD_FOREIGN_KEY_CHECKS=@@FOREIGN_KEY_CHECKS, FOREIGN_KEY_CHECKS=0 */;
15     /*!40101 SET @OLD_SQL_MODE=@@SQL_MODE, SQL_MODE='NO_AUTO_VALUE_ON_ZERO' */;
16     /*!40111 SET @OLD_SQL_NOTES=@@SQL_NOTES, SQL_NOTES=0 */;
17
18  ⊟--
19  |  -- Table structure for table `dru_actions`
20  |  --
21
22     DROP TABLE IF EXISTS `dru_actions`;
23     /*!40101 SET @saved_cs_client      = @@character_set_client */;
24     /*!40101 SET character_set_client = utf8 */;
25  ⊟CREATE TABLE `dru_actions` (
26  |    `aid` varchar(255) NOT NULL DEFAULT '0' COMMENT 'Primary Key: Unique actions ID.',
27  |    `type` varchar(32) NOT NULL DEFAULT '' COMMENT 'The object that that action acts on (node, user, comment, system or custom types.)',
28  |    `callback` varchar(255) NOT NULL DEFAULT '' COMMENT 'The callback function that executes when the action runs.',
29  |    `parameters` longblob NOT NULL COMMENT 'Parameters to be passed to the callback function.',
30  |    `label` varchar(255) NOT NULL DEFAULT '0' COMMENT 'Label of the action.',
31  |    PRIMARY KEY (`aid`)
32  L) ENGINE=InnoDB DEFAULT CHARSET=utf8 COMMENT='Stores action information.';
33     /*!40101 SET character_set_client = @saved_cs_client */;
34
35  ⊟--
36  |  -- Dumping data for table `dru_actions`
37  L--
38
39     LOCK TABLES `dru_actions` WRITE;
40     /*!40000 ALTER TABLE `dru_actions` DISABLE KEYS */;
41     INSERT INTO `dru_actions` VALUES ('comment_publish_action','comment','comment_publish_action','','Publish comment'),('comment_save_action','comment','comment
42     /*!40000 ALTER TABLE `dru_actions` ENABLE KEYS */;
```

Figure 10-22. *The resulting "dump" file from the MySQL Workbench data export process*

Summary

This chapter covered a large amount of information on how to work with the CMS website databases using AWS RDS and client tools. You started with an introduction to the RDS service and features, walked through the setup of an RDS database instance, which you then learned how to log into and manage from client tools loaded locally. You also walked through the full installation of Joomla, Drupal, and WordPress CMS installations using RDS as your data source. You learned just how quickly you can get a CMS website running in AWS using EC2 and RDS resources. Finally, you learned how to export data from AWS RDS so that you can use that export file as the source of an import on another database instance, whether it be locally hosted, within AWS, or elsewhere. In the next chapter, you are going to shift your focus and learn how to use another AWS service called CloudFormation to create your infrastructure with the use of code. This code will be an asset that you can update, put under source control, and use to rapidly deploy all the resources needed for your CMS website scenario in an organized deployment that will launch needed resources across all AWS services such as EC2, RDS, IAM, S3, and more!

CHAPTER 11

■ ■ ■

Building the Infrastructure

In the last chapter, I gave an overview the AWS RDS service along with how you can utilize the User Data field to provide commands to set up an EC2 instance at launch time. This is by far the easiest way to set up an instance, download necessary files, and prepare an instance for use. There is another method and service that can be used to manage your AWS infrastructure in a way that allows for easy deployment, updating, and redeployment: CloudFormation. In this chapter, I'll introduce AWS CloudFormation and explain the benefits of using it. You'll launch several versions of CloudFormation templates, each building on the previous one, and review a sample CloudFormation script that Amazon provides for deploying the WordPress CMS.

Infrastructure as Code

Managing infrastructure in the form of source code is not a new concept, but it is one that has been gaining acceptance across the Information Technology field in recent years. Amazon Web Services offers several services that allow you to define your infrastructure in what is referred to as a template. CloudFormation templates are created in JavaScript Object Notation (JSON) format, which is a lightweight, easy-to-understand way to organize data using a simple structure and key value pairs for data assignment. JSON is a text-based format, which makes it a quick way to exchange data between web servers and is efficient to process. JSON is similar to XML in readability and benefit for data storage and exchange.

JSON Data Format Example

JSON files are saved with the file extension json and use the MIME type of application/json. The following code is a simple example of the structure of an object called "users" in JSON format. The structure defines a "firstname" and "lastname" key for each "user" and stores the value for each key.

```
{"users":[
        {"firstname":"Jae", "lastname":"Nadon"},
        {"firstname":"Bob", "lastname":"Jones"},
        {"firstname":"Cindy", "lastname":"Matthews"}
        ]}
```

As you can see from the example above, JSON encloses key and value pairs in quotation marks separated by the colon character, and each object is enclosed in curled parenthesis. This is similar to how objects are defined in JavaScript.

© Jason Nadon 2017
J. Nadon, *Website Hosting and Migration with Amazon Web Services*, DOI 10.1007/978-1-4842-2589-9_11

The same example data structure is shown below in XML format for comparison:

```
<users>
        <user>
                <firstname>Jae</firstname> <lastname>Nadon</lastname>
        </user>
        <user>
                <firstname>Bob</firstname> <lastname>Jones</lastname>
        </user>
        <user>
                <firstname>Cindy</firstname> <lastname>Matthews</lastname>
        </user>
</users>
```

Both XML and JSON are text-based formats that can be classified as self-describing, meaning that the format of the data is human readable and easy to understand. In the above example, you will likely notice that JSON is more compact and, in my opinion, more easily read. Another key difference between the two formats is that XML needs an XML interpreter for the exchange of data where as JSON can be consumed by native JavaScript functions.

AWS CloudFormation Concepts

AWS CloudFormation uses the concepts of templates, stacks, and change sets to deploy infrastructure and allow for management of what is deployed. A template is a text file that defines the infrastructure, resources to be deployed, and the services to be used to deploy that infrastructure. A stack is a collection of resources from one or more template files that is managed as a single infrastructure entity. A change set is a version of a specific stack including changes made to the infrastructure. Since templates are at the core of your CloudFormation work, let's start by understanding how to define AWS resources in a JSON template that will deploy a single EC2 instance in a similar way as in previous chapters using the CLI EC2 `run-instances` command.

CloudFormation Template Structure

1. Statement Declaration (required): The opening and closing declaration of the statement containing optional and required components.

2. Template Format (optional): Defines the template format version that this template conforms to.

3. Parameters (optional): Key-value pairs that will be passed either interactively or through the template assignments to the CloudFormation Stack Launch Wizard when a launch is initiated.

4. Mappings (optional): Mappings can map a key value to a named list of data values based on the key value given. An example of a mapping is determining which EC2 AMI should be used in a specific region. CloudFormation can pull information on where the infrastructure is being launched and, based on that information, look into the mapping definitions in the template to see what value should be used.

5. Conditions (optional): Conditional statements can be added to a CloudFormation template to evaluate the value of parameters, mappings, or other conditions in order to perform a defined task. An example of when this might be used is if you want certain sections of the template to be processed if a condition value is met and others to be processed regardless of whether a condition value is met.

6. Resources (required): The resources section of the template lists the AWS resources to be deployed by CloudFormation.

7. Outputs (optional): Outputs can list the values of anything created by or within the referenced stack. These can be used to pass values from one template to another or to display information in the CloudFormation Stack Console to list information about resources that were created.

The easiest way to introduce the structure of a CloudFormation template is to reference the resources you created in the previous chapters using the AWS command line interface. Let's review the following statement and then create a similar template that can be deployed with CloudFormation:

```
aws ec2 run-instances --image-id ami-1e299d7e --count 1 --instance-type t2.micro --user-data
file://userdata_Joomla.txt --security-group-ids sg-5381752b --key-name nadonhosting
```

This command calls to the EC2 service and uses run-instances to launch one new virtual server instance from the AMI with an ID of ami-1e299d7e, it defines the type of instance as a t2.micro, passes the userdata_Wordpress.txt file at launch time, and associates a security group and key pair to be used with the instance.

Creating a New CloudFormation Stack

For you to launch this same instance using CloudFormation, you will first need to define a template where you request the resources to be created in a similar but different fashion. As you'll recall from previous chapters, passing user data at launch allows you to run commands only that one time. Since one of the main benefits of using CloudFormation is being able to update your stack of resources deployed, you'll need to adjust the way you call to load applications. No fear, though; once you have a base template defined in this chapter, you'll be able to see the benefit of being able to update and redeploy in the next chapter.

You'll start with the template declaration, the template format, and description statements and then a resources section that will simply launch an EC2 virtual server instance and associate it with your existing security group and key pair. There may be field values that you'll need to adjust to match your environment, such as security groups, ids, and key names.

```
{
    "AWSTemplateFormatVersion" : "2010-09-09",
    "Description" : "Creation of an EC2 Instance using CloudFormation",
    "Resources" : {
        "WebServer" : {
            "Type" : "AWS::EC2::Instance",
            "Properties" : {
                "ImageId" : "ami-1e299d7e",
                "KeyName" : "nadonhosting",
                        "InstanceType" : "t2.micro",
                        "SecurityGroupIds" : ["sg-5381752b"]
            }
        }
    }
}
```

The template above is included in this chapter's source files and is named CF_EC2_Stack.json. If you want to use CloudFormation to create this instance for you, the first thing you'll need to do is to log into the AWS Console.

Once logged into the AWS Console, click the Services menu and under the Management Tools section, select CloudFormation. This will bring you to the CloudFormation welcome page shown in Figure 11-1.

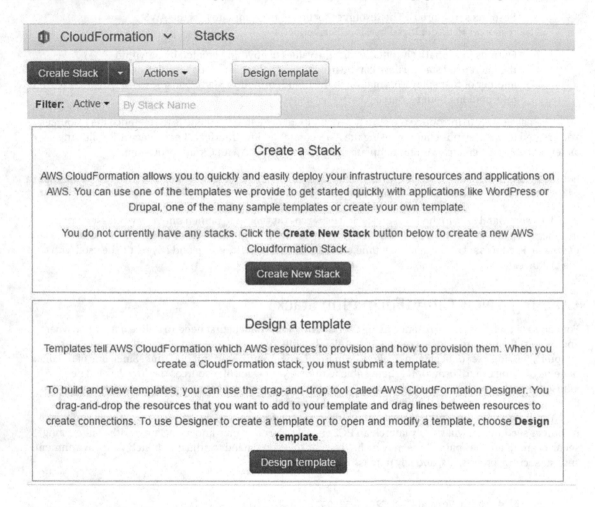

Figure 11-1. *The CloudFormation welcome screen with a call to action to create a new stack*

From the welcome screen, click the Create New Stack button to start the Create Stack Wizard. The first step of the wizard asks how you would like to create the template that will be used to create your infrastructure. In this case, you'll select the "Upload a template to S3" option and you'll select the CF_EC2_Stack.json file mentioned above. This will copy this file and store it in your S3 account under a new bucket that CloudFormation will use for storing information and templates. After selecting the json file to be uploaded, click the Next button to continue with the wizard.

The next step will ask you to name your stack. Let's call this stack "TestEC2." Enter the name for the stack and click the Next button.

The next step in the wizard will allow you to add information related to the stack creation such as tags for the stack, permissions, and notification settings. You will leave them on the default settings and click the Next button.

This will bring you to the last step where you can review the creation properties that you have specified for your infrastructure. AWS will also remind you that although there is no cost associated with the CloudFormation service, the infrastructure that it creates is real and is subject to charges the same as if you had deployed it in any other method, such as via the EC2 Launch Instance Wizard or via the AWS CLI. Once you've finished reviewing the information, click the Create button to start the CloudFormation stack creation.

The creation will immediately start and you can see the progress of the creation by clicking the Events tab, as shown in Figure 11-2.

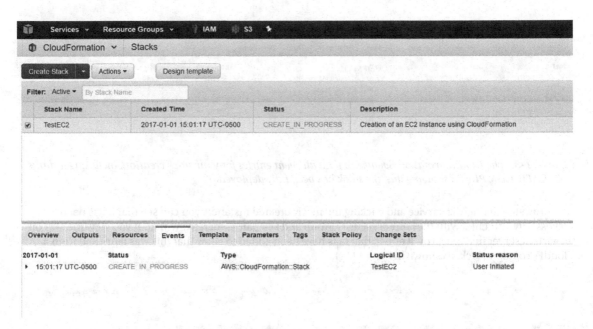

Figure 11-2. *The CloudFormation Events tab is shown for your newly launched stack*

As you can see in Figure 11-2, the stack has a status of CREATE_IN_PROGRESS while resources are being created. If you browsed to your EC2 Dashboard you would see that a virtual server instance has been launched and is in the midst of being created. Once the instance has been created, you'll see the stack status change to CREATE_COMPLETE, as shown in Figure 11-3.

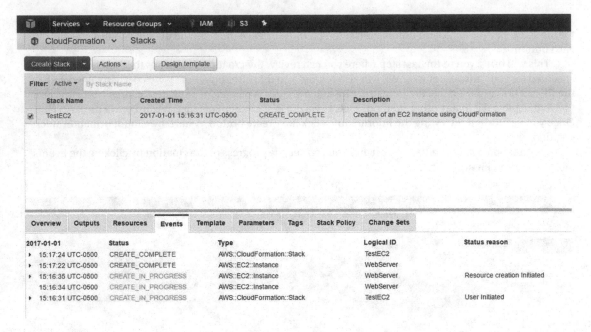

Figure 11-3. *The CloudFormation Events tab with all event entries for your stack creation, including a status of CREATE_COMPLETE showing that the stack has been fully deployed*

Browsing to the EC2 service and clicking the newly created instance, you can see that it has been successfully launched with the correct security group and key pair associated with it. If you view the tags on the virtual server instance, you'll notice that tags have been added to show that this was launched from a CloudFormation stack, as shown in Figure 11-4.

Figure 11-4. *The EC2 Dashboard with your new instance tag values selected, showing that this was launched from the CloudFormation Stack named TestEC2*

Deleting a CloudFormation Stack

Now that you have created a CloudFormation stack using a simple template that launched an EC2 virtual server instance, I'll show you how to delete the stack. This is a reminder of the concept of a CloudFormation stack as a single entity collection of infrastructure resources that can be managed as one. Although this example was extremely simple, if you had added more than just an EC2 resource (and you will use a sample template that does just that in the next section), when you choose to remove or delete a stack all the resources associated with it will be removed.

To delete an existing stack, navigate back to your CloudFormation dashboard in the AWS Console by clicking the Services menu and choosing the CloudFormation link under the Management Tools section.

When arriving at the CloudFormation dashboard you should be presented with a list of your current infrastructure stacks that have been deployed. Click the checkbox next to the stack you would like to delete and then click the Actions button. In the drop-down, choose Delete Stack, as shown in Figure 11-5.

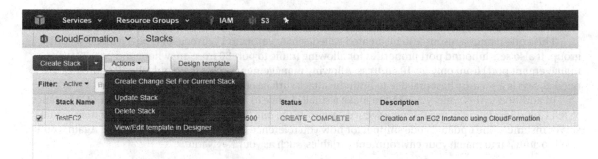

Figure 11-5. *The CloudFormation Dashboard with the TestEC2 stack selected and the Action menu expanded*

You will be prompted and warned that deleting a stack will delete all associated resources. Click the "Yes, Delete" button to proceed. After confirming that you want to delete the stack, CloudFormation will set the stack status to DELETE_IN_PROGRESS and once the deletion has been completed, you will no longer see the stack listed in the CloudFormation dashboard. All resources created by the stack will also have been deleted and will not be available within their respective dashboards.

Creating Multiple AWS Resources in a Single CloudFormation Template

In your first example of a CloudFormation template, you launched a single EC2 instance and associated it with an existing key pair for management and an existing security group. CloudFormation templates can be as simple or complex as you want them to be in terms of managing your infrastructure. In your first example, it made sense to simply associate the newly launched EC2 instance with existing resources in your AWS account. If the use case is to define the infrastructure for a small business website or to define a larger scale website infrastructure, your template may include much more than just a single EC2 instance; it may include the creation of IAM accounts and roles, networking resources such as VPCs, security group definitions for varying types of compute resources, S3 bucket creation as storage for resources that will be created, and much more. Creating a complex stack is out of the scope of this chapter but will be visited in the final web hosting scenario later in the book. For now, let's assume that you want to have CloudFormation create the EC2 instance for you as well as the security group that will be used by that resource.

For this example, I included the file CF_EC2_SecurityGroup_Stack.json in the chapter source files. The file will look similar to the example above, with the addition of the following code under the Resources section of the template, which will create a new security group. You will want to update the sample code where needed to specify resources in your environment; for example, the IP address that you're connecting from will need to be added to the port 22 configuration.

```
"WebServerSecurityGroup" : {
   "Type" : "AWS::EC2::SecurityGroup",
   "Properties" : {
   "GroupDescription" : "Enable HTTP access via port 80",
     "SecurityGroupIngress" : [
       {"IpProtocol" : "tcp", "FromPort" : "80", "ToPort" : "80", "CidrIp" : "0.0.0.0/0"},
       {"IpProtocol" : "tcp", "FromPort" : "22", "ToPort" : "22", "CidrIp" : "24.57.80.57/32"}
       ]
   }
}
```

This code names a resource to be created called WebServerSecurityGroup, of type AWS EC2 security group. It also sets inbound port properties for allowing traffic to port 80 from anywhere and port 22 (your management port) from only my IP address. Allowing management access from only the IP addresses that need access is a security best practice to limit the attack surface of your infrastructure.

In addition to this code, you need to make a small change to the code that will create your EC2 instance to tell CloudFormation to use this new security group as the one that gets associated with your new virtual server instance. The updated code snippet for how you reference this in the template is below. Again, you'll need to adjust it to match your environment variables, such as your KeyName.

```
"WebServer" : {
    "Type" : "AWS::EC2::Instance",
    "Properties" : {
    "ImageId" : "ami-1e299d7e",
    "KeyName" : "nadonhosting",
        "InstanceType" : "t2.micro",
        "SecurityGroups" : [ {"Ref" : "WebServerSecurityGroup"} ]
        }
    }
```

As you can see, you can use a "Ref" call to reference a resource in your CloudFormation template. As you launch this stack, the security group will be created and then the new EC2 virtual server will be launched and the referenced (and newly created) security group will be associated with the new EC2 instance. As a reminder, to create the stack, you'll browse to CloudFormation from the AWS Console Services menu, click Create Stack, and enter your stack information. After the launch of the stack has completed, browsing to your EC2 dashboard and inspecting the instance properties as shown in Figure 11-6 will show the newly created EC2 instance, the properly associated security group, and the proper inbound port settings as requested in your CloudFormation template file.

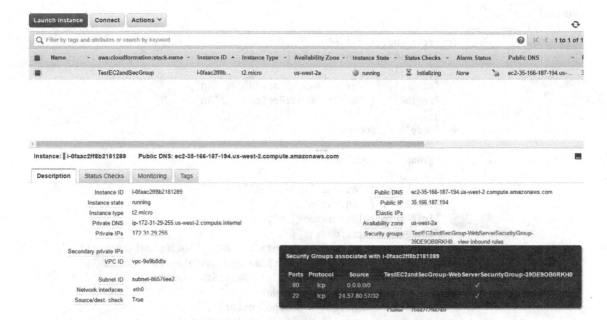

Figure 11-6. *Inspecting your EC2 virtual server instance to verify that proper settings have been associated and created from your CloudFormation template*

At this point, from within the CloudFormation dashboard, you can go ahead and delete the stack to remove the resources created from your account.

Application Installation in a CloudFormation Template

Now that you've seen how to create multiple resources in a CloudFormation template, let's move on to something a bit more complex. Let's look at how you add the steps similar to what you used in the User Data section of an EC2 instance launch in a CloudFormation template. The process is similar, but the code/tools used will be a bit different.

For this example, I have included the file CF_EC2_SG_WebApp_Stack.json in the chapter source files. I've added quite a bit of information in this file and it may seem overwhelming, but I'll focus on just the areas that I've added and go through an explanation of what the code additions address.

Starting at the top of the file, you will notice an addition of the Metadata section to your WebServer resource. In this section, you can define data about the steps to be done to your server. The code added to this section is below:

```
"Metadata" : {
        "AWS::CloudFormation::Init" : {
                    "configSets" : {
          "webapp_install" : ["install_cfn", "install_webserver"]
                                },
```

This code adds the section for Metadata, and creates a CloudFormation Init key that will be used by the CloudFormation service. In the Init key you can define a configSet, which can be thought of as a list of functions to run. Each function will be declared below and will list actions to be performed within them. From the code above you can tell that the webapp_install configSet is made up of two additional sections to be processed: install.cfn and install_webserver. Let's start by exploring install.cfn:

161

```
"install_cfn" : {
        "files": {
               "/etc/cfn/cfn-hup.conf": {
                      "content": { "Fn::Join": [ "", [
                      "[main]\n",
                      "stack=", { "Ref": "AWS::StackId" }, "\n",
                      "region=", { "Ref": "AWS::Region" }, "\n"
                      ]]},
                      "mode"  : "000400",
                      "owner" : "root",
                      "group" : "root"
               },
               "/etc/cfn/hooks.d/cfn-auto-reloader.conf": {
                      "content": { "Fn::Join": [ "", [
                      "[cfn-auto-reloader-hook]\n",
                      "triggers=post.update\n",
                      "path=Resources.WebServer.Metadata.AWS::CloudFormation::Init\n",
                                    "action=/opt/aws/bin/cfn-init -v ",
                      "       --stack ", { "Ref" : "AWS::StackName" },
                      "       --resource WebServer ",
                      "       --configsets webapp_install",
                      "       --region ", { "Ref" : "AWS::Region" }, "\n"
                      ]]},
                      "mode"  : "000400",
                      "owner" : "root",
                      "group" : "root"
                      }
               }
        }
```

This code adds necessary files for the CloudFormation Helper files needed to use with CloudFormation Init. As you explore the code, you can see how files on a file system are referenced and content is created within them using the join commands. You can also see how to set file permissions for the files. This is a standard code block needed to be able to use CloudFormation Init, so this was taken from AWS Sample templates. As you will remember, you have two sections within the web_install configSet definition, so once the above code has been completed, the process will move on to the install_webserver section. Let's explore that code addition now:

```
"install_webserver" : {
        "packages" : {
               "yum" : {
                      "php"           : [],
                      "httpd"         : []
               }
        },
        "services" : {
               "sysvinit" : {
                      "httpd"  : { "enabled" : "true", "ensureRunning" : "true" }
                      }
               }
        }
```

In this code, you can see how to launch your package manager "yum" by declaring it under the packages declaration. You can choose which packages to install. In the above example, you have only defined PHP (php) and the Apache Web Server (httpd). If you want to add additional packages, you can add them here. Under the package definitions is a "services" definition and in here you are asking CloudFormation Init to make sure that the httpd service is enabled and running before proceeding. Now that you have listed the two functions that will be processed by CloudFormation Init, let's examine how CloudFormation Init is initiated through adding a user data definition in the Properties declarations of your web server resource. Let's explore that code addition now:

```
"Properties" : {
        "ImageId" : "ami-1e299d7e",
        "KeyName" : "nadonhosting",
        "InstanceType" : "t2.micro",
        "SecurityGroups" : [ {"Ref" : "WebServerSecurityGroup"} ],
        "UserData" : { "Fn::Base64" : { "Fn::Join" : ["", [
                "#!/bin/bash -xe\n",
                "yum update -y aws-cfn-bootstrap\n",
                "/opt/aws/bin/cfn-init -v ",
                "        --stack ", { "Ref" : "AWS::StackName" },
                "        --resource WebServer ",
                "        --configsets webapp_install ",
                "        --region ", { "Ref" : "AWS::Region" }, "\n",
                "/opt/aws/bin/cfn-signal -e $? ",
                "        --stack ", { "Ref" : "AWS::StackName" },
                "        --resource WebServer ",
                "        --region ", { "Ref" : "AWS::Region" }, "\n"
        ]]}}
        }
```

In this code, you can see that the web server Properties definition looks much like your previous example in terms of which AMI, key pair, instance type, and security group you're using. You can see the addition of a User Data definition and in the user data you can see that you're running commands as you did when you used the CLI to launch an instance, but this time you're calling to the CloudFormation Init application (cfn-init) and referencing the configSet to run, along with information about the stack and region where the infrastructure is being deployed. The reason you're doing this rather than a single call of application installs in the user data definition is because there may be times where you need to update and redeploy your infrastructure, as you'll explore further in the next chapter. You can refer to what you're using in the user data definition above as a "hook" into CloudFormation for this specific resource that you're creating, which enables CloudFormation to manage the infrastructure and for you to define configSets to instruct CloudFormation on steps you'd like done to that infrastructure.

What we have discussed here captures all of the changes to the template except one. The final change you made was to implement a CloudFormation template named Outputs to help you see the public DNS name value of the EC2 virtual server instance that is being created in your template. The code snippet for this output is as follows:

```
"Outputs" : {
"WebsiteURL" : {
"Value" : { "Fn::Join" : ["", ["http://", { "Fn::GetAtt" : [ "WebServer",
"PublicDnsName" ]}]]},
"Description" : "Web Server DNS Address"
        }
}
```

In this code, you add the Outputs section to your template, and define an output called WebsiteURL that reaches out to the WebServer resource that is created in the template and references the value of the PublicDNSName of that resource. You then also define a description of this resource so that it's easier to read. After launching this stack template in CloudFormation, the process will process as you've seen other stack creation work and you'll see the stack status update from CREATE_IN_PROGRESS through to CREATE_COMPLETE. However, now if you look under the Outputs tab in the Properties section of the newly created stack, you'll see a link to the EC2 virtual server instance, as shown in Figure 11-7.

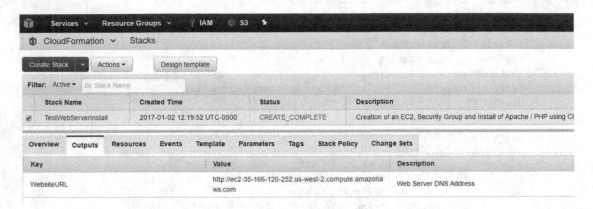

Figure 11-7. *Your newly launched CloudFormation stack with the Outputs tab selected and showing the URL of the EC2 resource that was launched as part of the CloudFormation template resources*

At this point, you can log back into CloudFormation from the AWS Console Services menu and delete the stack that you created to remove unnecessary resources and ensure that you don't have multiple EC2 instances running, which may result in extra AWS billing charges.

Amazon Sample CloudFormation Templates

At this point in the chapter I hope you're starting to see the power and flexibility of using CloudFormation to deploy infrastructure. In the next chapter, you will see the true benefit of being able to update infrastructure that has been deployed and the central management of these resources, but for now let's talk about a different type of resources, ones that Amazon offers for those looking to build their infrastructure using CloudFormation. Amazon has a variety of premade templates for your use and customization located at

`https://aws.amazon.com/cloudformation/aws-cloudformation-templates/`.

You can use them to learn more about how to define resources within the structure of a template or to customize and create complex templates used to launch your resources. Before I end this chapter, let's review one of the Amazon CloudFormation templates for deploying WordPress to an EC2 virtual server instance. The template has been included in this chapter's source files and is named `AWS_Wordpress_Sample_SingleInstance.json`. Since you've looked at the sections of the template file such as the statement declaration, format, resources, and outputs, let's look at the other sections used in this template.

The first section you'll explore is the Parameters section. Anything declared in this section will be requested from the account/user launching the CloudFormation template prior to stack creation.

```
"Parameters" : {

    "KeyName": {
      "Description" : "Name of an existing EC2 KeyPair to enable SSH access to the instances",
      "Type": "AWS::EC2::KeyPair::KeyName",
      "ConstraintDescription" : "must be the name of an existing EC2 KeyPair."
    },
```

You can think of each of the sections defined above in the template as a question that will be asked about the infrastructure to be created by CloudFormation. After the user enters these values, the data for each will be available to other parts of the CloudFormation template. The first section, shown in the code above, asks for the key pair that will be used to log into the resources created and defines it as "KeyName." The code shown below asks for the instance type to be used during the EC2 virtual server instance creation:

```
"InstanceType" : {
"Description" : "WebServer EC2 instance type",
"Type" : "String",
"Default" : "t2.small",
"AllowedValues" : [ "t1.micro", "t2.nano", "t2.micro", "t2.small", "t2.medium", "t2.large",
"m1.small", "m1.medium", "m1.large", "m1.xlarge", "m2.xlarge", "m2.2xlarge", "m2.4xlarge",
"m3.medium", "m3.large", "m3.xlarge", "m3.2xlarge", "m4.large", "m4.xlarge", "m4.2xlarge",
"m4.4xlarge", "m4.10xlarge", "c1.medium", "c1.xlarge", "c3.large", "c3.xlarge",
"c3.2xlarge", "c3.4xlarge", "c3.8xlarge", "c4.large", "c4.xlarge", "c4.2xlarge",
"c4.4xlarge", "c4.8xlarge", "g2.2xlarge", "g2.8xlarge", "r3.large", "r3.xlarge",
"r3.2xlarge", "r3.4xlarge", "r3.8xlarge", "i2.xlarge", "i2.2xlarge", "i2.4xlarge",
"i2.8xlarge", "d2.xlarge", "d2.2xlarge", "d2.4xlarge", "d2.8xlarge", "hi1.4xlarge",
"hs1.8xlarge", "cr1.8xlarge", "cc2.8xlarge", "cg1.4xlarge"]
    ,
    "ConstraintDescription" : "must be a valid EC2 instance type."
    },
```

In the above definition, you can see that the input expected is a string value and that the default value is set to t2.small. The user will be able to select any instance type from the list of defined AllowedValues and no other type. The next item that is defined asks for the IP address of where SSH connections will be coming from to manage resources:

```
"SSHLocation": {
  "Description": "The IP address range that can be used to SSH to the EC2 instances",
  "Type": "String",
  "MinLength": "9",
  "MaxLength": "18",
  "Default": "0.0.0.0/0",
  "AllowedPattern": "(\\d{1,3})\\.(\\d{1,3})\\.(\\d{1,3})\\.(\\d{1,3})/(\\d{1,2})",
  "ConstraintDescription": "must be a valid IP CIDR range of the form x.x.x.x/x."
},
```

In the above definition, the IP address will be entered as a string but there is also an AllowedPattern constraint imposed that uses regular expressions to make sure that the value entered matches an IP address range in the form of CIDR notation. It also sets a minimum and maximum length for the value as an additional data validation step. There are four additional items defined in the Parameters section of the template that use the same format as the code samples above; they ask the user for the WordPress database name, database user, database password, and database root password. This information is set in the

165

parameters so that this template can be used by different people but still collect the needed information to complete a WordPress CMS website and database setup.

Another reason that you may choose to use parameter definition is because you may **delegate** the responsibility to others within your AWS account **the ability** to launch resources using CloudFormation templates, but you may want to require them to stay within certain parameters of what type of infrastructure that they can launch. As you see from above, definition options such as AllowedValues will limit what can be launched by an account within the context of CloudFormation.

The next new section that you'll explore in the template is the Mappings section. This section is a key-value pair listing of possible keys and the value that should be associated with it when referenced. Two snippets of keys are defined as follows:

```
"Mappings" : {
    "AWSInstanceType2Arch" : {
        "t1.micro"    : { "Arch" : "PV64"   },
        "t2.nano"     : { "Arch" : "HVM64"  },
        "t2.micro"    : { "Arch" : "HVM64"  },

    "AWSRegionArch2AMI" : {
 "us-east-1":{"PV64" : "ami-2a69aa47", "HVM64" : "ami-6869aa05", "HVMG2" : "ami-648d9973"},
 "us-west-2":{"PV64" : "ami-7f77b31f", "HVM64" : "ami-7172b611", "HVMG2" : "ami-09cd7a69"},
 "us-west-1":{"PV64" : "ami-a2490dc2", "HVM64" : "ami-31490d51", "HVMG2" : "ami-1e5f0e7e"},
```

In the first key, the EC2 instance architecture is mapped to what should be used for each of the possible InstanceTypes that were defined in the Parameters section are listed. This means that if the user chose the instance type of t1.micro, the architecture used would be PV64 because of this mapping definition. In the second key, the instance architecture and the AMI to be used is mapped to the value of AWS region. If the CloudFormation template is launched in the Oregon AWS region, the values for us-west-2 will used. This means that if the user selected a t1.micro instance type, this mapping tells you that for the Oregon region (us-west-2) an instance type with an architecture of PV64 (the t1.micro instance) should use the AMI ID ami-7f77b31f as the base image to launch the EC2 resource. This should illustrate how the Mappings definition within a CloudFormation template is used to map keys to data values.

The above mappings are used in the Resources : WebServer : Properties section of your template sample, as shown by the following code snippet:

```
"Properties": {
"ImageId" : { "Fn::FindInMap" : [ "AWSRegionArch2AMI", { "Ref" : "AWS::Region" },
  { "Fn::FindInMap" : [ "AWSInstanceType2Arch", { "Ref" : "InstanceType" }, "Arch" ] } ] }
```

When fields or keys are defined in a Mappings section, they can be referenced by calling a function named FindInMap, as shown above. This function uses the key to find the value mapped to the key, and the code above is an example of single and multi-level mapping.

Summary

This chapter introduced using the AWS CloudFormation service to define architecture and resources to be deployed using templates. You walked through the creation of a very basic template that deployed a single resource to AWS, an Amazon sample template that can be used to deploy a single instance with WordPress CMS installed on it. CloudFormation is a service and AWS concept that could have an entire book written on it. I'll spend a bit more time talking about the management of infrastructure in the next chapter, and the knowledge from this chapter and the next will be foundational in terms of what is discussed in the third web hosting scenario of the book.

CHAPTER 12

■ ■ ■

Updating the Stack

In the last chapter, I discussed using CloudFormation and templates to deploy AWS infrastructure as code. You were introduced to the concept of a stack as a collection of infrastructure that is deployed and can be managed as a single entity. You walked through multiple template examples showing how to deploy a very simple template with one AWS resource all the way up to deploying a sample AWS WordPress template that deployed multiple applications on a single EC2 virtual server. In this chapter, I'll cover updating the stack and other management-related items. You'll use two AWS sample templates to see how to update an existing stack to move from being deployed to a single instance to a much more fault-tolerant solution using additional AWS resources and instances in multiple availability zones within a given region.

Managing the Deployment Code/Template

As you saw in the previous chapter, you can use a template that contains JSON-formatted text to deploy resources in the AWS platform using CloudFormation. Although the template used to launch a CloudFormation stack is available under the Template tab in the stack properties section of the CloudFormation dashboard, it is also recommended that you have a working copy saved in a safe location. This working copy will be used when you want to edit your resources because of an update or if for any reason you need to relaunch an exact copy of this stack elsewhere. There are multiple ways that you can approach backing up the code template. CloudFormation templates that you've uploaded in the previous chapter will be stored in S3 when used to deploy resources. An example of how the templates are stored in S3 is shown in Figure 12-1.

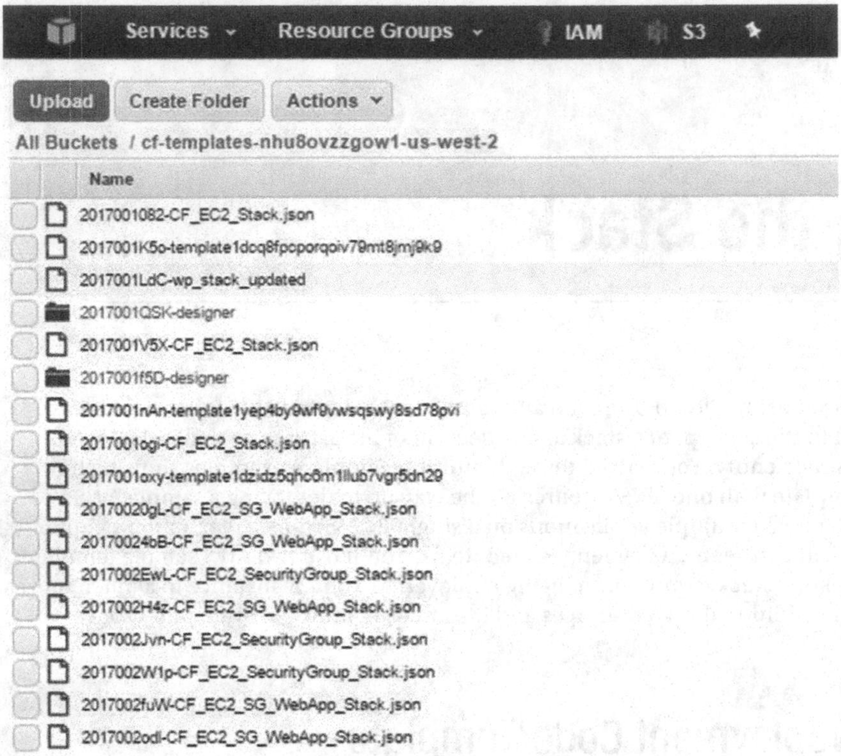

Figure 12-1. CloudFormation templates stored in S3 as part of the "upload a template" function for deploying AWS resources

Each time a CloudFormation stack is updated and redeployed, a copy of the current template used to deploy the resources will be saved in the S3 bucket that CloudFormation created and uses for template information. If you want to back up this bucket to another bucket, use the AWS CLI to sync the files between buckets. The command to sync between buckets is

```
aws s3 sync s3://mybucket-src s3://mybucket-target
```

Rather than syncing S3 buckets, you could just choose to create a new bucket of your own to hold backup information that you feel may be needed. If you want to save a bit of money, you can even switch the storage class to be "Standard - Infrequent Access" rather than the default storage class. The least costly option is to store the template files in offline storage, such as locally or a free cloud storage option like Google Drive.

Storing a single template, or even ten, is not going to take up a large amount of space. Some readers may be looking for a more robust option for storing their CloudFormation templates and code. The AWS platform has a solution for this in the form of the CodeCommit service. CodeCommit allows you to create secure code repositories in the cloud. The benefits of a code repository include versioning and the ability for multiple developers to be working on and checking in code that can then be deployed to your infrastructure. You can access CodeCommit from the Services menu of the AWS Console under the Developer Tools section.

Managing Access to Stack Updates

In the previous chapter, you logged into the AWS Console to deploy your CloudFormation stacks. Although this is a simple way to deploy the infrastructure, there may come a time when you have multiple templates and stacks that can be deployed and you may want to delegate the ability of performing updates to other IAM accounts or roles in your AWS account. As discussed in earlier chapters, AWS IAM allows you to create accounts, groups, and roles and to assign permissions by applying policies that have the access needed to perform tasks. For CloudFormation, you can create a role that acts on behalf of your account to launch resources, but when the account assumes that role, it is still the base permissions or policy applied to that account that is used to launch resources. This means that if you try to launch a CloudFormation template from an account that has limited permissions in a given resource, such as EC2, you may not be able to launch the resources within the stack. In terms of CloudFormation access, what you may choose to do is to limit certain accounts to only have read access to the CloudFormation service by attaching the policy to limit access via IAM to the group or account, as shown in Figure 12-2.

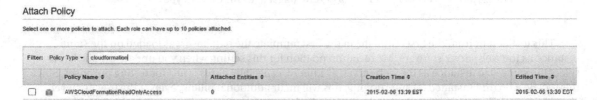

Attach Policy

Select one or more policies to attach. Each role can have up to 10 policies attached.

Filter: Policy Type ▾ cloudformation

	Policy Name ⬦	Attached Entities ⬦	Creation Time ⬦	Edited Time ⬦
☐	AWSCloudFormationReadOnlyAccess	0	2015-02-06 13:39 EST	2015-02-06 13:39 EST

Figure 12-2. The IAM AWSCloudFormationReadOnlyAccess policy is shown. This is a way to limit accounts or groups from launching stacks using CloudFormation

Although limiting accounts and groups may seem like overkill, CloudFormation is quite powerful and can easily launch a very large infrastructure into your AWS account, which could become a billing nightmare if one of your users did this without your knowledge.

Deploying the Sample Stack

In the previous chapter, you used the AWS WordPress CloudFormation template sample, which launched WordPress on a single EC2 instance. In this chapter, you'll launch that stack and then work through updating it to launch additional resources; the end result is a more scalable, fault tolerant infrastructure implementation.

The AWS WordPress Single Instance template is included in this chapter's source files: AWS_Sample_Wordpress_SingleInstance.json. Since I covered the launch of a stack in the previous chapter, I'll assume that you have successfully launched the stack, waited about 30 minutes after launch, connected to the instance, and walked through the WordPress installation.

Updating the Stack

Now that you have the WordPress Single Instance stack running, let's take a look at updating the stack to a multi-instance, multi-availability-zone sample template. The updated template is included in this chapter's source files: AWS_Sample_Wordpress_MutliInstance.json. Let's take a look at the template differences first to understand what is being defined in this updated template.

The first thing to notice is the inclusion of a DB instance class in the Parameters section. It asks for information at launch time and defines what instance type should be used as the EC2 virtual server instance that will be used to host your database resources.

```
"DBClass" : {
"Description" : "Database instance class",
"Type" : "String",
"Default" : "db.t2.small",
"AllowedValues" : [ "db.t1.micro", "db.m1.small", "db.m1.medium", "db.m1.large",
"db.m1.xlarge", "db.m2.xlarge", "db.m2.2xlarge", "db.m2.4xlarge", "db.m3.medium",
"db.m3.large", "db.m3.xlarge", "db.m3.2xlarge", "db.m4.large", "db.m4.xlarge",
"db.m4.2xlarge", "db.m4.4xlarge", "db.m4.10xlarge", "db.r3.large", "db.r3.xlarge",
"db.r3.2xlarge", "db.r3.4xlarge", "db.r3.8xlarge", "db.m2.xlarge", "db.m2.2xlarge",
"db.m2.4xlarge", "db.cr1.8xlarge", "db.t2.micro", "db.t2.small", "db.t2.medium", "db.t2.large"]
,
"ConstraintDescription" : "must select a valid database instance type."
},
```

This is different from the first template; in the first template the database was loaded on the same instance as the web server software. My recommendation for this setting when you update the stack is to select the same size instance as the web server, a t2.micro, especially if this is just for testing purposes. Since this will be a second instance up and running, this will incur additional billing, even at the free tier level.

The next difference is related to a question of whether you want to set up a multi-AZ MySQL RDS instance. If you choose "True" for this parameter, additional answers will need to be provided about the setup.

```
"MultiAZDatabase": {
 "Default": "false",
 "Description" : "Create a Multi-AZ MySQL Amazon RDS database instance",
 "Type": "String",
      "AllowedValues" : [ "true", "false" ],
      "ConstraintDescription" : "must be either true or false."
    },

  "WebServerCapacity": {
    "Default": "1",
    "Description" : "The initial number of WebServer instances",
    "Type": "Number",
      "MinValue": "1",
      "MaxValue": "5",
      "ConstraintDescription" : "must be between 1 and 5 EC2 instances."
    },

"DBAllocatedStorage" : {
    "Default": "5",
    "Description" : "The size of the database (Gb)",
    "Type": "Number",
      "MinValue": "5",
      "MaxValue": "1024",
      "ConstraintDescription" : "must be between 5 and 1024Gb."
    }
  }
```

As you can see in the above template code, you're going to be asked for three items in the Parameters section related to this decision: whether you'll use multi-AZ or not, the initial count of web servers to initialize (between 1 and 5), and the allocated storage for the database.

The largest changes to the template occur under the Resources section. In comparing the files, you'll notice that the first set of noticeable changes (shown below) have to do with adding an Elastic Load Balancer. A load balancer is an EC2 resource that accepts web traffic and forwards that traffic on to web server resources that can be as small as a single EC2 instance or a group of EC2 instances in a balanced fashion.

```
"ElasticLoadBalancer" : {
    "Type" : "AWS::ElasticLoadBalancing::LoadBalancer",
    "Properties" : {
        "AvailabilityZones" : { "Fn::GetAZs" : "" },
        "CrossZone" : "true",
        "LBCookieStickinessPolicy" : [ {
            "PolicyName" : "CookieBasedPolicy",
            "CookieExpirationPeriod" : "30"
        } ],
        "Listeners" : [ {
            "LoadBalancerPort" : "80",
            "InstancePort" : "80",
            "Protocol" : "HTTP",
            "PolicyNames" : [ "CookieBasedPolicy" ]
        } ],
        "HealthCheck" : {
            "Target" : "HTTP:80/wordpress/wp-admin/install.php",
            "HealthyThreshold" : "2",
            "UnhealthyThreshold" : "5",
            "Interval" : "10",
            "Timeout" : "5"
        }
    }
}
```

This template code will add the resource of an EC2 Elastic Load Balancer (ELB) that will accept traffic on port 80 (LoadBalancerPort) and forward it on to any instances behind the load balancer on port 80 (InstancePort). It also implements a cookie-based persistence policy. More information EC2 Load Balancers and their settings can be found at https://aws.amazon.com/elasticloadbalancing/. It is worth noting that AWS recently added an Application Load Balancer that offers many more features for web application load balancing than the Elastic Load Balancer, which you'll take a look at in the next section. Finally, an ELB Health Check is added to verify that there is always a response from one of the instances behind the load balancer for the URL (/wordpress/wp-admin/install.php).

The next differences that you'll notice have to do with the web server resources. In the new template, you're deploying multiple web servers, so the Resource section has been updated from defining a single web server resource to a WebServerGroup that has quite a few new properties that you haven't seen yet. I'll discuss some of them.

```
"WebServerGroup" : {
    "Type" : "AWS::AutoScaling::AutoScalingGroup",
    "Properties" : {
        "AvailabilityZones" : { "Fn::GetAZs" : "" },
        "LaunchConfigurationName" : { "Ref" : "LaunchConfig" },
```

```
      "MinSize" : "1",
      "MaxSize" : "5",
      "DesiredCapacity" : { "Ref" : "WebServerCapacity" },
      "LoadBalancerNames" : [ { "Ref" : "ElasticLoadBalancer" } ]
    }
```

First, the WebServerGroup is defined as an AWS Auto Scaling group that will use values passed from the Parameters section in terms of WebServerCapacity, and references that this group will sit behind the Elastic Load Balancer that was created earlier in the code template.

```
"UpdatePolicy": {
    "AutoScalingRollingUpdate": {
      "MinInstancesInService": "1",
      "MaxBatchSize": "1",
      "PauseTime" : "PT15M",
      "WaitOnResourceSignals": "true"
    }
  }
```

An Auto Scaling group update policy sets the minimum number of instances to be available in the Auto Scaling group and the maximum that can be launched in a batch. It also defines the wait time (PT15M, or 15 minutes) for a signal to be received from the instance before the Auto Scaling group takes action. If you're wondering about the method of the Auto Scaling group communication in terms of getting information about the instance, you'd be correct if you guessed CloudWatch.

Next, an Auto Scaling launch configuration is defined. This section defines what should be done when a new instance is launched by the Auto Scaling group. This will look very familiar (with the exception of the MySQL Server installation) as the previous template. These instance resources will still need MySQL client utilities, but won't require the server software since a MySQL RDS database instance will be part of the Resources definition.

This brings you to the last change to the template, which is the definition of the MySQL RDS Database resources.

```
"DBSecurityGroup": {
    "Type": "AWS::RDS::DBSecurityGroup",
    "Condition" : "Is-EC2-Classic",
    "Properties": {
      "DBSecurityGroupIngress": {
        "EC2SecurityGroupName": { "Ref": "WebServerSecurityGroup" }
      },
      "GroupDescription": "database access"
    }
  },
  "DBEC2SecurityGroup": {
    "Type": "AWS::EC2::SecurityGroup",
    "Condition" : "Is-EC2-VPC",
    "Properties" : {
      "GroupDescription": "Open database for access",
      "SecurityGroupIngress" : [{
        "IpProtocol" : "tcp",
        "FromPort" : "3306",
        "ToPort" : "3306",
```

```
            "SourceSecurityGroupName" : { "Ref" : "WebServerSecurityGroup" }
        }]
    }
},
  "DBInstance" : {
    "Type": "AWS::RDS::DBInstance",
    "Properties": {
        "DBName"              : { "Ref" : "DBName" },
        "Engine"              : "MySQL",
        "MultiAZ"             : { "Ref" : "MultiAZDatabase" },
        "MasterUsername"      : { "Ref" : "DBUser" },
        "MasterUserPassword"  : { "Ref" : "DBPassword" },
        "DBInstanceClass"     : { "Ref" : "DBClass" },
        "AllocatedStorage"    : { "Ref" : "DBAllocatedStorage" },
        "VPCSecurityGroups"   : { "Fn::If" : [ "Is-EC2-VPC", [ { "Fn::GetAtt":
                                  [ "DBEC2SecurityGroup",
"GroupId" ] } ], { "Ref" : "AWS::NoValue"}]],
        "DBSecurityGroups"    : { "Fn::If" : [ "Is-EC2-Classic", [ { "Ref": "DBSecurityGroup" } ], {
Ref" : "AWS::NoValue"}]]}
    }
  }
}
```

In this section of the template code, you're adding an AWS RDS database instance with the MySQL engine. Refer back to the Parameters section to find out whether this should be a multi-AZ setup and to get the database username, password, administrator password, and instance class to be used.

In addition, you also create a new security group based on a condition that is evaluated to find out whether you're in a virtual private cloud (VPC) network setup or if you're using EC2 Classic. EC2 Classic only comes into play if this AWS account had been set up years ago; it's not an option for new AWS accounts.

Understanding Impact

You now have the template code that you want to update your stack with and you understand that you'll be adding resources. It is important to understand that in the process of a stack update some resources can have changes done to them without impacting the service and disrupting website visitors while others will most definitely impact website visitors. In your situation, since you are creating an Auto Scaling group to hold your instance configuration, the existing EC2 virtual server resource that you have must be destroyed and a new instance will be launched as part of the new configuration definition. All data on that single EC2 instance will be lost, and since you're setting up a new RDS database instance, you'll need to walk back through the WordPress installation once the stack has been installed.

CloudFormation evaluates the current template and what changes are needed to update it to the new version of the template. There are three types of changes that will be made when updating a template. The first is a change that has no interruption. An example of this type of change is the addition of tags to an EC2 virtual server instance. In this case, CloudFormation can make the update without having to redeploy the resource. The second type is an update that causes some interruption. An example of this type of change is the creation of a new security group with differing inbound and outbound port configurations. The instance would experience a brief interruption as the newly created security group was applied to it and the old one was disassociated from it. The last type of change is the most disruptive and is referred to as replacement. In this type of update, CloudFormation is not able to update the asset in its current state, so it will destroy the current resource and replace it with the definition of the resource in the updated template file.

There is a process that protects you and gives you the opportunity to review the changes before implementing them. This process is called a Change Set. To update an existing stack, click the stack name from within the CloudFormation dashboard and then click the Action button and click "Create Change Set for Current Stack." On the next screen, shown in Figure 12-3, choose to upload the new version of your stack template and click the Next button.

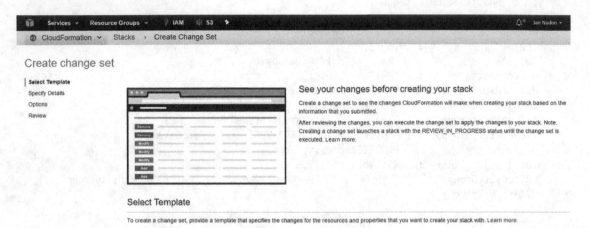

Figure 12-3. *Creating a new Change Set from the CloudFormation dashboard with the initial screen to update the template file used by CloudFormation*

You'll then progress through the Parameters section of the new stack template, as shown in Figure 12-4.

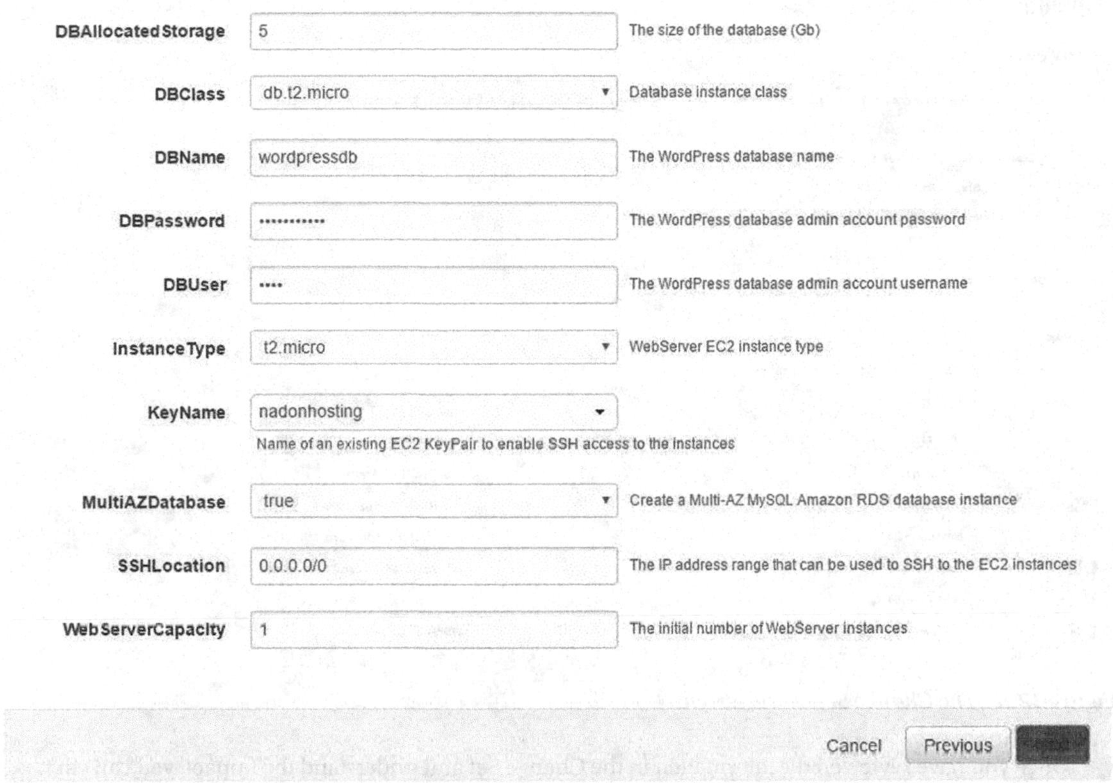

DBAllocatedStorage	5	The size of the database (Gb)
DBClass	db.t2.micro ▾	Database instance class
DBName	wordpressdb	The WordPress database name
DBPassword	•••••••••••	The WordPress database admin account password
DBUser	••••	The WordPress database admin account username
InstanceType	t2.micro ▾	WebServer EC2 instance type
KeyName	nadonhosting ▾	

Name of an existing EC2 KeyPair to enable SSH access to the instances

MultiAZDatabase	true ▾	Create a Multi-AZ MySQL Amazon RDS database instance
SSHLocation	0.0.0.0/0	The IP address range that can be used to SSH to the EC2 instances
WebServerCapacity	1	The initial number of WebServer instances

Cancel   Previous

Figure 12-4. *The new template parameters are requested as you walk through the update of your Change Set using CloudFormation*

After entering needed information and clicking the Next button to progress to the following step, you will be presented with a screen that allows you to review the changes to the resources; any resources that fall into the "replacement" category type of CloudFormation change will be identified in the review screen. An example of the screen is shown in Figure 12-5.

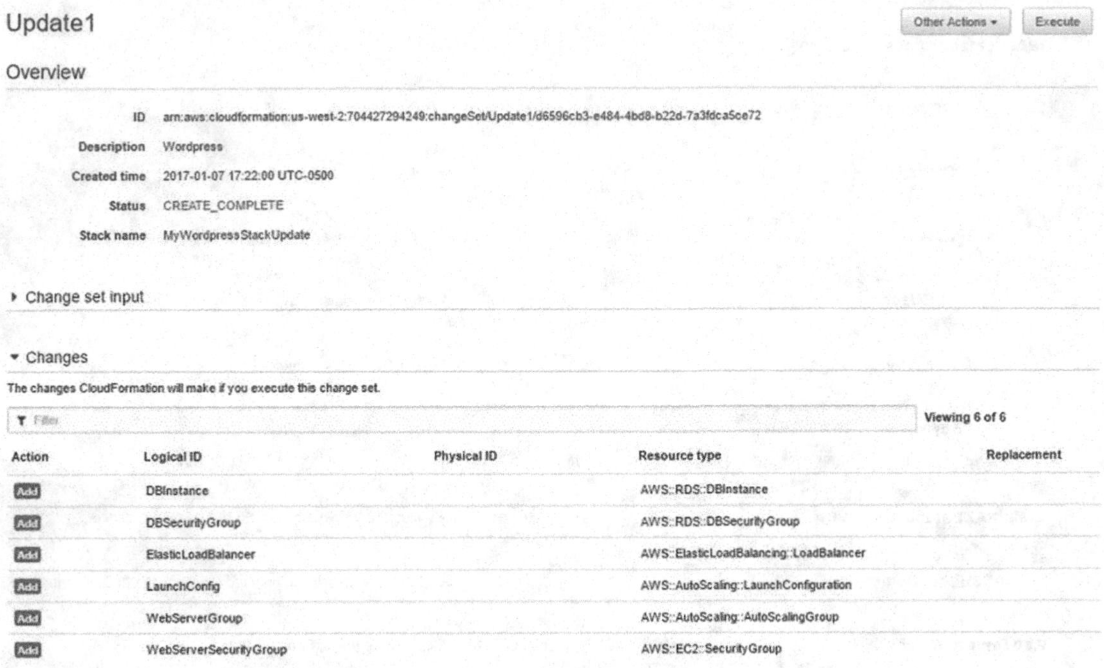

Update1

Overview

ID	arn:aws:cloudformation:us-west-2:704427294249:changeSet/Update1/d6596cb3-e484-4bd8-b22d-7a3fdca5ce72
Description	Wordpress
Created time	2017-01-07 17:22:00 UTC-0500
Status	CREATE_COMPLETE
Stack name	MyWordpressStackUpdate

▸ Change set input

▾ Changes

The changes CloudFormation will make if you execute this change set.

Viewing 6 of 6

Action	Logical ID	Physical ID	Resource type	Replacement
Add	DBInstance		AWS::RDS::DBInstance	
Add	DBSecurityGroup		AWS::RDS::DBSecurityGroup	
Add	ElasticLoadBalancer		AWS::ElasticLoadBalancing::LoadBalancer	
Add	LaunchConfig		AWS::AutoScaling::LaunchConfiguration	
Add	WebServerGroup		AWS::AutoScaling::AutoScalingGroup	
Add	WebServerSecurityGroup		AWS::EC2::SecurityGroup	

Figure 12-5. *The Change Set review screen*

Once you have reviewed the information in the Change Set and understand the impact, you can click the Execute button in the top right-hand corner to proceed with the stack update. You will be prompted by a confirmation window; click the Execute button a second time to complete the process.

Summary

CloudFormation and having a way to deploy your infrastructure in a way that is easy to reproduce quickly are key benefits of managing your Infrastructure as Code. This chapter covered ways that you can protect that code and how to update a deployed stack. You learned how to determine the impact of a stack update before proceeding with the update. Next, I'll summarize what you've learned in this section of the book and do a knowledge check and explore cost considerations for hosting a CMS platform website in Amazon Web Services.

Part 2: Hosting a Platform/CMS Website in Amazon Web Services Wrap-Up

In this section you learned about services related to hosting a platform/content management system-type website in AWS, including migration options, installation using Infrastructure as Code concepts, and the CloudFormation service to stand up and modify an infrastructure stack.

As with the static website hosting scenario, this knowledge check will summarize the services that you've used and give links to additional resources so you can learn more about these services and features. In addition, I will talk about cost considerations for the example CMS sites that you've worked with in this section.

Knowledge Check

CMS Website: You learned that a CMS is a content management system website that consists of static content, database, and application/dynamic resources. They are sometimes referred to as "platform" websites and I covered examples for the three most popular of these platforms: WordPress, Drupal, and Joomla.

AWS S3 (Simple Storage Service): You revisited AWS S3 usage as a major component for this hosting scenario because it will still play a major role in hosting not only static files, but also application files and the CloudFormation templates that define the infrastructure stack that will be launched.

AWS EC2 (Elastic Cloud Compute): You learned how to launch an EC2 virtual server instance through the AWS Console as well as how to use the AWS command line interface to launch resources. You learned about user data and how to install applications during launch time. You learned about security groups and how they control access to your EC2 resources. I introduced EBS (Elastic Block Storage) and covered how it can be used to create volume storage that you can attach to EC2 virtual server instances. You also learned how EC2-related resources can be defined in CloudFormation templates and launched and managed via that AWS service.

AWS RDS (Relational Database Service): You were introduced to the AWS RDS service and learned about the various databases that can be hosted in this fully-managed service. You learned how to set up MySQL database resources from the AWS Console and CLI as well as how to connect to these resources using client-side applications to manage your database resources. You learned how RDS can assist you by handling backups of your databases and even perform upgrades automatically to the platform hosting the databases.

AWS CloudFormation: You learned about the AWS CloudFormation service and how to define infrastructure using JSON/text files. You then learned how to use these definition files to launch an infrastructure stack and how it can be managed as a single unit of resources. You learned how to update and redeploy changes to the infrastructure stack and you learned that some stack updates are more disruptive than others.

Cost Considerations

As with your first hosting scenario, the static website, the scenario presented in this chapter will have similar cost considerations in terms of when to move to a new hosting platform such as AWS. In the first scenario, the benefit to hosting in AWS had to do with the high availability and durability of hosting your files in S3. When you think about a platform/CMS website, there will be additional cost for resources such as EC2 virtual server instances and RDS instances. These costs can range from being quite minimal and reasonable to being significant based on how much data is stored and how much traffic the website is handling. If you are hosting a very active site, you may need to deploy a larger infrastructure. The benefit of using the AWS platform in this case is that you are only charged for what you use and you have the ability to easily scale up to address the real-time need of your visitors. The AWS platform allows you to launch resources quickly and to test functionality with minimal expense. You have the ability to set up your infrastructure to scale automatically to meet the demand of your customers if you so choose. This flexibility and scalability is the selling point when looking at your web hosting platform. When launching a new site, you may not know if you'll get 100 visitors or 100,000 visitors, but you want to be able to deliver your content to the 100,000 visitors if they come. If you lock in with many smaller hosts, they will limit the amount of data (bandwidth) that they will deliver to your customers and you may need to manually intervene if website traffic grows unexpectedly.

In terms of realistic cost estimations when deploying a CMS website using EC2 and RDS resources, you can expect to pay anywhere from $4-$15 per month in hosting charges for a small-to-medium site. At the time of writing, Amazon recently launched a new service call LightSail that offers an easy way to setup a VPS that can be used to host your platform/CMS website. Hosting plans start at $5 per month and go up to $80 per month. Using this method, you're given a predefined set of resources to use based on the plan selected. It's very similar to other hosting providers and I believe that Amazon is offering this to directly compete at this level. My preference is to manage my own resources across the full AWS platform and pay for what I use, but your mileage may vary. You can find more information at https://amazonlightsail.com/.

PART III

Hosting an E-Commerce Website in Amazon Web Services

CHAPTER 13

■ ■ ■

Building Upon Your Foundation

Welcome to Chapter 13 and the start of the final hosting scenario. This scenario, which will be described in more detail in Chapter 14, will be a study of a hypothetical, full-service, e-commerce website that not only handles a high level of web traffic but also accepts payments for products and services sold through the website. I will build upon the foundation of knowledge that you've obtained from the past two hosting scenarios and explain concepts and functionality of AWS services and products that will enable you to deliver a website and services to your customers using the power and flexibility of the AWS platform. In addition to the discussion around the e-commerce hosting scenario, you'll also start looking at the features of the AWS platform that will appeal to those hosting enterprise architecture in data centers who are looking to extend their service catalog or infrastructure into the cloud.

Before I describe the architecture of the next hosting scenario, let's touch base on the concepts and AWS services that will be covered in this section of the book.

AWS Services Introduced/Used

- **AWS S3**: Amazon Web Services Simple Storage Service will be revisited a third time as your main storage location, although this time you'll also start managing a storage lifecycle for your S3 assets. You'll also use the AWS Glacier Storage Solution as a long-term archiving solution.

- **AWS EC2**: Amazon Web Services EC2 (Elastic Cloud Compute) Service will be used in this scenario. Your e-commerce website will be fully redundant and will support Auto Scaling to adapt your infrastructure based on your website traffic needs. This means that you'll have multiple EC2 virtual server instances running your web server application and available to serve your content. You'll learn AWS networking concepts including VPC (virtual private cloud), Elastic IPs and their use, and more, including a deeper look at web traffic load balancing using Elastic Load Balancers and Application Load Balancers.

- **AWS CloudFront**: You'll use Amazon Web Services CloudFront, the CDN (content distribution network) solution for efficiently delivering your website content to customers across the globe in a low-latency, geographically optimized way.

© Jason Nadon 2017
J. Nadon, *Website Hosting and Migration with Amazon Web Services*, DOI 10.1007/978-1-4842-2589-9_13

- **AWS RDS**: Amazon Web Services Relational Database Services, the fully managed service that enables you to leverage AWS infrastructure to host your database services and workloads, will be used again to host the databases needed for your e-commerce website. You will use third-party applications that need database resources to hold information about the products that you're selling as well as your customer database.

- **AWS Workflow Services**: You'll spend some time learning about the ability to extend your efficiency and interaction with your new infrastructure by using AWS Workflow Services including SNS (Simple Notification Service), SQS (Simple Queue Service), and code deployment options including Elastic Beanstalk, OpsWorks, and CodeDeploy.

- **AWS Security Services**: You'll learn about the various services and products that are at your disposal to help with infrastructure security, reporting, and compliance. Topics will include implementing SSL certificates on your website, as well as introductions to AWS Inspector, AWS CloudTrail, and AWS Trusted Advisor.

- **AWS Enterprise Solutions**: Lastly, you'll learn about AWS platform services, which enable you to extend your business into the cloud and deliver desktop workstations, enterprise mail, directory services, and document management to your employees. You'll also see how these services can be used to fill short-term needs for trainers or instructors.

Overview of Services

In addition to the information covered above, you'll explore the current service list offered by AWS at the time of writing this book and you'll learn about the release rate of new products and services from this cloud vendor (Figure 13-1).

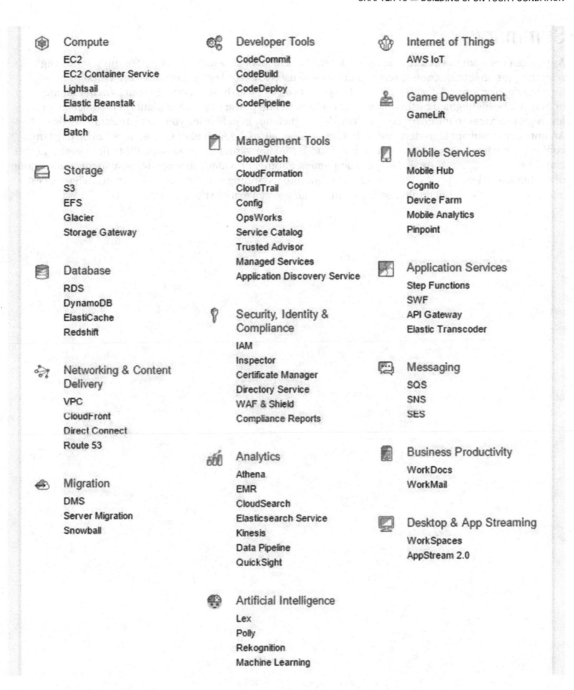

Figure 13-1. *A list of available AWS products and services at the time of writing*

Summary

As you can see from the description above, there will be a lot of information covered in this last hosting scenario plus an introduction to services that can be used to extend enterprise services. As you progress through the next several chapters, think of ways that you can use these services to your benefit that may or may not be highlighted by this book. The true benefit and power of the AWS platform is realized when leveraging services to improve your productivity or efficiency in delivering your infrastructure needs. An important concept to understand is that many, if not all, of the AWS platform services can be used in conjunction with each other to deliver a full cloud-based infrastructure or individually to fit a need, whether cloud-based, on-premise, or as a way to compliment another provider's services. My goal in this final section of the book is to leave you feeling confident in your understanding of how to use all current AWS services and to know the basics of implementing them so that you can explore them further.

CHAPTER 14

■ ■ ■

Enterprise Website Scenario

In this chapter, I will describe the infrastructure of your last web hosting scenario, the enterprise website. I will be describing the resources required to deliver a fault tolerant, highly available solution that leverages AWS services to scale up and down based on website traffic requirements. The solutions and website described in this section of the book will be based around a hypothetical business that has implemented an e-commerce website that sells products and services online. This business also uses its website as a way to drive new business, manage and measure customer engagement, and interact with customers across social media platforms. The focus in this hosting scenario is to deliver a great experience for website visitors and to ensure that transactions that occur are secure and that you protect your customer data and privacy.

I'll also discuss the need for this new business to launch a new product online and how you can manage the uncertainty of being able to accurately forecast your customer interest with an eye to understanding how AWS can help in this area. Let's start diving into this scenario as we have in previous ones, by describing the content, the assets or resources needed, and, in this case, an architecture design diagram that will help you understand the scenario further.

Website Content Overview

This hosting scenario will be focused on a hypothetical enterprise-level website that has e-commerce capabilities plus the requirement to support a small staff operation in a physical location. In your scenario, the website will have the following resources and requirements:

- **Home**: The home page will be the landing page for the website. This is the place where the majority of the advertising and "call to action" activity will occur for this website. It is also the front door to the e-commerce sections of the website content.

- **Products**: This section will have the sales information of the products that you are selling from your online store. As you'll see from the folder structure breakdown later in this chapter, there will be a few different product types. In this example, the business is selling various art works on the site.

- **Promotions**: This area of the site will hold information pertaining to monthly promotions and discounts that the business will offer to its customers.

- **Static Content**: This section of the website will hold your static assets, such as images and documents.

© Jason Nadon 2017
J. Nadon, *Website Hosting and Migration with Amazon Web Services*, DOI 10.1007/978-1-4842-2589-9_14

- **Store**: This e-commerce website scenario will most definitely have a shopping cart/online merchant component. Some may choose to implement a simple way to process payments and orders from a site such as PayPal, and others may choose to use a more complex online store solution like Magento. In your scenario, you will assume and plan for the latter. The installation of the Magento application will be installed in the Store directory within the site structure and you'll need to plan for not only database resources for your website but also for this component, which will hold your product inventory and all the details about it.

- **Contact**: The traditional contact page will also have a feedback form, your social media presence information, and physical store location information.

Website Asset Overview

Figure 14-1 shows the basic file structure of this website scenario. It includes resources that will be hosted on each of the web servers that are serving up the website content.

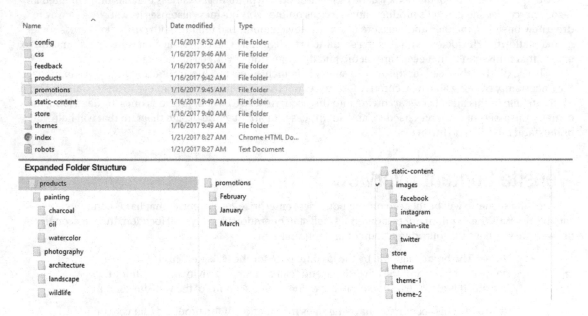

Figure 14-1. *The basic file structure for the web server of the enterprise website scenario*

Website Architecture Design

This section covers the architecture design for the website scenario. This design will deliver a highly available, fault tolerant website hosted in AWS and leveraging the built-in redundancy of having multiple availability zones (AZ) within a given AWS region.

When deploying resources such as EC2 instances or RDS database instances in AWS, you can select whether you'd like them to be placed in a specific AZ. In most cases, when you're standing up resources for testing or development, fault tolerance is not an issue at the top of your mind, so you usually just deploy a single resource to a single AZ within a single region. However, production-level websites and applications require fault tolerance, so for this website hosting scenario you will deploy multiple resources in multiple availability zones. Figure 14-2 provides an overview of the architecture of the website scenario.

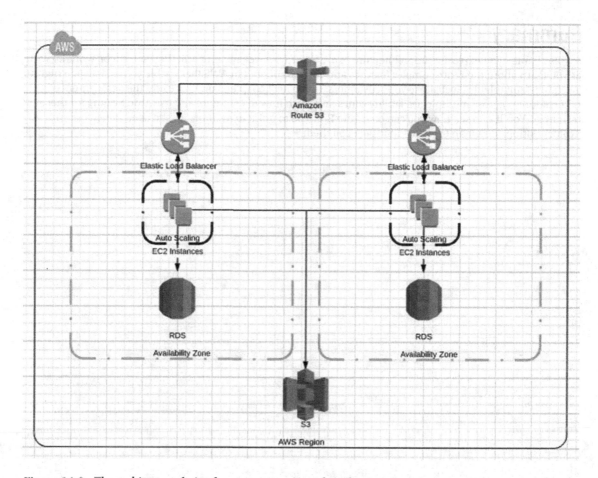

Figure 14-2. *The architecture design for your enterprise website hosting scenario*

As you see from Figure 14-2, you will front all of your web traffic using AWS Route53, which you'll remember is a highly available DNS service with a 100% SLA. From here, you'll have Route53 route your web traffic to a pair of redundant EC2 Elastic Load Balancers. The load balancers will pass the traffic on to your EC2 instances, which will be part of an Auto Scaling group configuration so that you can configure a minimum and maximum setting for how many web servers you want and allow AWS to handle scaling up the infrastructure for you on-demand as your resources become more utilized from web traffic or processing requests. Each EC2 Auto Scaling group will be inside an availability zone with an RDS database instance for that availability zone. You'll have the same infrastructure configured in a second availability zone for an additional level of fault tolerance.

Think of availability zones as data centers. This setup allows you to have EC2 and RDS resources in two locations so that if the infrastructure in one of them fails, you can route traffic to the second. EC2 resources in each AZ will communicate back to S3 for storage resources for the website content.

Summary

In this chapter, you explored the architecture of the enterprise website scenario that you will be working with as you learn about the more complex features and services offered in AWS that enable you to deliver a highly available, fault tolerant website to your customers. In the next chapter, you'll dive into the deployment of EC2 resources across multiple availability zones and learn how to configure and use Auto Scaling for these resources. You'll also see how you can configure Route53 to point to multiple Elastic Load Balancers and explore options for when to route traffic between them.

■ ■ ■

CHAPTER 15

EC2 Resources at Scale

In this chapter, I will walk you through the setup and configuration options to create the top section of the infrastructure resources described in Figure 14-2 in Chapter 14. This will include Route53 setup and configuration options to send web traffic to redundant Elastic Load Balancers, the creation of EC2 resources behind these load balancers in two availability zones, and RDS database resources across availability zones. I'll include a CloudFormation template at the end of this chapter that can be used to deploy an infrastructure that will model what was described in Chapter 14.

Multiple Levels of Redundancy

In the enterprise hosting scenario, your goal is to provide a highly available website to your visitors, one that has the ability to survive failure at multiple levels of the infrastructure stack. Infrastructure in the stack should be designed and deployed with failure in mind. When you launch a new virtual server instance within EC2, you should plan for that instance to have downtime or times when it will need to be redeployed. This is one of the reasons why it is worth the time investment to understand how to use tools like the command-line interface and AWS CloudFormation for easier deployment and management of these resources. In addition to being able to stand up resources quickly using the tools just mentioned, you should plan to have multiple resources available to serve your content. AWS offers regions for resources in a geographical area and availability zones as data center locations for resources within a given region. I discussed this concept earlier in the book, but it's worth talking about further to understand the design for using AZs and regions for redundancy.

Availability Zones and Regions

As mentioned, availability zones and regions are AWS location identifiers for your resources. An availability zone can be thought of as a data center location and there are at least two availability zones within each AWS region. Figure 15-1 illustrates the availability zones and regions available for your resources at the time of writing.

© Jason Nadon 2017
J. Nadon, *Website Hosting and Migration with Amazon Web Services*, DOI 10.1007/978-1-4842-2589-9_15

Code	Name
us-east-1	US East (N. Virginia)
us-east-2	US East (Ohio)
us-west-1	US West (N. California)
us-west-2	US West (Oregon)
ca-central-1	Canada (Central)
eu-west-1	EU (Ireland)
eu-central-1	EU (Frankfurt)
eu-west-2	EU (London)
ap-northeast-1	Asia Pacific (Tokyo)
ap-northeast-2	Asia Pacific (Seoul)
ap-southeast-1	Asia Pacific (Singapore)
ap-southeast-2	Asia Pacific (Sydney)
ap-south-1	Asia Pacific (Mumbai)
sa-east-1	South America (São Paulo)

Figure 15-1. The listing of current AWS regions with geographic name and code

In Figure 15-1, you can see at least two availability zones per location. The naming of these zones consists of the region code with an alphabetic identifier appended to the end. For example, the region "us-east-1" has the following availability zones: "us-east-1a," "us-east-1b," "us-east-1c," "us-east-1d," and "us-east-1e." This region is the original region that was set up and this is why it has so many availability zones. Most have two or three AZs per region, but the naming convention is the same across regions.

Each AWS region is isolated from the other, meaning that resources running in "us-east-1" are isolated from resources running in "us-west-2." If you were to launch all of your resources in a single AZ and this availability zone had an outage, all of your resources would be affected. If you launch resources in multiple AZs, you are considered redundant in that region. Availability zones in a given region are connected via low latency network connections and can easily route traffic between them when there is a failure of a resource in one. AWS gives you the full capability to launch and design your infrastructure to be redundant and fault tolerant, but it is up to you to make those design decisions and implement them for the design to be effective.

When designing architecture to be deployed and dealing with regions and AZs, you also need to consider the following factors:

- Not all AWS resources and services are available in all regions.

- AWS resources and services are scope based, in that they are delivered at the AZ level, the region level, or global.

For the first bullet point, it is important to understand that not all AWS resources and services are available in all regions. An example of this is the AWS Lambda service. At the time of writing this book, this service was not available in all regions. For the most current information on which services are available in which regions, please see the AWS Global Infrastructure Region Product page at https://aws.amazon.com/about-aws/global-infrastructure/regional-product-services/. This will help you determine if the products and services you need are available in the region where you want to deploy resources.

The second bullet point focuses on the fact that AWS resources are not all available to be deployed at the lowest level of scope, which is an AZ. EC2 instances, for example, are an AZ-level resource, which means you can deploy EC2 virtual server instances to a given AZ within a specific region. A security group, which as you know is used to control ingress and egress connections to a resource such as an EC2 instance, is a regional-level resource. This means that a security group can be created in a given region and applied to resources within that region, but not used to secure resources in a different region. The last type of resource scope is global; an example of a globally scoped resource is one that is used across regions and is usually tied to your AWS account.

A good example of a global resource that you've experienced in this book is the IAM account. An account created in IAM is a global resource; the keys associated with that account are also global in nature. This means that they are used across the account and are not tied to a specific region or AZ. On top of this, there are outliers that fall into multiple scope categories, such as the AWS S3 bucket. The bucket itself is created with regional scope and by default will have data redundancy built in because Amazon will make a copy of your data in each of the AZs within that region to help it meet the high availability SLA that it boasts for this product. Data will not be automatically copied to another region, though; remember that *region scope* means that the resource stays in the defined region. So if you want this extra layer of redundancy, you need to use tools to get it out of your implementation. The S3 bucket name, as you know from earlier in the book, is a global scope and is even larger than just your account; across the entire AWS platform it has to be unique.

If you're thinking that this is getting confusing, you're right. Some research is needed when you design your infrastructure in order to understand the level the resource is scoped at so that you can properly plan for resource redundancy at the right scope level. Thankfully, AWS documentation is an excellent resource for resource scope and locations. Here is documentation that explains at which level a variety of EC2 resources are scoped: http://docs.aws.amazon.com/AWSEC2/latest/UserGuide/resources.html.

Throughout this chapter I'll call out the resource scope and how you would achieve redundancy by deploying multiple layers of resources that can assist at the time of failure.

Elastic Load Balancing

In the infrastructure of this scenario, you've deployed two Elastic Load Balancers. Elastic Load Balancers are endpoint devices that handle web traffic and can balance that traffic between multiple EC2 virtual server instances. In 2016, AWS introduced a new type of load balancer with enhanced features and benefits called an Application Load Balancer. At this point, AWS started referring to the Elastic Load Balancer offering as a "Classic Load Balancer." A great comparison of the features of each load balancing type can be found at https://docs.aws.amazon.com/elasticloadbalancing/latest/userguide/what-is-load-balancing.html?icmpid=docs_elbv2_console#elb-features. One of the main benefits of the Application Load Balancer is the support for multiple ports.

For your example, you are going to deploy two Classic Load Balancers as a way to offer redundancy and you'll place your EC2 resources in auto-scaling group configurations in web server pools attached to each load balancer. In this section, you'll set up your two load balancers in a single region, as shown in Figure 15-2.

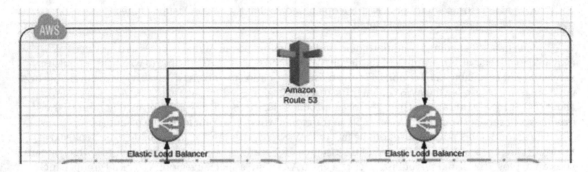

Figure 15-2. *Your domain, set up in Route53 DNS, will point to one of two possible load balancers based on a health check*

To set up your load balancers, log into the AWS Console and browse to the EC2 Dashboard. From here you'll select the Load Balancers link under the Load Balancing section in the left-hand navigation. Click the Create Load Balancer button and choose the Classic Load Balancer option. This will launch the wizard to walk you through creating the resource.

On the first screen, you will define the load balancer name. You will choose which network (VPC) you would like to deploy the load balancer within. VPCs are network resources that are scoped at the AZ level, meaning you can have multiple VPCs in each AZ. In your example, you will deploy your resources to the same VPC so that they will live in the same public IP address space. Lastly, you'll configure listener ports on the load balancer. Since your load balancers will only handle web traffic, you'll leave the default settings of Port 80 listening on the load balancer and forwarding to Port 80 on the EC2 virtual server instances.

In the next step of the wizard, you can choose to apply a security group configuration to the load balancer. I've chosen not to associate a security group with the load balancer.

In the third step of the wizard, you will be prompted with information saying that your load balancer does not have a "secure" listener, such as listening for traffic over HTTPS using SSL (Port 443). Just click the button without taking action and proceed to the next step in the wizard.

Step four is shown in Figure 15-3. In this step, you configure health check settings for EC2 virtual server instances that will receive traffic from the load balancer. Configuring these settings allows the load balancer to tell whether an instance is in a healthy state and ready to receive traffic.

Services ▾	Resource Groups ▾	IAM	S3	
1. Define Load Balancer	2. Assign Security Groups	3. Configure Security Settings	**4. Configure Health Check**	5. Add EC2 Instances	6. Add Tags	7. Review

Step 4: Configure Health Check

Your load balancer will automatically perform health checks on your EC2 instances and only route traffic to instances that pass the health check. If an instance fails the health check, it is automatically removed from the load balancer.

Ping Protocol	HTTP ▾
Ping Port	80
Ping Path	/index.html

Advanced Details

Response Timeout ⓘ	5 seconds
Interval ⓘ	30 seconds
Unhealthy threshold ⓘ	2 ▾
Healthy threshold ⓘ	10 ▾

Figure 15-3. *Step four of the Load Balancer Creation Wizard: configuring EC2 health check settings*

Configuration changes to the health checks can be made after the creation of the load balancer in the Settings tab, which means that you have the opportunity to adjust them at a later time if fine-tuning is needed.

In the next step of the Load Balancer Creation Wizard you will add your EC2 virtual server instances that you want this load balancer to balance traffic between. Figure 15-4 shows that you have two web servers currently set up. Each of them has the same configuration but live in separate availability zones. So if AWS had a failure of services in the "us-west-2a" availability zone, the EC2 server in the "us-west2c" availability zone would still be available to serve traffic. By checking the "Enable cross zone load balancing" checkbox, this load balancer will be able to send traffic between these two availability zones.

Figure 15-4. *Selecting which EC2 instances to load balance traffic between, showing EC2 instances currently set up in separate availability zones*

Although Figure 15-4 shows that the web traffic will be load balanced between only two instances, you can set up as many as you'd like to have the traffic balanced across. You could also set up load balancers in multiple regions, which load balances traffic in multiple availability zones, if you want to add an additional layer of fault tolerance. Setting up the infrastructure in this manner will protect against a regional failure rather than just an availability zone failure. However, for this example, let's keep it simple and have two load balancers set up in the same region, which will load balance across instances in multiple availability zones.

In the final step of the wizard, you can add any tags that you'd like to create for the load balancer resource. Similar to tagging other resources, it makes sense to add any tagging information that would make it easier from a reporting perspective. Tagging resources as internal or external, or production or development, can help as the deployed infrastructure grows in size.

After you've added any tags that you want, click the "Review and Create" button to review your load balancer configuration. After reviewing the information for accuracy, click the Create to create your new load balancing resource.

It's worth calling out that while there are other ways to load balance web traffic between instances, AWS load balancers are easy to set up and an effective way to manage and balance the traffic. They offer additional benefits such as supporting multiple protocols and SSL. They do come at a significant cost, however. Each load balancer deployed will cost approximately $15 per month, so be sure that you're prepared for the cost that this level of redundancy will bring.

Now that you know how to place a load balancer in front of multiple EC2 virtual server instances to balance web traffic between them, let's look at how you can use another feature of AWS to scale the amount of EC2 virtual server instances automatically up or down based on how busy the resource is in terms of activity.

Auto Scaling Introduction

AWS Auto Scaling is a feature that allows you to define a set of conditions that will scale up or down your EC2 resources to match the instance requirements for those conditions. Setting up Auto Scaling is a multiple-step process that has you first create a launch configuration and then define an Auto Scaling group. I'll describe the process in detail below.

Since Auto Scaling is a feature of AWS EC2, you can access the setup of the groups and launch configuration settings from the EC2 Dashboard in the AWS Console. In the left hand navigation you'll find an Auto Scaling section, as shown in Figure 15-5.

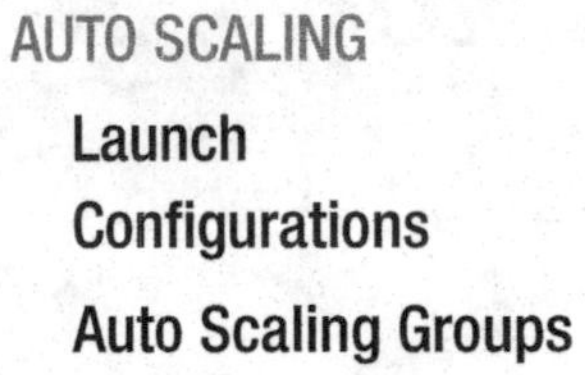

AUTO SCALING

Launch

Configurations

Auto Scaling Groups

Figure 15-5. *The Auto Scaling section of the EC2 Dashboard is shown*

The first step is to create a launch configuration. The launch configuration of an Auto Scaling group is very similar to launching a new EC2 virtual server instance. In the Launch Configuration Wizard you will choose the AWS AMI to be used, the virtual server instance size, and the configuration details including storage and security groups to be used. You'll also name the launch configuration. To start the wizard, click the Launch Configurations link in the left-hand navigation of the EC2 Dashboard and then click the Create Auto Scaling Group button. This will bring you to the welcome screen of the wizard, which defines the two parts of the process mentioned above and that a launch configuration will first need to be created. Click the Create Launch Configuration button to move to the first step of the Launch Configuration Creation Wizard, as shown in Figure 15-6.

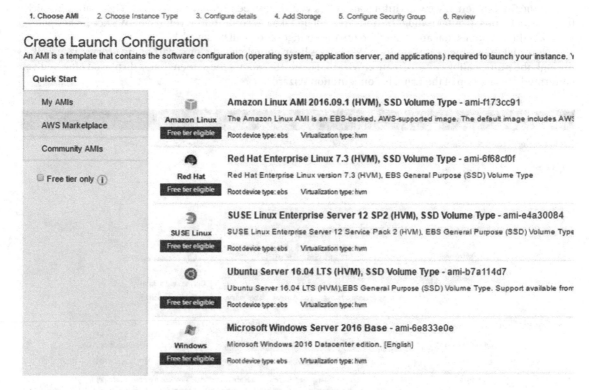

Figure 15-6. *The first step of the Launch Configuration Creation Wizard, also showing the rest of the steps in the process. This process is very similar to the Launch EC2 Instance Wizard since it handles much of the same configuration details.*

In the first step, you will choose which AMI to use when launching new instances within your Auto Scaling group. For this example, you'll choose the Amazon Linux AMI that is free tier eligible. Click the Select button next to the instance to move on to the next step. In the second step, you will choose the instance size of the instances to be deployed in your Auto Scaling group. For this example, you'll again stay with the free tier eligible option and choose t2.micro. After selecting the radio button next to the instance size choice, click the "Next: Configure Details" button to move on to the third step in the wizard.

The third step asks you for a launch configuration name and has an Advanced Details section, as when launching new instances, where you can put user data configuration and select IP configuration options. For this example, you can use the UserData.txt source code included in this chapter's resources to simply load the Apache Web Server and PHP application. Once you've entered this data, click the "Next: Add Storage" button to move on to the next step.

In the fourth step, you define storage configuration options for your new instances. Leave the default setting and click the "Next: Configure Security Group" button.

In the fifth step, you can choose to have a new security group created or apply the settings of an existing security group to the instances launched by your Auto Scaling group. In this example, choose the web server security group that already exists because it has the ports that you want open (web traffic on Port 80 from anywhere and administrative access via Port 22 from only your IP address). Once you've chosen this existing security group, click the Review button to get to the last screen of the Launch Configuration Creation Wizard.

In the final screen, review the information that you've entered through the wizard. When satisfied, click the "Create Launch Configuration" button. You will be asked to confirm that you have AWS access key pairs to access the resources that are created before the configuration will be saved.

Now that the Launch Configuration Wizard has been completed, the next part of the process is to walk through the Auto Scaling Group Creation Wizard. Figure 15-7 shows the screen that is displayed after you've confirmed the last step of the Launch Configuration Wizard.

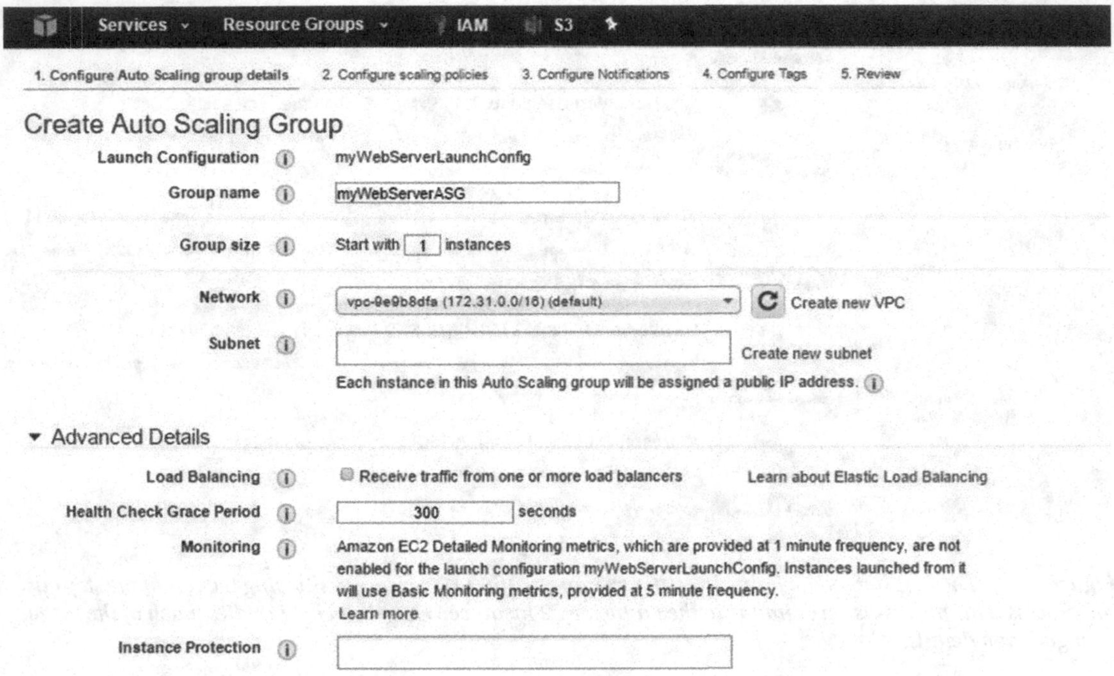

Figure 15-7. *The first screen of the Create Auto Scaling Group Wizard is shown. Your launch configuration name is automatically entered from the previous wizard.*

In the first step of the Auto Scaling Group Creation Wizard you're asked to define a name for your group and a minimum size for the group. Leaving this option set at "1" means that you'll always want to have at least one instance in the group. This is the preferred setting. You also have to choose which subnet you want to use for your Auto Scaling group, or you can create a new one. In addition, under Advanced Details you can choose to receive traffic from one or more load balancers. Since you set up load balancers earlier in the chapter, you can select this option. The Health Check Grace Period tells your Auto Scaling group how long to wait between the action of scaling up or down resources within your group. Setting this too low could result in additional resources being created unnecessarily. The default setting is acceptable for this example. Click the "Next: Configure Scaling Policies" button to proceed to the next step.

In step two, you can define whether you want the group to be set to be static at the size you define, or to scale based on definitions that you can configure. Choose the radio button for "Use scaling policies to adjust the capacity of this group." When you choose this you'll be presented with the configuration screen shown in Figure 15-8.

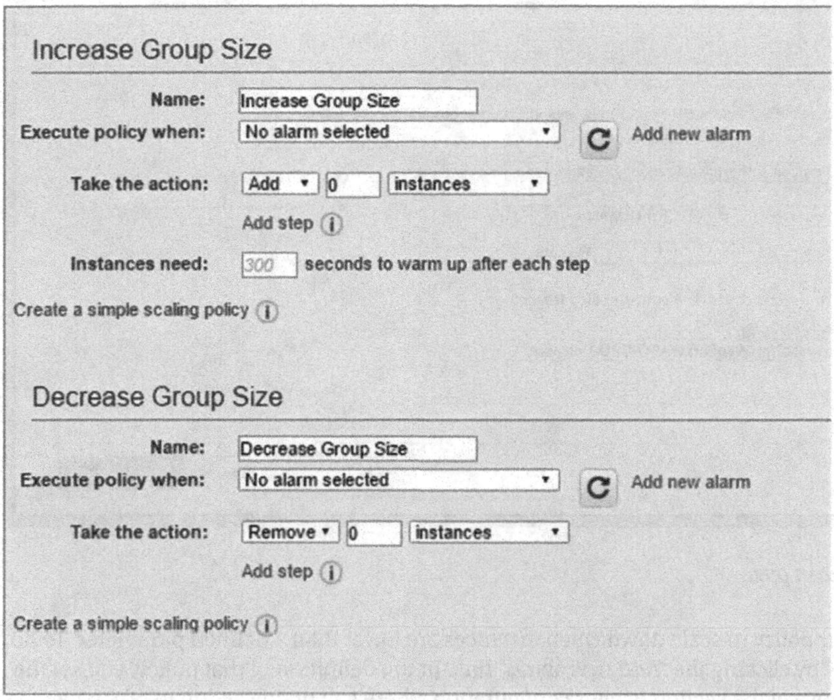

Figure 15-8. *The options for scaling policies*

In the scaling policies settings, the most important option is the "Scale between" configuration at the top of the screen. This tells the minimum and maximum number of instances that will be created within your Auto Scaling group. For your example, you will limit this to a maximum of three instances. This means that no matter the performance of the instances in the Auto Scaling group, it will not grow past three instances without manual intervention. Although this seems counterintuitive, this is a way to protect against growing the group indefinitely and ending up costing a bunch of dollars in resources created without you knowing.

In this part of the wizard you can set up CloudWatch Alarms that will be used to evaluate whether EC2 instances need to be added or removed from the auto scaling group. Any instances that are added will use the launch configuration that you set up in the previous wizard. Figure 15-9 shows how you can configure a policy to scale up by one instance when the CPU of existing instances in the auto scaling group reach 80% or greater.

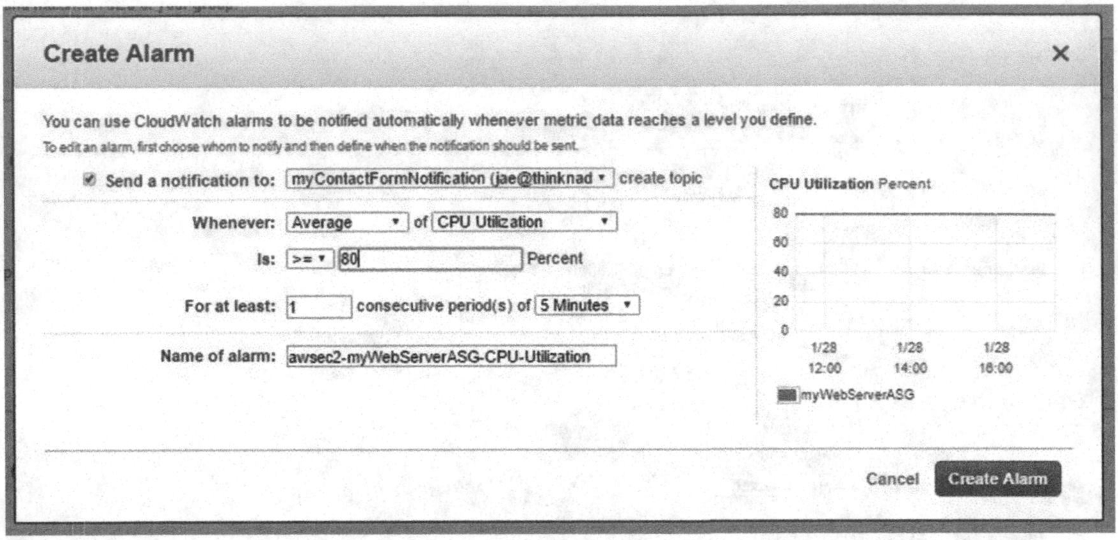

Figure 15-9. *The Create Alarm page*

You can define a similar policy to scale down when instances are lower than a defined parameter. To do this, you create a new policy by clicking the "Add new alarm" link. In the definition of that policy, you set the number of instances to remove in the section of your configuration where you define action to take when the alarm triggers. You could choose to do the opposite of above and scale down instances in the group when all of the instances have an average CPU utilization of 20% or lower.

Scale up parameters are defined in the "Increase Group Size" section and scale down parameters are defined in the "Decrease Group Size" section. Once you have defined your scaling policies and any alarms that you'd like to create, you can click the "Next: Configure Notifications" button.

In the next step of the wizard, you set up how you are notified of Auto Scaling group activity. This step is important because you will want to know whether your hosted environment has arrived at a point where resources are being scaled up. Most times you will be aware of when this may happen, such as a marketing campaign launch or some other activity that you've been involved in that is driving additional traffic to your website. In this step, you can use existing or set up new SNS topics for messages to be delivered to when Auto Scaling activities occur. As a reminder, when you set up a new topic, you need to subscribe to that topic to receive notifications. Once you have set up your notification details, you can click the "Next: Configure Tags" button to move on to the next step, which allows you to add any tags to the Auto Scaling group. When you are satisfied with the tags defined, click the Review button to move to the last screen of the Auto Scaling Group Creation Wizard.

The last step allows you to review your configuration and to create the Auto Scaling group with your defined parameters and launch configuration. Since you have defined a minimum of one instance in the group, an EC2 virtual server instance will be launched with your launch configuration details immediately. From there, the Auto Scaling group will monitor your CloudWatch metrics defined to watch the CPU utilization to know when it should add more resources to the group. Each EC2 resource will use the same AMI, instance size, and user data as defined in your launch configuration settings.

Route53 Routing Configuration Options

Similar to Auto Scaling policies, you can define DNS traffic policies within Route53. In these policies you can choose to have health checks that you've set up in earlier chapters evaluated, and if they are found unhealthy, apply a failover rule that will direct traffic from a primary region endpoint to a secondary region endpoint. Since Route53 has a global scope, these region endpoints can be in the same region or in unique regions, adding an additional layer of redundancy.

The easiest way to define a Route53 traffic policy is through the graphical editor found on the Route53 Dashboard in the AWS Console. Log into the AWS Console and browse to the Route53 Dashboard. Once there, you will see the Traffic Policies link under the Traffic Flow section. Click that link and then click the "Create traffic policy" button to launch the GUI.

In your scenario, you have a single domain that you want to point at two load balancers, which balance traffic between two EC2 Auto Scaling groups scoped in unique availability zones. To set this up in Route53, you'll first be asked to name your policy. Use "myDNSTrafficPolicy" for this example.

Leave the default selection on the Start Point set to IP Address and then click the "Connect to" link and choose the Failover Rule option. This will add a failover rule configuration, as shown in Figure 15-10.

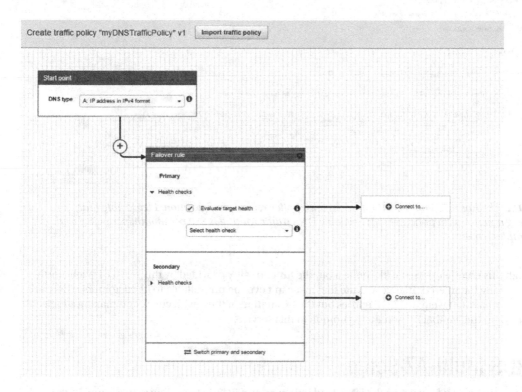

Figure 15-10. *The Route53 traffic policy GUI with a failover rule added*

The failover rule allows you to configure primary and secondary traffic routes based on DNS health checks. Earlier in the book you set up a DNS health check for your primary domain, so set the configuration to evaluate that health check on both routes. You do this by checking the "evaluate health check box" and choosing your health check from the drop-down menu.

In the primary route, click the "Connect to" button and choose the New endpoint option. In the New endpoint box, under Value, choose the Classic Load Balancer option, and then select the first load balancer you have set up. You can then do the same for the secondary route, but this time choose your second load balancer. This configuration will test the health check, and if the primary route is healthy, it will send traffic along that route. If the health check is unhealthy, it will evaluate the health check of the secondary route, and if healthy, it will send traffic along that route.

When completed, click the Create Traffic Policy button. This will bring you to a page that asks which hosted zone and DNS records should be created for this policy. Please note the message in Figure 15-11: adding these records will incur significant charges. Adding a traffic policy and the records needed to implement it is $50 per month, per policy and record set.

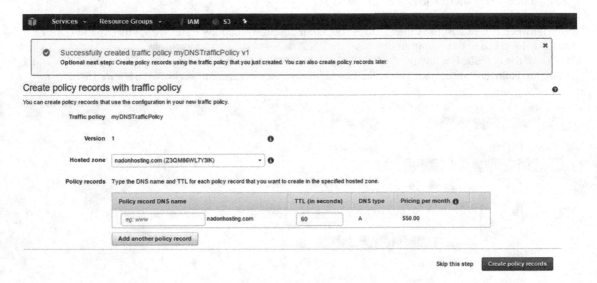

Figure 15-11. *The Route53 Policy creation screen with policy record configuration. Please note that implementing a policy with policy records to enable DNS traffic routing is $50 per month, per policy and record set implemented*

Although this charge may seem like quite a bit, the functionality provided by this service is well worth the cost, especially for an e-commerce website that just can't ever be unavailable to its customers. There are other ways to implement weighted DNS entries but the evaluation of the health check and making a logical decision based on the feedback is something unique to this service.

AWS RDS Multi-AZ Setup

In the sections above, you focused on the DNS, load balancer, and EC2 Auto Scaling group setup. In this last section, I'll talk about configuration options within AWS RDS to support the multi-availability zone configuration shown in Figure 15-12.

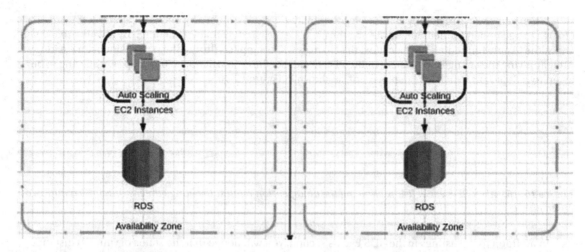

Figure 15-12. *A look at the availability zone section of the architecture design described in Chapter 14*

In previous chapters you set up AWS RDS as a single availability zone deployment. In this section, you'll modify the RDS database instance to be multi-AZ configured. Log into the AWS Console and browse to the RDS Dashboard. Figure 15-13 shows that the RDS instance that you configured in earlier chapters is not currently deployed to multiple availability zones.

Status	▾	CPU	Current Activity	Maintenance	▾	Class	▾	VPC	▾	Multi-AZ ▾
available		1.02%	0 Connections	None		db.t2.micro		vpc-9e9b8dfa		No

Figure 15-13. *AWS RDS instance configuration summary with the Multi-AZ option set to "No"*

To change this database instance to deploy to multiple availability zones, click the Instance Actions button and choose Modify. This will bring up the main configuration details for the RDS database instance. Under the Instance Specifications section, choose "Yes" under the Multi-AZ drop-down menu shown in Figure 15-14.

Instance Specifications

DB Engine Version	MySQL 5.6.27 (default) ▾
DB Instance Class	db.t2.micro — 1 vCPU, 1 GiB RAM ▾
Multi-AZ Deployment	No ▾
Storage Type	General Purpose (SSD) ▾
Allocated Storage*	5 GB

Figure 15-14. *AWS RDS instance configuration detail screen showing whether the instance will be a multi-AZ deployment*

When you choose to deploy to multiple availability zones, you must also choose whether you want this change to be applied immediately or during the next change window that you defined. By default, unless you check the "Apply Immediately" checkbox, the changes will be applied during the next maintenance window. After applying the changes requested, in the RDS Events section you will notice that steps are starting to be taken to redeploy as a multi-AZ deployment, as shown in Figure 15-15.

Type	Date	▾	Event
Instances	January 28, 2017 at 3:00:14 PM UTC-5		Applying modification to convert to a Multi-AZ DB Instance

Figure 15-15. *AWS RDS event listing showing the modification request to change the instance into a multi-AZ DB instance*

In addition to the listings in the RDS Events section, you will notice that the status of your DB instance will change from "Available" to "Modifying" until redeployment is completed. After the deployment to multiple availability zones is complete, the status of your RDS instance will go back to "Available" and the multi-AZ configuration summary will be set to "Yes." To see additional configuration options about the RDS multi-AZ deployment, click the Instance Actions button and then choose the See Details option.

Summary

In this chapter, you learned how to use features of Route53, EC2, and RDS to support multi-availability zone architecture deployments, which are the basis for highly available, fault tolerant websites hosted on the AWS platform. You mastered EC2 Auto Scaling and saw how policies can be created to add or remove resources based on a defined CloudWatch metric such as CPU utilization. This introduction just scratches the surface of what can be configured in terms of having AWS service react to situations that arise in your deployed infrastructure, but it does show the power of the platform and how it can be leveraged to respond to your website requirements in an on-demand fashion. In the next chapter, you'll learn about content lifecycle management, backup, and additional storage options, including how to migrate large amounts of data into AWS.

CHAPTER 16

■ ■ ■

Content Lifecycles, Management, and Backup

In this chapter, you'll revisit your friend AWS S3 and look at backup strategies. You'll also take a closer look at other storage options on the AWS platform for storing your data. As your hosting presence, site, and files grow over months and years, you'll need a plan for backing up data that is important, moving data that is less frequently accessed or not as relevant as it once was to less costly storage, and evaluating expiring data that is no longer needed. The process of doing these steps is referred to as *the content lifecycle* and the AWS platform has a way for you to manage your data and content from the start of the lifecycle to its end of usefulness.

I'll also introduce AWS Glacier and AWS Snowball as storage solutions that can help with storing and importing large data sets into the AWS Platform.

Managing Content Lifecycles in S3

Throughout this book you've been introduced to and revisited features within AWS Simple Storage Solution (S3). As discussed in the beginning of the book, the goal is to introduce you to what I feel are the most useful basic features of each service and to give you the confidence to explore the advanced features more in-depth as you start using the platform for your environments. In this third hosting scenario I presented the enterprise website scenario, a business that not only supports and hosts a highly available, fault tolerant e-commerce website in AWS but wants to be able to use other services on the platform in order to be as effective as possible.

Content lifecycles refer to the effective lifespan of a piece of data. The start of the lifecycle is when the data is created and the end of the lifecycle is when the data is deemed no longer of value. Lifecycle management features are accessed through your S3 Dashboard and specifically at the bucket properties level. Figure 16-1 shows the structure of your e-commerce content in S3.

© Jason Nadon 2017

J. Nadon, *Website Hosting and Migration with Amazon Web Services*, DOI 10.1007/978-1-4842-2589-9_16

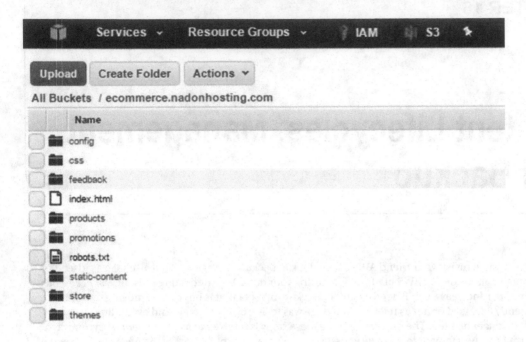

Figure 16-1. *The e-commerce website root is shown in the S3 bucket created for your content*

For the examples in this chapter you'll focus on the promotions folder since it will hold pages that are specific for a given month. As you take a look at the properties of the promotions folder in Figure 16-2, you can see the different storage class types called out.

Figure 16-2. *The S3 folder properties for your promotions folder. On the right-hand side you can see the Storage Class setting for the folder object*

By default, objects (including buckets and folders) created in S3 use the Standard storage class. You've seen the other types mentioned earlier in this book, but I didn't spend much time talking about them. Let's take a look at the three storage classes now.

The **Standard** storage class is the default storage type for all S3 objects. This class offers the highest level of durability in terms of SLA at "eleven nines" or 99.999999999% durability and "four nines" or 99.99% availability. This storage class is used for general storage where items are accessed frequently. Behind the scenes, AWS replicates your data across its own infrastructure to make sure that your data is there when you need it. As it relates to your promotions folder, this class is the default setting for all objects (bucket, folder, and object) contained within it, so there are no changes to be considered until you learn more about the other class types.

Standard - Infrequent Access is the next level of storage class available for S3 objects. This class offers the same level of durability and one less "nine" or 99.9% availability. This class is best for data that is still needed in terms of accessibility, but less frequently. This class has a lower per-GB fee for storage of objects, but also has a per-GB fee for retrieval of objects of this class. In terms of your promotions folder, it would make sense to have your current month promotions set as Standard, but you could change the storage class to Standard - Infrequent Access once the current month promotions have passed.

Reduced Redundancy Storage (RRS) is the third storage class types for S3 objects. This class offers less durability in terms of SLA with a "four nines" or 99.99% durability. It has the lowest per-GB cost of the three storage classes and may be a good option for files that are stored in multiple locations and are easily replaced. As noted in the AWS documentation, the level of durability is still approximately 400 times more durable than that of a typical disk drive. There is no retrieval fee for objects that use this class. The amount of replication that happens behind the scenes is not the same level as with Standard class object types, and this class is designed to survive the failure of a single location or availability zone.

There is another storage class, but I look at it as more of an AWS product/service, and that is **AWS Glacier**. Glacier is a very low-cost storage solution for objects that do not need to be accessed frequently and is an excellent as an option for long-term backup. There is a retrieval fee per GB for data stored in Glacier and there is a longer expectation in terms of how quickly the object will be restored and available for retrieval. You'll see how Glacier fits into your lifecycle management options shortly.

At any time you can change the storage class of your object in S3 via the Object Properties screen. Manually moving data between classes is something that is quite effective in terms of cost savings; however, if you want to perform this process in a more automated fashion, you can use content lifecycle rules to accomplish the same over time.

If you take a look at the Object Properties settings, you'll note that with no lifecycle policy applied to it, the expiration date and expiration rule are blank, as shown in Figure 16-3.

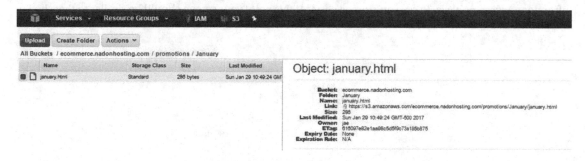

Figure 16-3. *The S3 object properties for an object within your promotions folder shows that the expiry date on the object is set to "None" and the expiry rule is set to "N/A"*

Lifecycle management policies, referred to as rules, are accessed from within the Properties menu of the S3 bucket on which you'd like to set the policy. If you browse to the S3 bucket properties you will see a drop-down section within the properties options called Lifecycle. Expand that section to view the available options for this feature, as shown in Figure 16-4.

Figure 16-4. *The S3 bucket properties for your e-commerce content with the Lifecycle section expanded*

From within this section you can add a new lifecycle policy for your bucket by clicking the Add Rule button. This will start the Lifecycle Rules Wizard that will guide you through the process.

There are three major steps in the Lifecycle Rules Wizard. The first step asks you to choose a rule target. You have the option of having all the content in the bucket have the policy applied to it, or you can enter a prefix to apply the policy against. In your example, you want to apply this against the `promotions` folder, so you'll enter the prefix `promotions/`. Entering this will mean that this lifecycle rule will apply to all objects that have that prefix, which can also be expressed as any objects within this S3 folder.

Click the Configure Rule button to move to the second step, which asks you for details about what you'd like to do in terms of lifecycle management of the target objects. For your example, you'll keep it simple and just check the three checkboxes next to "Transition to Standard - Infrequent Access," "Archive to the Glacier storage class," and "Permanently Delete." When you select the checkboxes, a default value will be added to each of the steps in the lifecycle. The default settings move objects from the Standard class to the Standard - Infrequent Access storage class after 30 days after the object is created. Thirty days after the object has been moved to Standard - Infrequent Access storage it will then be moved to the AWS Glacier storage class. Lastly, 425 days after the object was created it will be permanently deleted. You can choose to have all of these steps as a natural progression for deleting unused content or a subset of them, such as moving to Standard - Infrequent Access, as a way to save on storage costs. At this point your screen should be similar to that shown in Figure 16-5.

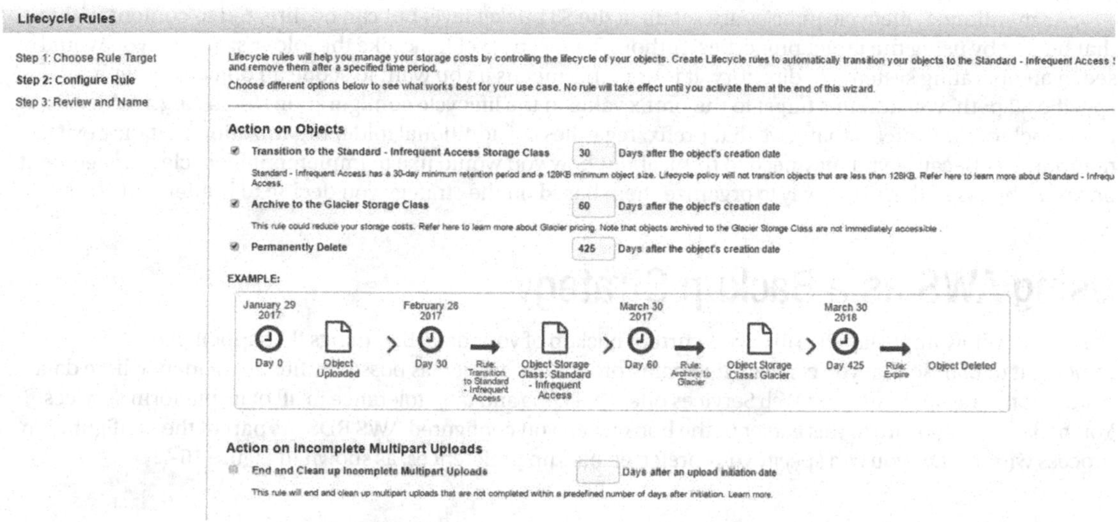

Figure 16-5. *The second step of the Lifecycle Rule Creation Wizard is shown with default settings for moving objects from Standard to Standard - Infrequent Access, then to AWS Glacier, and then permanently deleting the object*

On the last step of the wizard you will be asked to name the lifecycle rule and will have the opportunity to review the lifecycle management of the objects to which it will be applied, as shown in Figure 16-6.

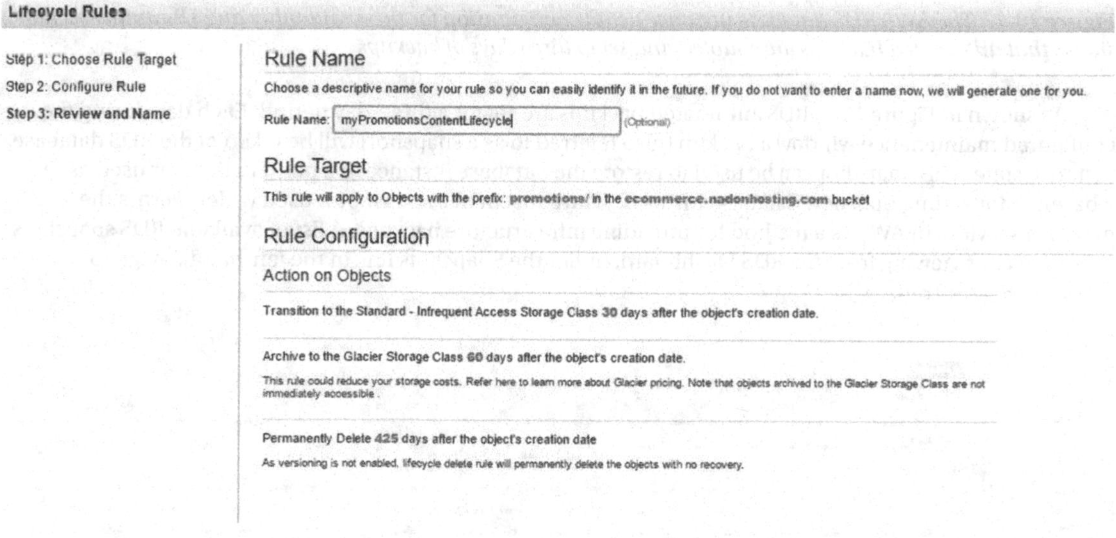

Figure 16-6. *The final step in the Lifecycle Rule Creation Wizard is shown summarizing settings and the rule to be applied*

As mentioned, lifecycle policies are set up at the S3 bucket level but can be directed to content within that bucket by using the target properties. Although an S3 bucket looks like the folder structure you would see in an operating system file directory, it is not. This means if you want to scope all objects under a specific S3 path, you add this target to the prefix value in the lifecycle configuration. Including a folder name includes all objects that have that prefix, regardless of additional folder organization that may exist. I mention this because you may need to think about how you would like to implement lifecycle management on your objects and the best way to organize them based on the strategy you decide to implement.

Using AWS as a Backup Strategy

We all know how important it is to have a current backup of your data. Bad things do happen and it is important to plan so that you can return to being productive as soon as possible after an incident where data restoration is needed. Amazon Web Services offers backups and fault tolerance in all of its platform services. You had some exposure to this earlier in the book when you configured AWS RDS. As part of the configuration process within RDS, you can specify your preferred backup preferences, as shown in Figure 16-7.

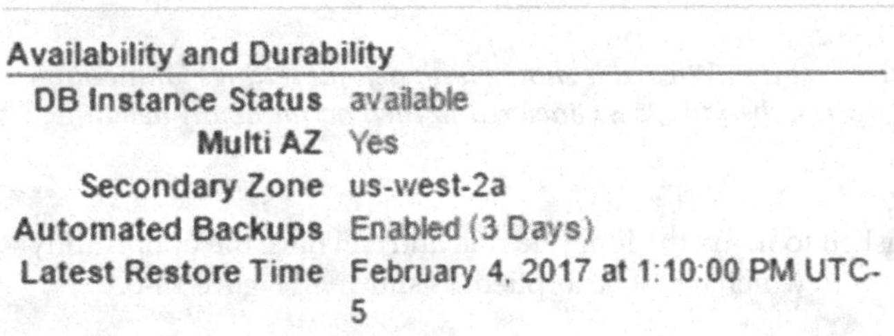

Availability and Durability

DB Instance Status	available
Multi AZ	Yes
Secondary Zone	us-west-2a
Automated Backups	Enabled (3 Days)
Latest Restore Time	February 4, 2017 at 1:10:00 PM UTC-5

Figure 16-7. *The AWS RDS database instance detail configuration for the Availability and Durability section shows that automated backups are enabled and set to three days of backups*

As shown in Figure 16-7, RDS automated backups are set for a three-day period. Each day during the configured maintenance window a backup (also referred to as a snapshot) will be taken of the RDS database instance state. This snapshot can be used to restore the database instance to a point in time, or used as a baseline for setting up a new database instance. The concept of a snapshot is used widely across the platform services in AWS as a method for providing infrastructure backups. A list of available RDS snapshots is available for viewing from the RDS Dashboard, under the Snapshots link in the left-hand navigation, as shown in Figure 16-8.

Figure 16-8. *AWS RDS snapshot listing shown from within the RDS Dashboard view*

Backup options exist for all platform infrastructure services. Copies of CloudFormation templates are stored on S3. S3 buckets can be copied across regions to provide redundancy and data protection. EC2 uses the concept of snapshots for backing up data volumes attached to EC2 Virtual Server instances. To access this, you can log into the EC2 Dashboard and under the Elastic Block Store section, click the Snapshots link. From here you can click the Create Snapshot button to create a new snapshot manually. You will be presented with a screen similar to the one shown in Figure 16-9, which will capture information about the snapshot you would like to create and for which volume you would like to create a snapshot.

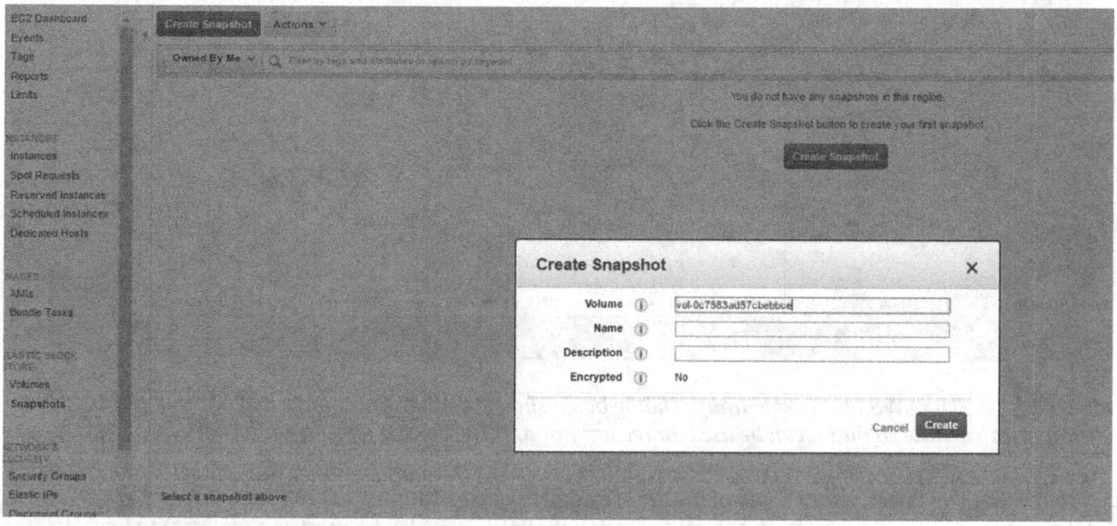

Figure 16-9. *The AWS EC2 EBS volume snapshot creation screen*

In addition to doing this manually, you can also choose to script this process using the AWS command line interface or other development and administration tools. Taking a snapshot of an EBS volume is a simple process and is an incremental backup based on the last successful snapshot. This allows you to do point-in-time restores of the data if needed. The following link is to online documentation from AWS of a tutorial on how to set up automatic snapshots of EBS volumes using CloudWatch:

http://docs.aws.amazon.com/AmazonCloudWatch/latest/events/TakeScheduledSnapshot.html

EC2 Virtual Server instances can also be backed up for later use/restoration. In this case, the backup process is referred to as *taking an image* of the server instance state. Taking an image of an instance is accessed through the Action menu from the EC2 Dashboard. Browsing under the Image menu option, you'll find the link/option for Creating an Image. Choosing this will launch the Create Image dialog box shown in Figure 16-10.

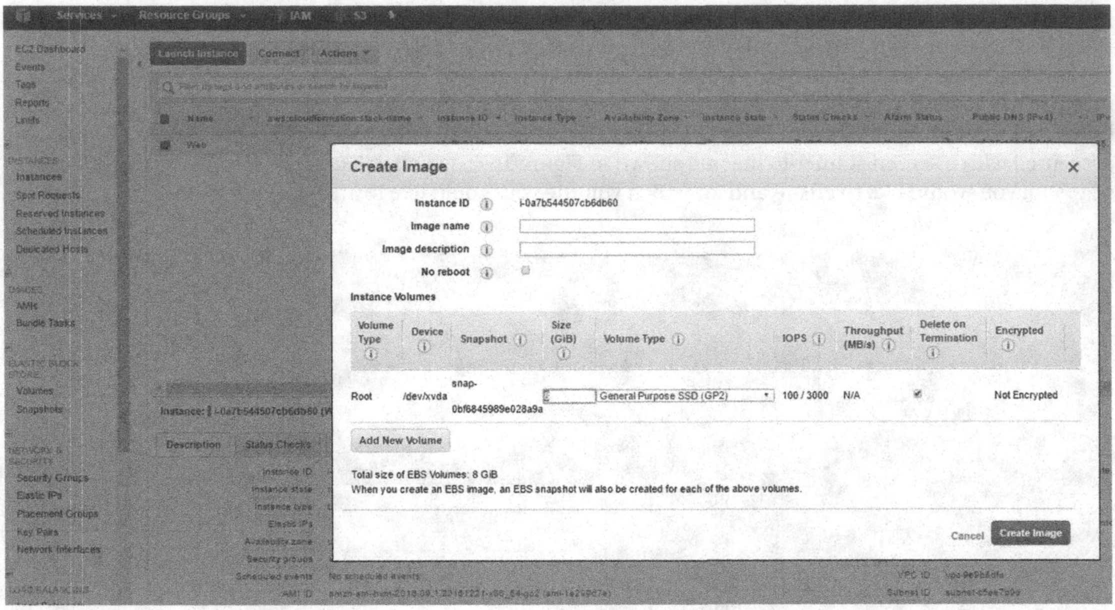

Figure 16-10. *The AWS EC2 Create Image Dialog box is shown. Creating an image will back up the EC2 virtual instance state so that it can be used for recovery or as the basis of a new virtual instance*

Now that I've talked about some of the infrastructure backup options that AWS provides for your infrastructure services in the cloud, I should mention that AWS can also be used as a platform to back up important information from your home or business. In early chapters, I showed you how to create S3 buckets and how to use the AWS CLI to sync local folder content with the S3 bucket. This same methodology can be used to scheduled tasks and network share locations on your business network. A contextual use case for this type of backup is backing up customer orders, shared documentation, and company marketing assets or training material. AWS S3 is an excellent, low-cost, highly available option for your backup storage, but if you're looking for something that is even lower cost, AWS Glacier may be a better fit for your storage needs.

AWS Glacier

AWS Glacier is described by Amazon Web Services as a "secure, durable, extremely low-cost cloud storage" and at the time of this writing was priced at $0.004 per GB per month. Although the storage cost is very low compared to other providers or the option to store the data on disk, there are other considerations to ponder before using this service.

First, there is no user interface for the service available from the AWS Console. If a UI is something that you prefer, there are options available, such as CloudBerry Lab Explorer, which I introduced in the first section of the book. Second, there is a retrieval fee for accessing data and retrieving it from Glacier. Third, when you want to access specific data, you initiate a request to retrieve it; based on the type of request, it could take as little as 5 minutes or as long as 12 hours to be accessed.

The price of this service makes it an excellent option for long-term data archival of important information; however, the considerations mentioned above may make this option unattractive to some people. Earlier in this chapter I explained how you can add the use of AWS Glacier into the lifecycle management of objects that you're storing. It is worth talking a bit about the options for retrieving the data if you choose to use the service.

In terms of setting up AWS Glacier, the object storage lifecycle management options are one way to move data into Glacier. Other than that, you can access AWS Glacier from the AWS Console, but in there you will only be able to set up vaults and notifications. Vaults are a collection of archive artifacts stored in AWS Glacier. Archives are a collection of objects, usually packaged in compressed format such as in ZIP or TAR format.

There are three types of retrieval requests that can be initiated through the AWS Glacier, but all of them are initiated through either a third-party provider application, the AWS SDKs, or AWS CLI. The three available types are Expedited, Standard, and Bulk.

Expedited requests will be retrieved in the shortest amount of time, but are meant for datasets that are no larger than 250MB in size and they should be available within 1-5 minutes. Within the option of expedited requests you can select whether you want the data in on-demand fashion, which will be best effort, or as provisioned storage as more of a dedicated resource format (the data will be there for as long as you need it). The difference between these two is really in how you will be charged for the storage resources that are housing the data you are asking to be retrieved. Yes, you must pay for the storage to hold the data that you're asking to be restored.

Standard requests are the most typical use case and you will be notified when the requested data is available for access. You can access the archive data via third party tools, the AWS SDK, AWS CLI, or even stand up an EC2 instance to access the data.

The last type of request is the Bulk request and these are reserved for the largest datasets. Retrieval time for these archives can take up to 12 hours, but seeing as this could cover up to petabytes of data, this timeframe is quite acceptable in most cases.

More information about AWS Glacier and the product features and usage can be found on the AWS product documentation website at https://aws.amazon.com/glacier/.

Getting Large Datasets into AWS

There may be times when you need to get a large amount of data or resources migrated from your location into Amazon Web Services. There are a couple key services that may assist with these tasks.

AWS has a **Database Migration Service** (DMS) that will help you migrate and replicate your data from your on-premise database system into the AWS platform. The process requires at least a source database, replication instance, and a target database. Database conversion tools are available to help you to migrate from one platform to another, including modifying the data schema of the database. More information on the service can be found at https://aws.amazon.com/documentation/dms/.

For migrating server instance resources, the AWS platform offers the AWS Server Migration Service. This service helps you move your virtual server infrastructure from your location to the cloud. The most popular Windows and Linux operating systems are supported by the service, and this is a great option when the goal is to move a server from being hosted on-premise to AWS. More information about this service can be found in the AWS documentation at http://docs.aws.amazon.com/server-migration-service/latest/userguide/server-migration.html.

If the resource that you need to move into AWS is a large amount of raw data, the AWS Snowball service may be the best fit for you. Snowball is an ultra-secure option for migrating large amounts of data from your site into AWS. The device will be shipped to your location, ready to be plugged in and accessed by your network and computing resources. Snowball devices come in 50TB and 80TB sizes, allowing you to transfer data to them locally and then ship them back to AWS. Then AWS will migrate that data to its storage resources and make it available to you. For data sets larger than 10TB, this process is often much more cost/time effective than trying to transfer the data via the Internet, and it is definitely more reliable and secure. More information about AWS Snowball can be found at https://aws.amazon.com/documentation/snowball/.

Summary

In this chapter, you considered multiple options for managing content lifecycles within AWS as well as backup options for infrastructure services used in the platform and for data that you have may have on-site in your home or business. You also learned about the multiple data and resource migration services that Amazon Web Services offers to help you get your resources into the cloud. In the next chapter, you will focus on the AWS workflow tools and services that you can use to help you extend your reach and productivity.

■ ■ ■

CHAPTER 17

Extending Your Reach with Workflow Services and Development Tools

In this chapter, I will discuss some of the AWS services that can assist you with extending your website and web presence by helping to perform processing tasks on your behalf. Some of the development tools introduced include using CodeCommit and CodeDeploy as ways to create and manage deployment pipelines. I'll also talk about using CloudWatch and Simple Notification Service (SNS) to monitor your infrastructure health, and I'll introduce AWS Simple Queue Service (SQS).

Monitoring the Health of Your Services

At this point in the book you've come a long way in terms of knowledge about the many AWS services that the Amazon Web Services platform offers. You've set up infrastructure resources using services like EC2, S3, and RDS that are core components of your website hosting. You've learned how CloudWatch can be used to gather basic metrics for RDS and EC2 and you've seen how well the CloudWatch service is integrated into the dashboard screens for each service. You had a sneak peek at how powerful this tool can be in assisting you with reacting to changes in your infrastructure needs when you configured your first Auto Scaling group earlier in this section of the book. CloudWatch was the conduit that monitored the CPU utilization of your EC2 instances and, based on thresholds set in a CloudWatch alarm, would take action to either scale up and launch additional EC2 virtual server resources or scale down and remove EC2 virtual server resources that were no longer needed based on server load.

CloudWatch alarms can tell you when to take action on a given situation based on measured metrics. CloudWatch can be used in other ways to monitor and gather information from your AWS resources. For example, CloudWatch can be used to gather log data from your EC2 instances. By default, the data collected about an EC2 virtual server instance has to do with the performance of that infrastructure within the AWS platform. Figure 17-1 shows a sample of the data collected by default, which is available through the EC2 Dashboard, under the Monitoring tab.

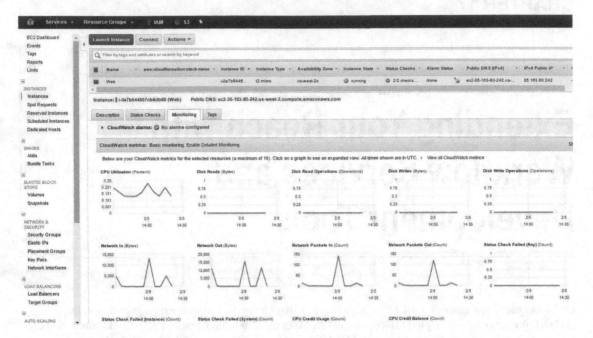

Figure 17-1. *EC2 Dashboard with CloudWatch basic metrics shown for a specific EC2 instance*

While the metrics shown in Figure 17-1 are very good for giving you a time-based view of how your infrastructure is performing, there may be a time when you want to collect more information from a resource.

CloudWatch Monitoring Options

CloudWatch offers multiple forms of monitoring that you can choose to implement to help with the monitoring of your infrastructure and services. The first was discussed in the previous section and is the basic monitoring option. This is included in some fashion in most of the AWS platform services dashboard screens to give a glance of the performance metrics of those services implemented. You can also access all of the metrics collected by the basic CloudWatch monitoring through the CloudWatch dashboard in the AWS Console under the Metrics link in the left-hand navigation.

By default, CloudWatch basic monitoring metrics are collected on a five-minute interval. For most resources, this is sufficient; however, there are services within the platform that allow for more granular monitoring via CloudWatch. EC2, for example, is one of those services that allows for detailed monitoring to be enabled on a virtual server instance. This can be specified while setting up the instance or can be enabled after the instance has been created. To enable detailed monitoring for an instance, browse to the EC2 Dashboard, choose the Instances link in the left-hand navigation, select the Instance for which you would like to enable detailed monitoring, and click the Actions button to open up the Options menu, as shown in Figure 17-2. From here, choose CloudWatch Monitoring and Enable Detailed Monitoring.

Figure 17-2. *EC2 Dashboard with the CloudWatch Monitoring Options menu expanded*

Enabling the CloudWatch detailed monitoring this way could be quite time consuming if you need to enable it on multiple instances. Thankfully, you can use the following command to enable detailed monitoring on an instance using the CLI:

```
aws ec2 monitor-instances --instance-ids <instance-id>
```

This command will make a call to your given instance to enable detailed monitoring. It will return a status of "pending" while it is changing the instance from basic to detailed monitoring. Issuing the command a second time will show a status of "enabled" when complete. If you want to disable monitoring on that instance, you can use the following command:

```
aws ec2 unmonitor-instances --instance-ids <instance-id>
```

To verify that detailed monitoring is enabled, you can click one of the monitoring graphs presented in the Details Monitoring tab. When the graph is displayed you will note that the interval for the monitoring data is now available at 1-minute rather than 5-minute intervals. An example of this change is shown in Figure 17-3.

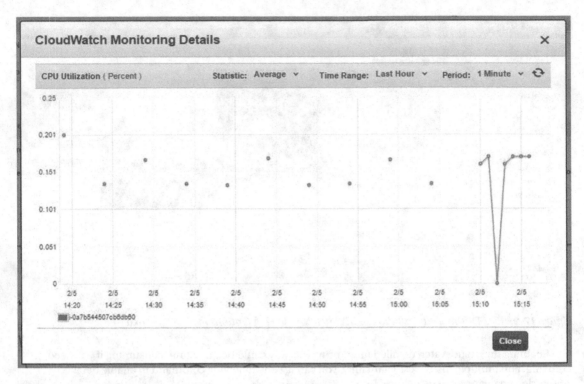

Figure 17-3. *CloudWatch metrics for a specific instance after updating from basic monitoring to detailed monitoring*

EC2 is not the only AWS service that offers this enhanced level of monitoring. A full list of all CloudWatch metrics available and the interval at which data collected can be delivered is available at http://docs.aws.amazon.com/AmazonCloudWatch/latest/monitoring/CW_Support_For_AWS.html.

Now that you have enabled detailed monitoring for your EC2 instance, you can use CloudWatch to set alarms to report or take action on metric data values and thresholds you feel are worthy of being notified about. You can create graphs to view a graphical representation of your CloudWatch metrics over time. You can collect these graphs into collections known as CloudWatch dashboards for easier viewing and aggregation of your data.

In addition to collecting and viewing data in the above method from CloudWatch, you can also gather additional metrics and data from CloudWatch on EC2 instances by deploying the CloudWatch Logs Agent to your EC2 instance. Although the process of installing the Logs Agent is a bit outside of the scope of this book, I feel that doing so to monitor and capture events written to web application logs such as Apache Server may be relevant, so I'm including a link to the Quick Start guides, which walk through setting up the CloudWatch Log Agent on existing instances or how to include this on new EC2 instances at launch time: http://docs. aws.amazon.com/AmazonCloudWatch/latest/logs/CWL_GettingStarted.html.

CloudWatch Rules

As you now know, CloudWatch alarms can be used to notify you or take action when a metric measurement has crossed a threshold set within the alarm. There is another way for CloudWatch to take action on resources and this is through the use of CloudWatch rules. CloudWatch rules can be accessed through the CloudWatch dashboard under the Rules link on the left-hand navigation.

Rules can be created to match an event pattern for a given resource or can be scheduled to occur on a timeframe, like that of a Linux-based cron schedule. An example of a pattern-based event rule is shown in Figure 17-4.

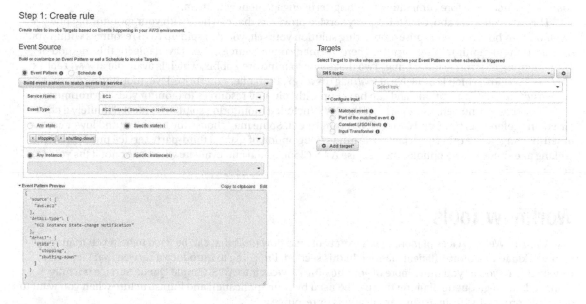

Figure 17-4. *CloudWatch rule configuration for an event pattern on an EC2 instance*

In the above configuration, you are using a pattern match event on EC2 resources. The event type is set to "EC2 Instance State-change Notification" and will look for a change in state on any of your EC2 resources to send a Simple Notification Service (SNS) message to a topic that you configure. SNS is a topic/subscription-based service provided by AWS to handle communication and notification between services. This can be used as an endpoint for communication from all services such as EC2, CloudWatch, Lambda, and many others across the platform. Not only can it be used in your AWS account to receive notifications from services that you are using, but it can be used as a platform service itself, creating an endpoint for messaging services from applications, SMS, and more. The full scope of SNS and how it can be used is outside of this book, but here's a link to the Getting Started Guide for SNS:

`http://docs.aws.amazon.com/sns/latest/dg/welcome.html`.

SNS can be used as your endpoint for all of your monitoring notifications, enabling you to set up topics by resource, region, or any other grouping you prefer and then subscribing to the topic to be instantly notified. Since SNS is also an AWS service, there are CloudWatch metrics that can be monitored and data that can be analysed, such as messages per topic, notifications delivered, and more.

External/Third-Party Monitoring Options

The previous section discussed how you can use CloudWatch as a monitoring solution for your services and infrastructure in AWS. CloudWatch is definitely not the only option for enterprise monitoring of your resources. There are many third-party applications that offer cloud monitoring services. A few examples that come to mind are DataDog and AppDynamics. DataDog is available from www.datadoghq.com/ and has a nice list of application integrations to help you receive notifications about infrastructure health in applications you may already use frequently, such as Slack. AppDynamics is available from www.appdynamics.com/ and is well designed for monitoring application stacks and the health of the application components. Both of these providers have free trials that can be used to test their services and reporting on your infrastructure before committing to a long-term engagement with them.

The two examples above are third-party service providers that can help with your monitoring; however, if you want to host your enterprise monitoring solution yourself, you can spin up AWS resources within your AWS account to monitor infrastructure. There are many open-source options available for this method of implementing enterprise monitoring. Two that come to mind are Zabbix, which is available at www.zabbix.com/, and Nagios, which is available at www.nagios.org/. Both offer enterprise-level monitoring for your infrastructure and applications, and can be set up with minimal resources to monitor your environment.

Choosing self-hosted, third-party, or the AWS-included monitoring solution is most definitely a choice based on preference, time, and cost-based commitment. Some may choose the flexibility and lower cost of self-hosting, while others will prefer the time saving option of using a third-party service provider. While looking at either of these options, you can use AWS CloudWatch and evaluate whether or not it fits your needs.

Workflow Tools

The Amazon Web Services platform has a variety of workflow tools that can be used to help you manage your workload in a more efficient manner. In this section, I'm going to introduce a service that I feel may be valuable to you as you move more of your hosting services into AWS. Simple Queue Service is a fully managed message queue platform that can be used by your application and infrastructure when you want to decouple processing from existing applications or resources.

Simple Queue Service can be accessed via the AWS Console, under the Services menu. It can be found in the Messaging section. SQS uses queues to organize and process messages sent to them. There are two main types of message queues that can be set up, Standard and FIFO.

Standard messaging queues are those where the processing of messages and throughput are most important to the applications using the queue. FIFO messaging queues are focused on processing messages as they are sent to the message queue in the exact order that they are received in. FIFO stands for "First In, First Out." The configuration of a queue is a very simple process and the only real setting that you are required to enter is the queue name. Figure 17-5 shows the configuration screen for setting up a new message queue.

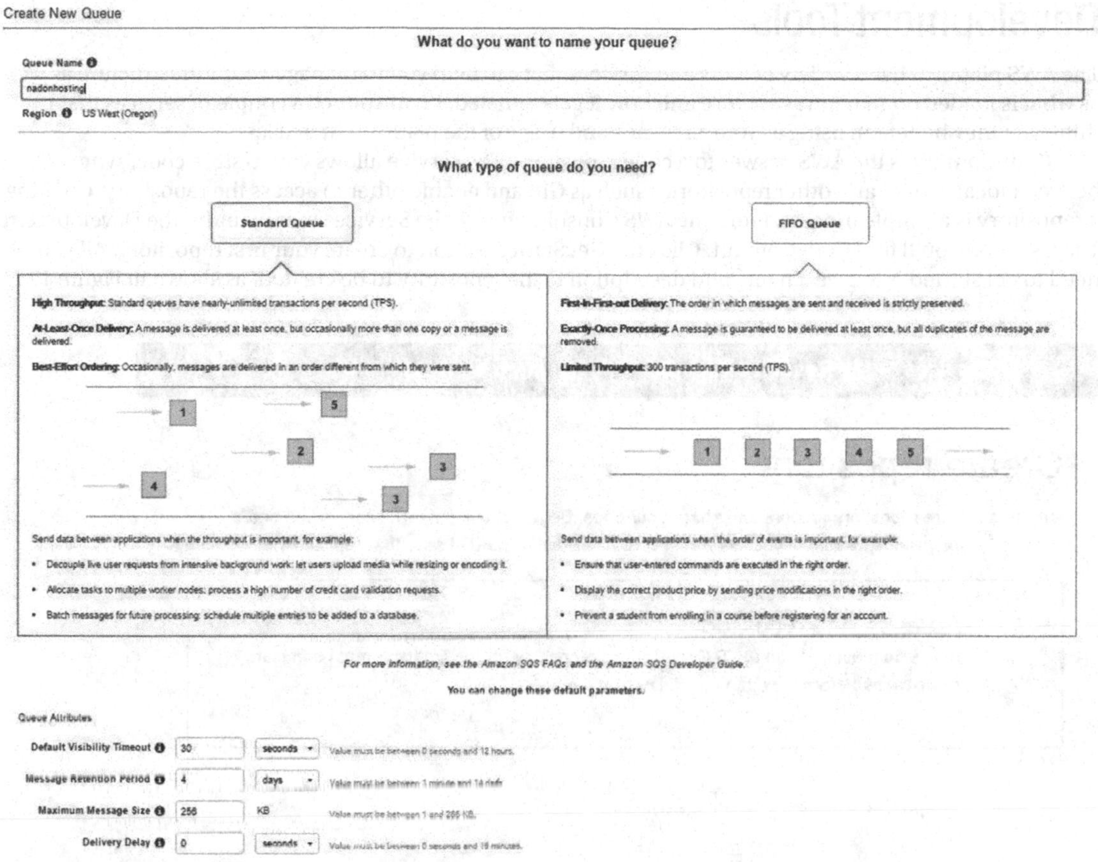

Figure 17-5. *The Simple Queue Service configuration screen is shown with the two main types of message queues, Standard or FIFO*

The main use case for SQS is to assist with decoupling applications that rely on using messaging to carry information about work to be performed. A simple example for your e-commerce website might be using this service to handle order processing with a third-party vendor. Your website code could use one of the SQS SDKs to connect to it as an endpoint and send order information accepted from your website to the SQS queue. You could use pull or push services to get information from this same message queue for processing. The message itself may contain information needed for successful processing of the order such as a ZIP code, which could be used to calculate and arrange shipping pickup for a product that has been ordered through the website.

The possibilities are limitless in terms of how the service can be used, but the best way to describe the use case is as a service that can connect two systems via an information exchange between them. SQS enables data to be passed from one system to another so that the system collecting the data can be as effective as possible without adding workflow overhead to that system.

Development Tools

The AWS platform has a variety of tools and services that can help you to manage your infrastructure as well as what is loaded on that infrastructure and how it gets updated. I'll introduce a couple of services that I think you may benefit in using as your presence and usage of the platform increases.

CodeCommit is the AWS answer to a code repository. The service allows you to store code; sync between local, cloud, and other repositories such as Git; and enable other to access the repository. Creating a repository is a simple process. From the AWS Console, choose the Services menu; under the Development Tools section you'll find CodeCommit. Click the Get Started button to create your first repository. All you need to get started is to give a name and description to the repository to be created, as shown in Figure 17-6.

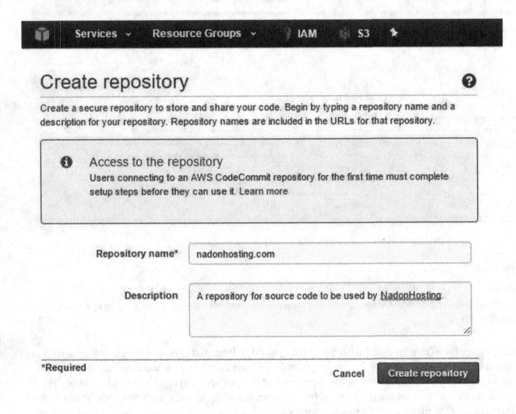

Figure 17-6. *The first screen in creating a repository in AWS CodeCommit*

The next step in setting up your repository is to connect to it to sync up data from your local machine. After you've clicked the Create Repository button in the previous step, you will be presented with a screen similar to the one shown in Figure 17-7. This will be specific to your operating system and will give you some brief instructions on the next steps to start working with CodeCommit. At the bottom of the screen is a context-sensitive link for more detailed steps that walk through the rest of the setup.

Follow the steps below to connect to your repository from your local computer.

Connection type ● HTTPS
○ SSH

Operating system ○ Linux, MacOS, or Unix
● Windows

Prerequisites

1. Install Git (1.7.9 or later supported) without the Git Credential Manager utility. If you don't have Git installed, install it now.
2. Install the AWS CLI.
3. At the command line, type aws configure and configure the AWS CLI with your IAM user access key and secret key.
4. Attach an appropriate AWS CodeCommit managed policy to the IAM user. Learn more

Steps to clone your repository

1. At the command line, paste the following commands:

```
git config --global credential.helper "!aws codecommit credential-helper $@"
git config --global credential.UseHttpPath true
```

2. Clone your repository to your local computer and start working on code:

```
git clone https://git-codecommit.us-west-2.amazonaws.com/v1/repos/nadonhosting.com
```

I want more detailed instructions

Close

Figure 17-7. *Once your repository is created, the next step is to connect to it and perform an initial sync of the local data to your CodeCommit repository*

After you've set up your connection and done your first commit, you will be ready to use this tool to store and version your source code. This service gives some nice visualization in terms of activity performed with the repository and makes it easy to share access to your repository to anyone that will need to access it. Users will perform the same steps that you did to connect with the repository, and you can use IAM to control access just as you can across all AWS resources.

Whether you have your code stored in AWS CodeCommit or an external repository, there are another two tools that can assist with the deployment of code to the infrastructure in AWS. CodeDeploy and CodePipeline are also found under the Developer Tools section in the AWS Console Services menu.

CodeDeploy can be used to configure and deploy an application to AWS resources. You configure the application stack to be deployed and configuration details for that specific stack. Think of it as CloudFormation for applications. You specify application details and the deployment model in the configuration wizard. The deployment models used are "in-place" (where infrastructure that is currently in use will have your code deployed to it) or "blue/green" (where your code will be deployed to a new set of infrastructure that is not currently used in production and then "phased" into use after the code is deployed as the current infrastructure is no longer used). Figure 17-8 shows the deployment type configuration screen when starting to set up CodeDeploy for the first time.

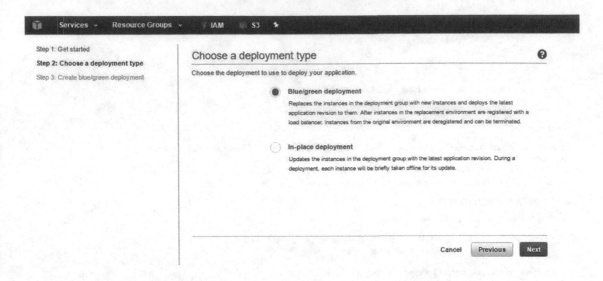

Figure 17-8. *The CodeDeploy Configuration Wizard is shown with the second step of choosing a deployment type. The options are "in-place" or "blue/green."*

The final step in the CodeDeploy wizard will ask you to confirm which infrastructure will be used to receive the deployment. If you choose a blue/green deployment, there may be additional infrastructure that will need to be set up to seamlessly move between the first version of code and the newly deployed version. The convenience of this option definitely has cost associated with it in terms of infrastructure requirement.

AWS CodePipeline takes the code deployment a step further and enables full orchestration of steps to be performed when updating versions of code, applications, or resources defined in AWS. This tool allows you to build a plan for deploying, testing, and releasing updates to your infrastructure, allowing you to build in checks that will automatically roll back if any step in the process fails.

A pipeline is a collection of tasks that build, deploy, and test your code. The process of creating a new pipeline in AWS CodePipeline is a multi-step process where you first define a name for the pipeline. After defining a name, you specify where you source files for the build are located. This can be in AWS CodeCommit, Git, or even files living in an S3 bucket. The next step is to define your build provider. Many people integrate or have built jobs using Jenkins and this is supported, as is AWS CodeBuild and Solano CI. There is also an option to use the pipeline with no build integration; however, if you choose this option, you will need to define a deployment provider, which is the next step. The deployment provider specifies what tool to use to deploy infrastructure needed when you run your build. If you chose a build provider in the previous step, then this is not required; however, if you didn't select a build provider in the previous step, choosing a deployment provider is required. The options for deployment providers are all AWS-based services: CloudFormation, CodeDeploy, or Elastic Beanstalk. Once you have selected which provider for build/deployment, you will then set up an AWS Service Role for performing your pipeline deployments and reviewing the initial configuration. Once your pipeline has been created, you can edit the configuration and build in monitoring of events, creation of stages, and building out complex deployment scenarios with built-in testing for your applications. The use of CodePipeline is outside of the scope of this book, but AWS documentation is available to help you get started setting up your first pipeline using S3 at `http://docs.aws.amazon.com/codepipeline/latest/userguide/tutorials-simple-s3.html`.

Summary

This chapter covered a wide range of additional AWS services that can be used to extend your capabilities when hosting your enterprise website in AWS. Some of these services can be utilized and of benefit even if you're not hosting your website on AWS but you are looking for ways to build in monitoring and methods or tools for doing continuous integration and deployment. In the next chapter, you will take a look at options for securing your website communication and content. You'll also review best practices for hosting on the AWS platform.

CHAPTER 18

■ ■ ■

AWS Security and Securing Website Communication

In this chapter, you will explore security options within the AWS platform. You'll start by using Secure Socket Layer (SSL) to secure your e-commerce website traffic and then you'll move into other topics that focus on the security and best practice reporting available for your infrastructure resources.

Securing Your Website Communication

Hosting an enterprise level e-commerce website on the Internet will certainly have you giving thought to ways to secure the communication that happens between your customers, employees, and the website resources that you have available. The most popular web transport protocol for securing web-based traffic is Secure Socket Layer (SSL). This protocol secures the communication between a client computer and your website by encrypting the data passed between them. To support this secure connection and encryption between the client browser and your website, the client must have a browser that supports SSL communication and the website must be able to host an SSL endpoint. These two points in the connection are referred to as the termination points, and when communicating via SSL, any traffic passed between these points will be encrypted, adding a layer of security to the communication that doesn't exist when communicating over a non-secure connection.

Non-secure web traffic connections can happen over many protocols, but the one that most will be familiar with is the application layer protocol HyperText Transfer Protocol (HTTP). This is the protocol that is used by default for web server applications and by default communicates over port 80. Figure 18-1 shows a standard web browser connected to a website over a non-secure connection via HTTP.

Figure 18-1. *A browser client with a standard, non-secure connection to www.bing.com over the HTTP protocol*

This connection is referred to as a non-secure connection because data that is passed between the client browser and the web server is not encrypted and is sent in plain text. This means that if someone analyzed the packets of data passed between these two points they would be able to interpret the data sent very easily. This could include non-sensitive data, but could also include things like usernames and passwords.

© Jason Nadon 2017

J. Nadon, *Website Hosting and Migration with Amazon Web Services*, DOI 10.1007/978-1-4842-2589-9_18

Most enterprise level websites, including the one in this hosting scenario, have username/password logins to gain access to certain parts of the website and will likely be selling products as well. In both of these situations, it is recommended to secure the web traffic between client and server to minimize the risk of sensitive data being accessed by anyone that shouldn't have access to this information.

In Figure 18-2, you can see the website shown in Figure 18-1 now connected via the secure HTTPS protocol.

Figure 18-2. *A browser client with a secure connection to* `www.bing.com` *over the HTTPS protocol*

In Figure 18-2, you can see that the browser client recognizes that this connection is a secure one and identifies it as such by putting the word "Secure" with a padlock icon next to it. This communication happens over a different port than the non-secure traffic; it occurs over port 443.

So how can you have both secure and non-secure connections on the same website? This is a valid question and the answer is really a question of website purpose and usage. The transmission of encrypted data requires some administrative overhead in terms of data being transferred and the time it will take to process and unencrypt that data. For this reason, data that is not sensitive in nature is most optimally transmitted via the non-secure HTTP protocol. For data and communication that has an opportunity to contain sensitive data, the HTTPS protocol is preferred. In the use case where both of these protocols are needed, this means that the website must support non-secure and secure connections. This can also be expressed as connections over HTTP and HTTPS or communications over port 80 and port 443 (although these are standard/default port values, which technically can be changed on the website end of the connection configuration, but let's not concern ourselves with that right now).

At this point, you now understand that your website must support both non-secure and secure connections between your server resources and your customers, but what are the options for implementing this in AWS? Whether in AWS or hosted elsewhere, the requirements as stated above are the ability for the client browser and the website to support both protocols. By default, all web server applications, including the one you've been using throughout this book, support non-secure connections over HTTP/port 80. You've already implemented this in your static website hosting example using S3, and in your platform/CMS hosting example using the Apache Web Server application hosted on an EC2 resource. You also implemented an Auto Scaling group using an Elastic Load Balancer earlier in this section's enterprise e-commerce hosting scenario with the HTTP protocol enabled and listening on port 80. Figure 18-3 shows the latter configuration option, with HTTP-based traffic connecting on port 80 on the ELB and port 80 on the EC2 resources behind the ELB.

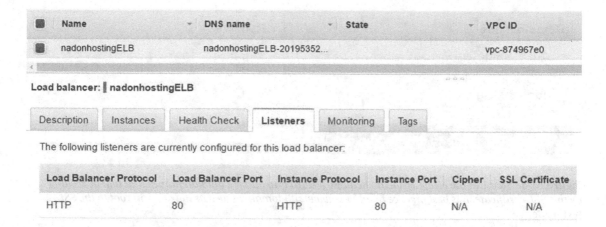

Figure 18-3. *EC2 Elastic Load Balancer listener configuration is shown with the default non-secure application protocol HTTP listening on port 80*

While the web server software (Apache Web Server) on your EC2 instances can be configured to support secure HTTPS connections, an easier method is to implement SSL at the Elastic Load Balancer layer.

As mentioned, secure connections encrypt data being passed between the client browser and the termination point at the server level. If you implement your SSL connection at the ELB level, this becomes your termination point in front of the web servers (EC2 instances) that are behind this load balancer and means that the load balancer will handle the termination of the SSL connection as well as the hosting of an SSL certificate, which is needed as part of the encryption process.

The act of acquiring an SSL certificate for most websites involves working with your hosting provider or a third-party SSL Certificate Authority such as Symantec to procure a specific SSL certificate that can be used to encrypt traffic between your customers and your website. This procurement process involves defining the domain name of your website to be secured, your contact information, and the payment for the SSL certificate. On average, basic SSL certificates can range between $50 and $100 depending upon your SSL certificate provider.

In AWS, this process is a bit more simplified and can be provided for resources hosted on the AWS platform at no charge. Let's walk through the process of procuring and adding a SSL certificate for the domain you've been working with in this book, www.nadonhosting.com.

AWS Certificate Manager

AWS Certificate Manager (ACM) is an Amazon Web Services platform resource that allows you to procure and manage SSL certificates to be used on your infrastructure. For resources hosted within the AWS platform, such as Elastic Load Balancers and CloudFront distributions there is no charge for procuring the SSL certificate.

To access ACM, browse to the Services menu in the AWS Console and under the "Security, Identity and Compliance" section heading, click Certificate Manager and click the Get Started button if this is your first visit to this AWS resource.

When creating your first SSL certificate you will need to provide the name of the domain to be secured. In your case, you specify www.nadonhosting.com and then you click the "Add another domain to this certificate" to also add in the root of this domain name, which is nadonhosting.com. Figure 18-4 shows the information filled into the text boxes presented in the New Certificate Request Wizard.

Figure 18-4. *Step 1 in the New Certificate Request Wizard is to add the domain names that will be secured by this SSL certificate. It is best practice to add the www subdomain as well as the domain root to the SSL certificate*

The next step is to review the information and then complete the submission request by clicking the "Confirm and Request" button. By default, AWS will email the domain registrant and administrative contacts for approval of the issuance of this SSL certificate for this domain. If you are not sure who the contacts are for your domain, you can find this information out using a website such as www.whois.net. This tool will allow you to enter any domain name and find out information that is publically available through the domain's registration record. A search of the nadonhosting.com domain produced the output shown in Figure 18-5.

WHOIS LOOKUP

 nadonhosting.com is already registered*

Whois Server Version 2.0

Domain names in the .com and .net domains can now be registered
with many different competing registrars. Go to http://www.internic.net
for detailed information.

Domain Name: NADONHOSTING.COM
Registrar: AMAZON REGISTRAR, INC.
Sponsoring Registrar IANA ID: 468
Whois Server: whois.registrar.amazon.com
Referral URL: http://registrar.amazon.com
Name Server: NS-1215.AWSDNS-23.ORG
Name Server: NS-1734.AWSDNS-24.CO.UK
Name Server: NS-352.AWSDNS-44.COM
Name Server: NS-754.AWSDNS-30.NET
Status: ok https://icann.org/epp#ok
Updated Date: 28-sep-2016
Creation Date: 28-sep-2016
Expiration Date: 28-sep-2017

>>> Last update of whois database: Sat, 11 Feb 2017 14:17:11 GMT <<<

Figure 18-5. *Result of a search for the nadonhosting.com domain using http://www.whois.net*

Figure 18-5 shows the information returned from the domain public information record. This domain was registered in AWS since the registrar is listed as Amazon Registrar, Inc. It was created in September of 2016 and the name servers being used to host the DNS records for this domain are also AWS resources. This search didn't return the administrative contact email, but this is because I chose for this information to be kept private. Your domain WhoIs search may return similar or additional information based on the configuration set when you registered your domain through the registrar you used.

After clicking the "Confirm and Request" button in the wizard, a list of the email addresses that will receive the certificate validation request will be listed. The next step is to access one of the validation emails and to approve the certificate request.

Once this has been completed, AWS will issue the SSL certificate and allow it to be used from within your AWS account. It is important to understand that AWS ACM certificates can only be used on resources within the AWS platform and cannot be exported out and used outside of the platform. Another noteworthy item is that ACM and the request for certificates can be done via the AWS Console or via the CLI. The request for these certificates happens within the East region, but certificates procured there can be used on infrastructure across your AWS account.

Once you have approved the validation email for the requested domains, you will see that your certificate has been issued in AWS ACM, as shown in Figure 18-6.

Figure 18-6. *AWS ACM showing the issued SSL certificate for www.nadonhosting.com with the additional domain of nadonhosting.com*

Once the SSL certificate has been issued, it is ready for use within your AWS account. This means that if you want to add SSL to your existing ELB, you can now do so by adding the new port listener and associating the above registered SSL certificate. To add a new listener, browse to your EC2 Dashboard in your AWS Console, click the Load Balancers link in the left-hand navigation, select the ELB that you would like to edit, and then click the Listeners tab. Click the Edit button and then choose the Add button. From the dialog presented, choose HTTPS Secure HTTP under the protocol drop-down list, leave the ports as the default selection, and then click the Change link under the SSL column. From this dialog, you can associate an existing certificate from ACM or IAM, or upload a new certificate to be used with this load balancer resource. Figure 18-7 shows your selection to use the SSL certificate that you just requested.

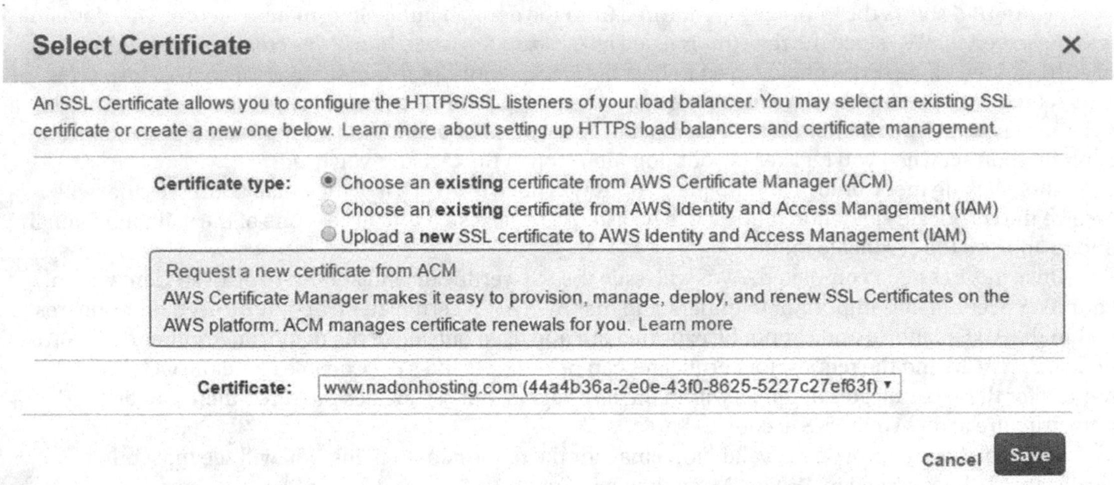

Figure 18-7. *Adding the new SSL certificate*

Once you click the Save button above, the ACM SSL certificate will be associated with the load balancer. Click the Save button again to save the listener configuration changes made to add the HTTPS listener to the load balancer. Once completed, you will now see two listeners configured on your load balancer, as shown in Figure 18-8.

Figure 18-8. *HTTP and HTTPS listeners being configured for this load balancer*

Now that your load balancer is listening and terminating a connection on the HTTPS application protocol using an ACM SSL certificate, traffic sent between a client browser and the address `https://www.nadonhosting.com` will be encrypted and has an extra layer of protection for any sensitive data that you may choose to send along that path.

AWS Security and Best Practices Resources

Now that you have a way to secure your sensitive website communication data such as logins, passwords, and e-commerce processes, let's discuss some of the other tools and resources that AWS has to help with security and best practices.

IAM

AWS Identity and Access Management should be the first place you think of when you think about AWS security. This is the resource I introduced in the beginning of the book, and it is used to manage access to your AWS account and resources within it. Early in the first hosting scenario I talked about the best practices to secure your root account and I want to mention it here again because I feel that it is important enough to do so. If your AWS root account is compromised, the owner of it controls all the keys to the kingdom and can cause a lot of havoc and lost revenue, or even incur operating costs by launching a bunch of AWS resources on your behalf.

CloudTrail

CloudTrail is an auditing resource that keeps track of all API calls that happen within your AWS account and holds metadata about each of these changes including what resources were affected and who affected them. CloudTrail is not on by default; it must be turned on through the AWS Console by configuring the first trail. Browse to the AWS Services menu and under the Management Tools section, click the CloudTrail link. Fill out information to configure your first trail and to store the trail information in S3. There is no charge for the first trail, which can be configured to monitor your entire account; however, additional trails do come at a charge. Also, the S3 storage that will be used to store your trail data will fall under normal S3 pricing. Figure 18-9 shows the configuration screen for your first CloudTrail.

Turn on CloudTrail

Trail name*	nadonhosting
Apply trail to all regions	● Yes ○ No ❶
Create a new S3 bucket	● Yes ○ No
S3 bucket*	nadonhosting-trails ❶
Log file prefix	❶
	Location: /
Enable log file validation	● Yes ○ No ❶
Send SNS notification for every log file delivery	○ Yes ● No ❶

Figure 18-9. AWS CloudTrail configuration screen showing the S3 bucket to be created to store CloudTrail data

Once created, CloudTrail will start tracking all API calls within your account. These calls are tracked whether they are done from within the AWS Console or done via the CLI. This gives you a full audit trail to find out what resources have been accessed, created, changed, removed, and by whom. It is a powerful tool that many forget to enable, but is highly recommended as a relevant tool for hosting on the AWS platform.

AWS Config

AWS Config is a management tool that, similar to CloudTrail, gives you a record of changes that have been performed against your AWS resources. AWS Config is focused around configuration management and change control, so the information presented is more directed from an asset perspective rather than all API calls, as with CloudTrail. In terms of an enterprise hosting scenario, AWS Config can be a useful resource to provide rulesets around change management for your AWS resources to show compliance.

AWS Trusted Advisor

AWS Trusted Advisor is a best practices analyzer that runs at the account level within AWS and analyzes your accounts and resources within AWS and reports on best practices that should be implemented. An example is the EC2 security groups that are open to anyone or if your AWS root account is not using multi-factor authentication. In addition to security best practices as the previous two examples illustrate, the tool will also report on performance optimization that can be achieved, such as applications that are running on underutilized EC2 instances. An example of the reporting overview screen is shown in Figure 18-10.

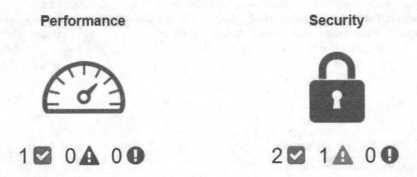

Figure 18-10. *AWS Trusted Advisor's Performance and Secuity overview reporting is shown from within the Trusted Advisor dashboard*

In Figure 18-10, there is a summary at the top of the Trusted Advisor dashboard that shows checks that are OK or have warnings and issues. This resource is a very valuable one and should be used at the beginning of your AWS hosting journey and at regular intervals thereafter.

AWS Inspector

AWS Inspector is an agent-based security tool that can be used to run against EC2 resources to report back on security vulnerabilities and give information on how to remediate them. The process for using AWS Inspector is to load the agent on resources that you would like scanned and then to set up scheduled assessment scans to run against those resources. You can limit not only the scheduled time, but how long the assessment scans run and analyze the resource. This fine-tuning means that you can gather information about the resources with minimal overhead and impact on your operation of them.

Summary

This chapter covered how to set up secure communication between your e-commerce website visitors and your website. It also introduced a variety of security and best practice-related resources that the AWS platform offers. AWS has a strong stance on security and compliance, and takes it quite seriously. Although you ultimately have a large share of responsibility for keeping your resources secure, the platform itself is designed with security in mind and makes it easy to implement stronger control and monitoring than you will see available on other hosting platforms.

CHAPTER 19

■ ■ ■

AWS Enterprise Applications

In this chapter, I will introduce the last of the services that I will discuss in this book. These services are focused on enterprise or corporate customers that are looking for ways to integrate their processes and workflow into the cloud. AWS has positioned the services and products that it offers in a way that makes it easy for a company to have a hybrid approach to their enterprise infrastructure needs, keeping main functions on-premise and using AWS to achieve scale and agility when needed. In this chapter, I'll introduce AWS Directory Services, WorkMail, WorkDocs, and Workspaces as products and services that you may want to look into as options for enterprise productivity applications.

Directory Services

As a company grows, its need for IT services and resources also grows. The organization, authentication, and tracking of these services and resources are usually handled within the company by means of a directory services application. A directory service contains data about objects and resources. Microsoft Active Directory is an example of a popular directory services application, and over the years there have been many others, including Novell Directory Services. Amazon Web Services offers its own directory services on the AWS platform.

To access AWS Directory Services, browse to the Services menu in the AWS Console and under the "Security, Identity and Compliance" section, click the Directory Service link. From here you'll be presented with the welcome splash page that offers up choices about what types of directory services the AWS platform supports.

First, there is the option to create a new cloud-native directory service using AWS Cloud Directory. Using this directory service you will choose a sample AWS schema for the data to be organized in your directory or you can upload a custom schema. Figure 19-1 shows the list of sample schemas currently included on AWS.

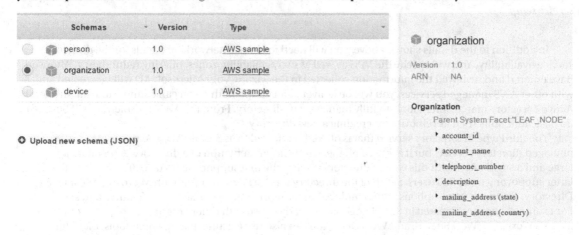

Figure 19-1. *AWS Cloud Directory schema sample options are displayed, with the organization sample selected to show data type information*

© Jason Nadon 2017

J. Nadon, *Website Hosting and Migration with Amazon Web Services*, DOI 10.1007/978-1-4842-2589-9_19

The schema of the sample selection called organization is displayed to the right-hand side of the screen. This shows you what type of information can be stored about each object within the directory. If the three samples given do not fit your needs in terms of information stored, you can also upload your own custom schema in JSON format.

This example is the easiest way to get started with using directory services in the cloud. However, you may already have directory services implemented on-site within your company. In these situations, AWS has a couple of services that can be used to help you migrate or connect to your existing directory services.

AWS Microsoft AD is a fully managed directory service that is hosted in AWS based on and compliant with Windows Server 2012 Active Directory. Fully managed offerings, such as this one and RDS, remove the administrative burden that comes with self-hosting and management of the instances. In this case, you can focus on the creation of the users and objects within the directory and not on managing directory service server instances. Similar to AWS Cloud Directory, setting up Microsoft AD in AWS is done through a simple, short wizard that first asks for specifics around the directory service, shown in Figure 19-2.

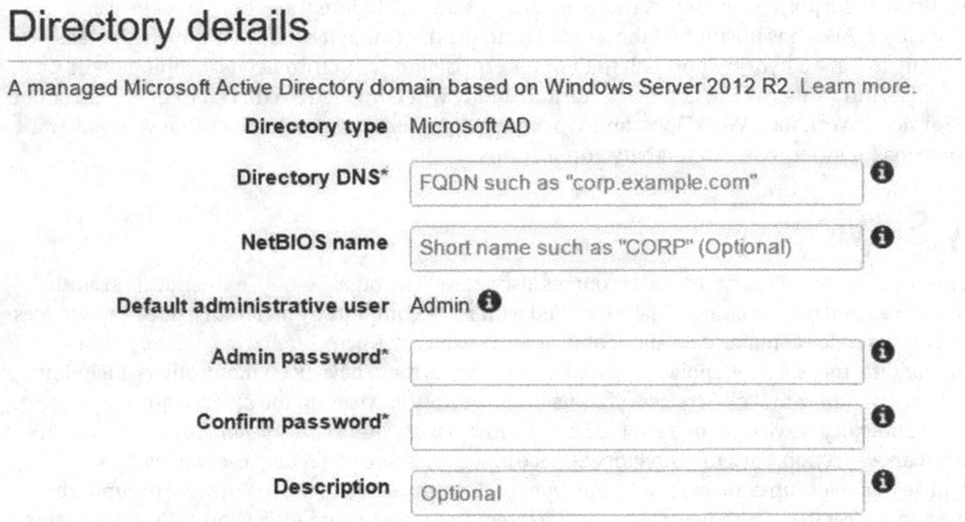

Directory details

A managed Microsoft Active Directory domain based on Windows Server 2012 R2. Learn more.

Directory type	Microsoft AD
Directory DNS*	FQDN such as "corp.example.com"
NetBIOS name	Short name such as "CORP" (Optional)
Default administrative user	Admin
Admin password*	
Confirm password*	
Description	Optional

Figure 19-2. The AWS Microsoft AD Setup Wizard asks for the directory service details to finish the managed service setup

In addition to the details shown above, you will need to choose networking details for the directory service availability. You will specify the VPC as well as two availability zones, offering redundancy. After you have entered and reviewed the information collected in the wizard, your Microsoft AD will be created and, as with other AWS managed services, you will be delivered an endpoint that you can connect to with Microsoft Active Directory management tools to fully manage your directory. From the AWS console you will be able to do basic functions such as removing or creating a new directory.

The third type of directory service that is offered is referred to as Simple AD, and this is also a fully managed directory service, but it is based off the Samba implementation of a directory. AWS offers a large and a small offering in this type of directory service, the first supporting up to 5,000 users and the latter supporting up to 500 users. Setup of the directory service is as simple as with Microsoft AD or Cloud Directory. There are more options with Simple AD in terms of built-in management features and services. For example, accounts created in Simple AD will be ready to use with other enterprise-level services such as AWS WorkMail, WorkSpaces, and WorkDocs. You can also use existing management tools, including Microsoft-based ones to manage the directory service through the endpoint delivered after setup.

That covers the three types of directory service that you can implement within AWS, but there is also a service called AD Connector that allows you to connect an AWS instance to your on-premise Active Directory. This will allow for accounts to be synchronized between the cloud and your installation, and gives you the opportunity to use directory services to manage access to your objects within the directory. Accounts in the cloud can be given access to your on-premise infrastructure and vice versa. This enables you to run in a hybrid mode and extend services to the cloud when it makes sense to do so, as well as to test before making a large commitment.

AWS allows you to try out any one of the above services for 750 hours as part of the free-tier level. This gives you one month to test drive the service that you feel would best suit your organizational requirements.

AWS WorkMail

WorkMail is Amazon Web Services fully hosted mail service for enterprise email communication and calendaring. The service supports desktop, web-based, and mobile connectivity to mail accounts. The use of the WorkMail service must be allowed via IAM policies (the same as with other AWS services) for an AWS account to be able to use the resource. The setup process for WorkMail involves the creation of an "organization" and it will create a Simple AD resource for you to manage your users/organizational object in as the most efficient and integrated directory service option. As long as you are using WorkMail you will not incur additional charges for the AWS Simple AD resource or other resources that get set up as part of the WorkMail setup process. Let's walk through the setup process for the domain we've been using throughout this book to give you a sense of the work needed to set up WorkMail for your domain. From the AWS Console, choose the Services menu and find the WorkMail link under the section called Business Productivity. After clicking the WorkMail link, click the Get Started button to launch the WorkMail setup wizard, as shown in Figure 19-3.

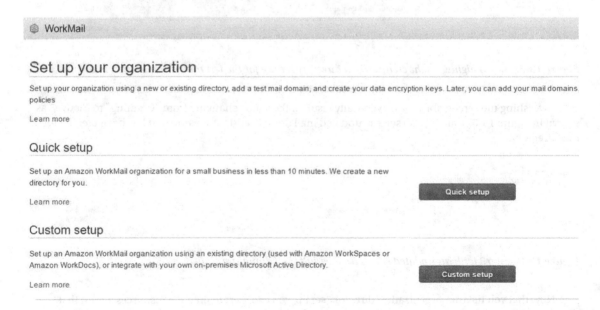

Figure 19-3. AWS Microsoft WorkMail Setup Wizard offers Quick or Custom setup options. Use the Custom option when you already have a directory service that you would like to use with WorkMail

You are going to choose the Quick setup option because this will set up a Directory Services (Simple AD) to be used with the WorkMail and other business productivity/enterprise applications in AWS. Click the Quick Setup button to move forward to the next step of the setup process.

In the next step, you'll enter a test domain to be used for configuring your WorkMail endpoint in AWS. Enter "nadonhosting" as the unique prefix test domain identifier, as shown in Figure 19-4.

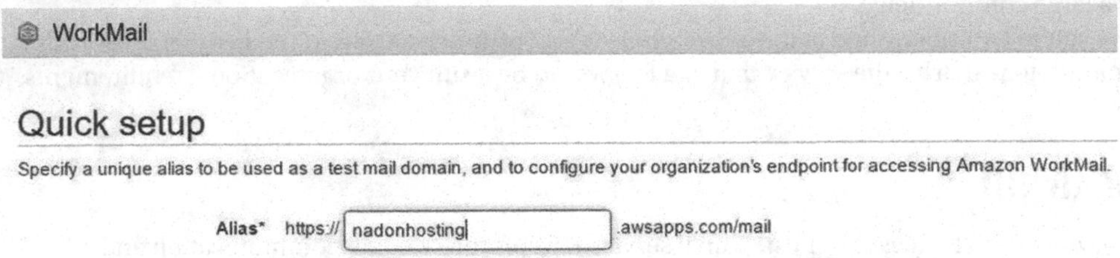

Figure 19-4. *Step 2 asks for a test domain to be used to configure the WorkMail endpoint*

Once you have entered your value in the text input field, click the Create button to start the directory service creation. This process can take approximately ten minutes to complete. Figure 19-5 shows the new directory with a status of "Creating" and shows the type of directory that is being created for you by AWS.

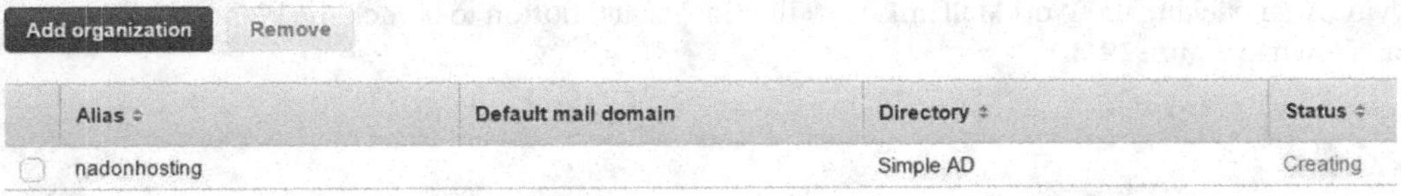

Figure 19-5. *Step 3 highlights the creation of a directory service for the test mail domain used in Step 2*

Refreshing the screen above will eventually result in the status changing from "Creating" to "Active," as shown in Figure 19-6. You will also see the updated mail domain endpoint value that has been created for this directory.

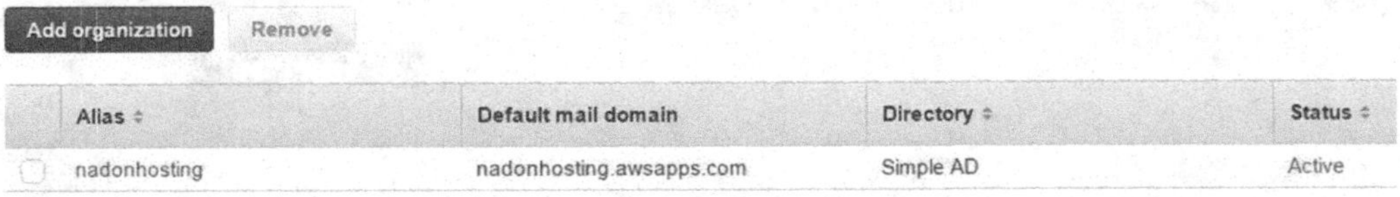

Figure 19-6. *Step 3 with an updated status and default mail domain specified*

Now that you have an organization directory set up, you can start to manage resources within that directory. Click the organization name to navigate to the organization management screen. You will notice that a set of default accounts have been created for your directory, as shown in Figure 19-7.

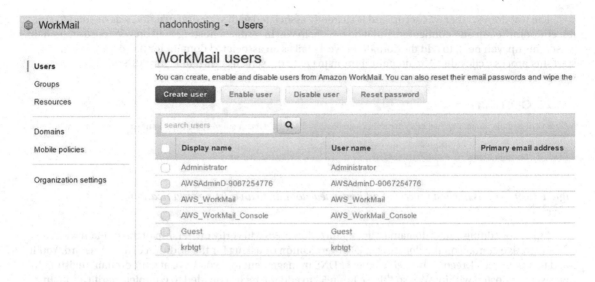

Figure 19-7. *AWS Microsoft WorkMail Management screen shows the default accounts in the directory service that was created for your organization*

From the AWS WorkMail Organization Management screen you can see the default accounts that have been created for you in the directory service that was created for your organization. These accounts include the Administrator account (disabled by default) and a host of other accounts that are used for application services by the WorkMail product. These accounts are system accounts and cannot be removed. As shown in Figure 19-7, in the left-hand navigation of the WorkMail Organization you can manage users, groups, resources, and domains to be used with this organization, mobile policies, and general organizational settings.

Since the goal of this exercise is to set up a mail account on your custom domain, let's click the Domains link in the left-hand navigation. This will list your current domains associated with this organization, as shown in Figure 19-8. As you'll see below, the only domain currently associated is the test domain that you specified in Step 2 of the WorkMail Setup Wizard.

nadonhosting ▾   Domains

WorkMail domains

You can add or remove email domains or make them the default.

Add domain   Remove   Set as default

Domain ▲	Domain status ⇕	Default domain
nadonhosting.awsapps.com	Verified	Default

Figure 19-8. *A list of all associated domains for this organization*

The test domain that was set up and is currently associated with your organization was needed to get the endpoint set up and configured, but it doesn't help you in terms of hosting mail on your custom domain. To set this up, you need to add the domain to WorkMail as an associated domain for this organization. To start this process, click the "Add domain" button to get to the screen shown in Figure 19-9.

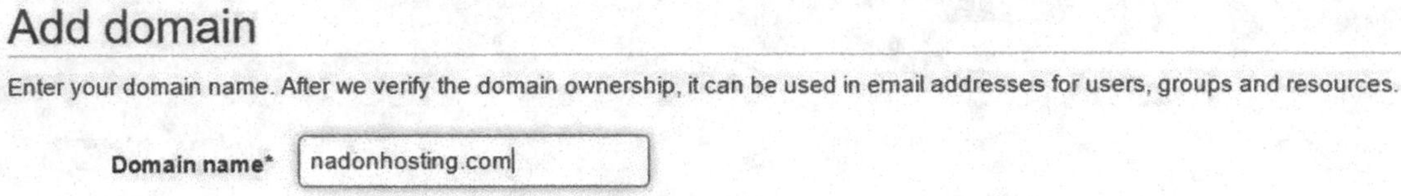

Add domain

Enter your domain name. After we verify the domain ownership, it can be used in email addresses for users, groups and resources.

Domain name*   nadonhosting.com|

Figure 19-9. This is the first process in adding a new domain to an existing organization

As part of adding a new domain to an organization, AWS will verify ownership of the domain with the administrative contact on the domain via DNS verification by asking for the addition of a TXT record. You'll need to add this TXT record through whatever DNS management tool you have at your domain registrar. In my case, I'm hosted within AWS, so I'll use Route53 to add the record needed to complete verification. In addition to the TXT record for verification purposes, the second step of the process will also tell you what other DNS records need to be set up on the domain for you to be able to send and receive email with it. The additional records needed are shown in Figure 19-10; you'll again use Route53 to set these records up in the domain DNS record.

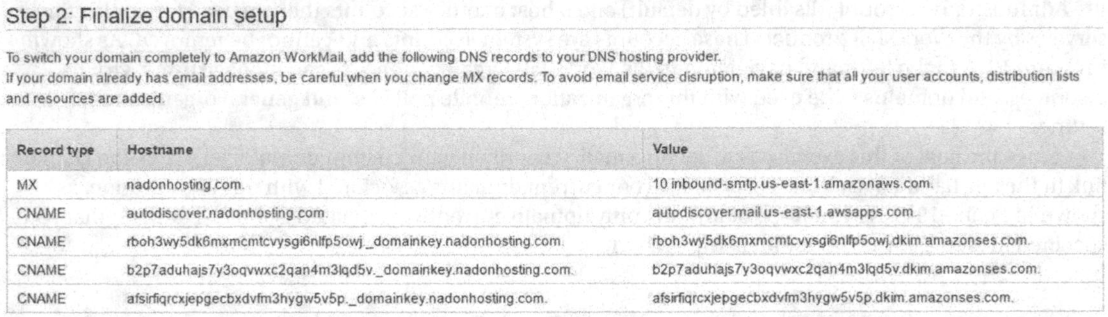

Step 2: Finalize domain setup

To switch your domain completely to Amazon WorkMail, add the following DNS records to your DNS hosting provider.
If your domain already has email addresses, be careful when you change MX records. To avoid email service disruption, make sure that all your user accounts, distribution lists and resources are added.

Record type	Hostname	Value
MX	nadonhosting.com.	10 inbound-smtp.us-east-1.amazonaws.com.
CNAME	autodiscover.nadonhosting.com.	autodiscover.mail.us-east-1.awsapps.com.
CNAME	rboh3wy5dk6mxmcmtcvysgi6nlfp5owj._domainkey.nadonhosting.com.	rboh3wy5dk6mxmcmtcvysgi6nlfp5owj.dkim.amazonses.com.
CNAME	b2p7aduhajs7y3oqvwxc2qan4m3lqd5v._domainkey.nadonhosting.com.	b2p7aduhajs7y3oqvwxc2qan4m3lqd5v.dkim.amazonses.com.
CNAME	afsirfiqrcxjepgecbxdvfm3hygw5v5p._domainkey.nadonhosting.com.	afsirfiqrcxjepgecbxdvfm3hygw5v5p.dkim.amazonses.com.

Figure 19-10. This is information that will need to be added to your domain DNS for WorkMail to function as expected

An SES (Simple Email Service) policy will be set up to allow this domain to be able to send/receive email within the Amazon Web Services platform. Amazon takes email setup and security quite seriously; resources that are hosted in the platform send mail from infrastructure managed by AWS. Therefore, it is important in terms of shared responsibility that those using the infrastructure resources are not using them for inappropriate functions such as creating and sending unsolicited email.

After adding the needed records to the nadonhosting.com domain DNS, you can refresh the screen and see that domain status had changed to "Verified." After the domain has been verified, go back to the main WorkMail Domain Management screen, select the nadonhosting.com domain, and click the "Set as default" button to make this domain the default domain for the organization. Figure 19-11 shows the list of domains now associated with this organization and their status.

WorkMail domains

You can add or remove email domains or make them the default.

> Successfully set the default to domain to 'nadonhosting.com' for the organization 'nadonhosting'.

Add domain	Remove	Set as default

Domain ▲	Domain status ⬍	Default domain
☐ nadonhosting.awsapps.com	Verified	
☐ nadonhosting.com	Verified	Default

Figure 19-11. A list of associated domains for the organization and their status

Now that the domain is associated with the organization, you can create a user within the organization so that you can then enable the WorkMail service for them. To do this, move to the Users section of the WorkMail Management interface and then click the Create User button to start the New User Setup Wizard. The information collected for a new user is shown in Figure 19-12.

Users

Add the details for your new user

User name*	jnadon	❶
First name	Jason	
Last name	Nadon|	
Display name*	Jason Nadon	❶

* Required information

Figure 19-12. AWS Microsoft WorkMail User Management new user screen

The first step collects basic information such as the user name for the account, first name, last name and a display name. Once you have entered this information, you'll move to the next step, which is shown in Figure 19-13.

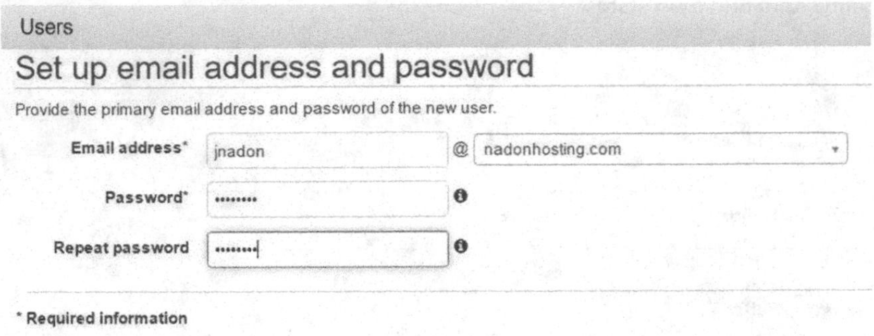

Users
Set up email address and password
Provide the primary email address and password of the new user.

Email address*	jnadon	@ nadonhosting.com ▾
Password*	••••••••	❶
Repeat password	••••••••	❶

* Required information

Figure 19-13. *Step 2 is where you can select the email address/domain to be associated with the user*

In the second step of adding a new user you will specify which domain this email address will be associated with and you'll set up a new password for the account. Once you specify these details, you can click the Create button to add the user. Figure 19-14 shows your user added to the existing list of users associated with this organization and that WorkMail is now enabled for this user.

	Display name	User name	Primary email address	Status
	Administrator	Administrator		Disabled
	AWSAdminD-9067254776	AWSAdminD-9067254776		System User
	AWS_WorkMail	AWS_WorkMail		System User
	AWS_WorkMail_Console	AWS_WorkMail_Console		System User
	Guest	Guest		System User
	Jason Nadon	jnadon	jnadon@nadonhosting.com	Enabled

Figure 19-14. *WorkMail is now enabled for the new user*

Now that the new account exists and has been enabled, let's test logging into the web interface and sending and receiving email using the account.

You will find your webmail interface listed under your Organizational settings tab, as shown in Figure 19-15.

Organization settings

You can view the organization's details and edit its settings.

| General settings | Migration settings | Journaling settings | Interoperability settings |

Information to set up mobile device or Microsoft Outlook can be found in the Amazon WorkMail User Guide.

Organization ID	m-55e3937adf4b4d21bb06a3cb913820f7
Organization Alias	nadonhosting
Directory ID	d-9067254776
Directory Type	Simple AD
Web Application	☑ https://nadonhosting.awsapps.com/mail

Figure 19-15. *The Organizational settings screen lists your WebMail interface in the Web Application field*

Using the link shown in Figure 19-15 you can log in with your new account and password using the webmail interface. Note that you don't need to use the email address, just the account name and password to log in. In my case, the user name is jnadon. Figure 19-16 shows the WorkMail web application interface after successfully logging into it.

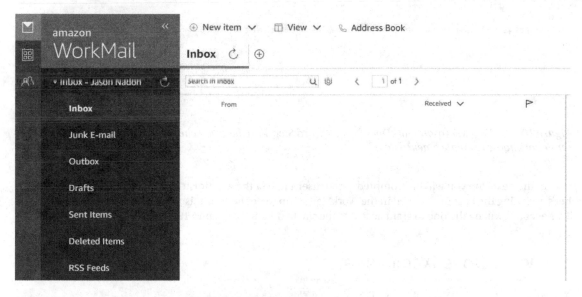

Figure 19-16. *AWS Microsoft WorkMail Web Application Interface*

Now that you can successfully access the AWS WorkMail interface, you can start using all the features such as email and calendaring. Accounts created for an organization will have the capability to connect via a desktop mail/calendaring application such as Microsoft Outlook via a webmail interface hosted by AWS and accessible via the console, or via a mobile device application that is registered with your directory service.

In terms of pricing, at the time of writing this book, each mailbox account is $4 per month and includes 50GB of mail storage. If used in conjunction with WorkDocs, the cost goes up $2 per month per user, but users will have an allowed 1TB of document storage each. You can set up 25 users for a 30-day trial period, but at the end of the 30 days you will be charged for all users still in an active state.

AWS WorkDocs

WorkDocs is Amazon Web Services fully managed enterprise document storage solution. This service offers document storage as well as the collaborative features of an online document management suite. You can easily collaborate on documents with multiple team members, track comments and feedback, route documents for review, and improve productivity while being able to track and report on work completed. WorkDocs storage is accessible after you walk through the process of setting up a WorkDocs site for your organization. Access is controlled in a way that is similar to WorkMail in that users managed in a directory service are granted access to your document storage location and applications.

Similar to how WorkMail was set up, if you want to set up a WorkDocs site, you should browse to the AWS Console Services Menu and choose the WorkDocs link under the Business Productivity heading. Once you access the welcome screen for WorkDocs, click the Get Started button to start the WorkDocs Site Setup Wizard.

The first step in the process will ask you to choose the AWS Directory Service for use with WorkDocs. Since you created one for use with WorkMail above, chose it, as shown in Figure 19-17.

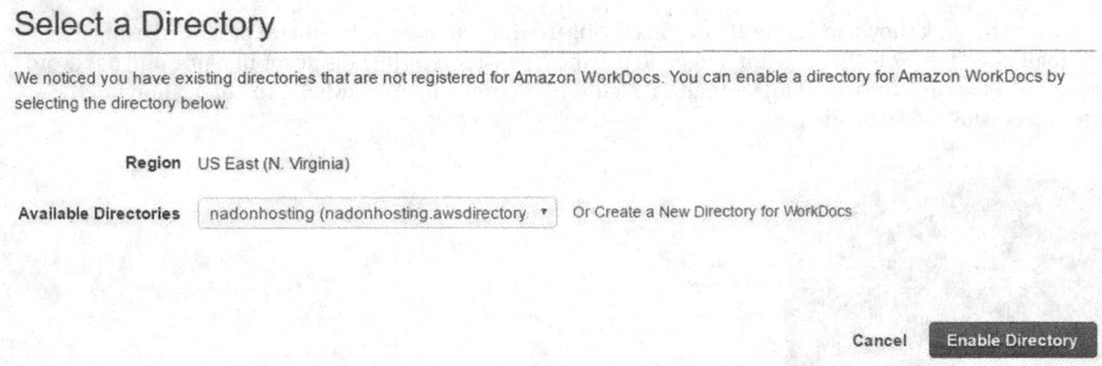

Select a Directory

We noticed you have existing directories that are not registered for Amazon WorkDocs. You can enable a directory for Amazon WorkDocs by selecting the directory below.

Region   US East (N. Virginia)

Available Directories   nadonhosting (nadonhosting.awsdirectory ▾)   Or Create a New Directory for WorkDocs

Cancel   Enable Directory

Figure 19-17. *AWS Microsoft WorkDocs Setup Wizard Step 1 is where you choose your existing directory service or choose to create a new one*

In the next step you will be prompted for the username of the Administrator account for WorkDocs. Let's assigning the account created in the WorkMail setup to be the Administrator for the WorkDocs site. This account will be the one to grant access to the site to others (see Figure 19-18).

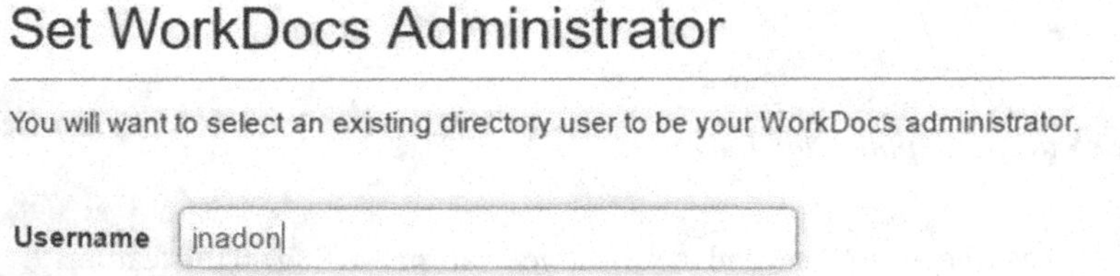

Set WorkDocs Administrator

You will want to select an existing directory user to be your WorkDocs administrator.

Username   jnadon|

Figure 19-18. *Step 2 is where you choose the Administrative user for your WorkDocs site*

After you enter the account name, the site will begin to be provisioned for you and an email will be send to the Administrator user to give them information about the WorkDocs site. Figure 19-19 shows the setup wizard's final screen.

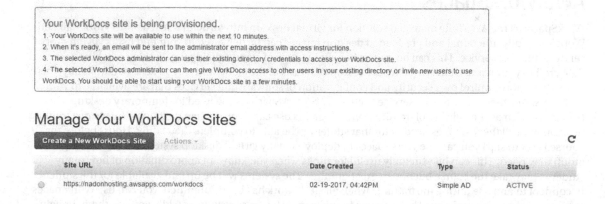

Your WorkDocs site is being provisioned.
1. Your WorkDocs site will be available to use within the next 10 minutes.
2. When it's ready, an email will be sent to the administrator email address with access instructions.
3. The selected WorkDocs administrator can use their existing directory credentials to access your WorkDocs site.
4. The selected WorkDocs administrator can then give WorkDocs access to other users in your existing directory or invite new users to use WorkDocs. You should be able to start using your WorkDocs site in a few minutes.

Manage Your WorkDocs Sites

Create a New WorkDocs Site	Actions ▾			C
Site URL	Date Created	Type	Status	
○ https://nadonhosting.awsapps.com/workdocs	02-19-2017, 04:42PM	Simple AD	ACTIVE	

Figure 19-19. *The final step offers information about your site provisioning*

After the provisioning of the site is complete, you'll be able to log into your WorkDocs site. The web application interface of WorkDocs is shown in Figure 19-20.

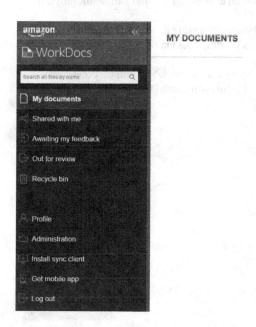

Figure 19-20. *The WorkDocs UI is shown with the left-hand navigation options highlighted*

Almost any file format can be stored in WorkDocs, and the platform has a built-in preview function that allows you to view a document even if you don't have the software loaded that created the document.

In terms of pricing, at the time of writing, WorkDocs pricing is $5 per month per account/user. Bundled with WorkMail, AWS charges $6 per month per account for a savings of $3 per month, per account.

AWS WorkSpaces

WorkSpaces is the AWS fully managed solution for virtual desktop infrastructure. Just as with WorkMail and WorkDocs, fully functional and pre-loaded desktop images can be delivered to your end users via directory services and this service. This can be quite a benefit in terms of standardizing the working machines delivered to your team. Delivering a work desktop that runs in the cloud and can be accessed from anywhere allows you more control over security and configuration of software and services that are available to your end users. Another use case for a service such as AWS WorkSpaces is the need for temporary desktop resources, such as the delivery of training content. In this use case, you can create a single image of a training desktop with all the resources needed for that student to be able to complete their study. Hours before the course is set to start you can use WorkSpaces to deploy as many virtual desktop systems as the training group may need. This can be extremely useful for times when you know an approximation of how many students may take the course but not an exact number. The systems will be up and available for the students to connect to and use during the training; when all study work has been submitted, you can use WorkSpaces to unprovision those desktops. The net value is only paying for these resources while you use them. Imagine instead delivering the same training on-site where you must plan for 20 desktop computers to be physically set up and software installed across them so that configuration matches and each is ready for the students. You might have to get this set up days before the class, and acquiring this hardware may become costly and time consuming.

As an added benefit, WorkSpaces can be configured to deliver a virtual desktop with additional preloaded software such as Microsoft Office to your end users for an additional fee that can be included in the pricing model.

It is easy to get started with WorkSpaces. There are a few choices that you can make if you just want to try out the service for testing purposes. First, you can access AWS WorkSpaces via the AWS Console Services menu, under the section heading "Desktop and App Streaming."

From here, click the Get Started button to move into the WorkSpaces wizard. You will be presented with a screen similar to Figure 19-21; it will ask you which type of setup you would like to continue with for configuration.

Get Started with Amazon WorkSpaces

Choose an option below to set up your WorkSpaces.

Quick Setup

Quickly launch WorkSpaces for an individual or small group of cloud-based users in less than 20 minutes.

Learn More

[Launch]

Advanced Setup

Launch WorkSpaces using advanced options-including using your on-premises directory and existing Amazon VPC.

Learn More

[Launch]

Figure 19-21. *In the AWS WorkSpaces Setup Wizard, the first choice is which type of setup configuration you would like to select*

You are presented with a choice of Quick or Advanced setup. Advanced setup is a better choice when you have tested out the service and have decided that you are ready to implement it in your organization. The Quick setup will allow you to select a number of workspaces to be delivered and provision them for you in the quickest manner with little administrative overhead. The Quick Setup Wizard will ask you for the desired workspace bundle that you would like to deploy and whether you would like it as a monthly or hourly billed resource. Subsequently, you will enter user detail information for each workspace to be created/provisioned. The general setup steps under the Quick setup choice are as follows:

- Create the IAM resources needed to provision network interfaces for workspaces.

- Create the network resources needed to organize and hold your workspaces.

- Simple AD creation and setup that will hold directory service information for your workspaces. This will include the creation of a directory service Administrator account.

- Create the workspaces specified in the configuration step of the wizard.

- Each user is notified via email of their workspace information and next steps to connect to the workspace that has been provisioned.

In terms of pricing for this service, you do have the option of paying for each workspace in a monthly period, where unlimited use is allowed, or by an hourly period. The hourly rate also includes a monthly flat rate and a per hour rate. Pricing details can be found at https://aws.amazon.com/workspaces/pricing/.

Summary

This chapter introduced a few of the enterprise-level applications and services that the AWS platform offers to help you extend your business productivity. Although they may not be a fit for all readers of this book, it is worth knowing that these types of services exist and are available to you if you choose to use Amazon Web Services as your web hosting platform. There are few other vendors in the world today that offer the amount of features and services within a single, cloud-based platform that are as accessible as AWS. I hope that this chapter introduced some concepts that may give you reason to learn more about these options and investigate how to implement a hybrid strategy to allow for infrastructure growth using the scalable and highly available resources of AWS.

Part 3: Hosting an E-Commerce Website in Amazon Web Services Wrap-Up

In this section, I will cover items related to hosting an enterprise-level e-commerce website as the last of the three of your web hosting scenarios.

As I have done previously, I will now include a Knowledge Check where I summarize the services that you've used and give links to additional resources so you can learn more about these services and features. In addition, I will talk about cost considerations for the example e-commerce website as well as all the additional services that I covered.

Knowledge Check

CMS Website: CMS is a content management system website that consists of static content, database, and application/dynamic resources. These are sometimes referred to as "platform" websites and you saw examples for the three most popular of these platforms: WordPress, Drupal, and Joomla.

AWS S3 (Simple Storage Service): You revisited AWS S3 usage as a major component for this hosting scenario because it will still play a major role in hosting not only static files, but application files and your CloudFormation templates that define the infrastructure stack that will be launched.

AWS EC2 (Elastic Cloud Compute): You learned how to launch an EC2 Virtual Server Instance through the AWS Console as well as how to use the AWS command line interface to launch resources. You learned about user data and how to install applications during launch time. You learned about security groups and how they control access to your EC2 resources. You saw how EBS (Elastic Block Storage) can be used to create volume storage that you can attach to EC2 virtual server instances. You also learned how EC2 related resources can be defined in CloudFormation templates and launched and managed via that AWS service.

AWS RDS (Relational Database Service): You were introduced to the AWS RDS service and learned about the various databases that can be hosted in this fully-managed service. You learned how to set up MySQL database resources from the AWS Console and CLI as well as how to connect to these resources using client-side applications to manage your database resources. You learned how RDS can assist you by handling backups of your databases and even perform upgrades automatically to the platform hosting the databases.

AWS CloudFormation: You learned about the AWS CloudFormation service and how to define infrastructure using JSON/text files. You then learned how to use these definition files to launch an infrastructure stack and how this can be managed as a single unit of resources. You learned how to update and redeploy changes to the infrastructure stack and you learned that some stack updates are more disruptive than others.

Cost Considerations

As with the first hosting scenario, the static website, the scenario presented in this chapter will have similar cost considerations in terms of when to move to a new hosting platform such as AWS. In the first scenario, the benefit to hosting in AWS had to do with the high availability and durability of hosting your files in S3. When you think about a platform/CMS website, there will be additional cost for resources such as EC2 virtual server instances and RDS instances. These costs can range from being quite minimal and reasonable to being significant based on how much data is stored and how much traffic the website is handling. If you are hosting a very active site, you may need to deploy a larger infrastructure to handle the need. The benefit of using the AWS platform in this case is that you are only charged for what you use and you have the ability to easily scale up to address the real-time need of your visitors. The AWS platform allows you to launch resources quickly and to test functionality with minimal expense. You have the ability to set up your infrastructure to scale automatically to meet the demand of your customers if you so choose.

This flexibility and scalability is the selling point when looking at a web hosting platform. When launching a new site, you won't know if there will be 100 visitors or 100,000 visitors, so you want to be in a situation where you can meet and deliver your content to the 100,000 visitors if they come. Many smaller hosts will limit the amount of data (bandwidth) that they will deliver to your customers and you may need to manually intervene if website traffic grows unexpectedly.

In terms of realistic cost estimations when deploying a CMS website using EC2 and RDS resources, you can expect to pay anywhere from $4-$15 per month in hosting charges for a small-to-medium site. At the time of writing, Amazon recently launched a new service call LightSail that offers an easy way to set up a VPS (Virtual Private Server) that can be used to host your platform/CMS website. Hosting plans start at $5 per month and go up to $80 per month. Using this method, you're given a predefined set of resources to use based on the plan selected. It's very similar to other hosting providers and I believe that they are offering this in order to directly compete at this level. My preference is to be able to manage my own resources across the full AWS platform and pay for what I use, but your needs may be different, so check out the LightSail offerings at `https://amazonlightsail.com/`.

CHAPTER 20

■ ■ ■

Additional Resources

This section of the book provides you with some additional resources for topics that were introduced in earlier chapters but where the structure of the book did not allow for in-depth investigation or instruction. The resources are organized by category and include resources for connecting to and managing AWS resources, training, and important AWS concept documentation.

Managing AWS EC2 Resources

You deployed AWS EC2 resources in Chapter 8 using the AWS Console and CLI, and although I included the necessary code to launch the instance and install the needed web server resources, I didn't go into great detail about how to log in and manage these resources using remote management software. For this reason, I'm including the link to AWS documentation for using IAM access keys to access your instances remotely and manage resources on them.

Connecting to Linux Instances

The following link describes the process of connecting to an EC2 Linux instance:

http://docs.aws.amazon.com/AWSEC2/latest/UserGuide/AccessingInstances.html

Connecting to Windows Instances

The following link describes the process of connecting to an EC2 Windows instance:

http://docs.aws.amazon.com/AWSEC2/latest/WindowsGuide/connecting_to_windows_instance.html

Amazon Web Services Support Options

As you start using AWS to host your website and infrastructure resources there may come a time when you need to reach out for assistance. AWS Free Tier includes a basic level of support, and you also have the option of purchasing higher levels of support that offer better response timeframes and access to additional support resources. The following link has a comparison of support options on the AWS platform:

https://aws.amazon.com/premiumsupport/compare-plans/

© Jason Nadon 2017
J. Nadon, *Website Hosting and Migration with Amazon Web Services*, DOI 10.1007/978-1-4842-2589-9_20

Additional Website Content Resources

The resources below will help with content hosted on your website and would be considered more of intermediate level resources on the topics mentioned.

JavaScript

In the first hosting scenario I mention that JavaScript can be used to extend your static website to create an interactive one. While this is true, the client browser must have JavaScript enabled to take advantage of this benefit. There may be times when your website visitors have disabled JavaScript in their web browser and you must handle this in a way that offers a seamless interaction for the website visitor. There are multiple ways to do this and there wasn't room to cover them all in the book. The following is a link to a discussion that offers multiple options for displaying content for those that have JavaScript enabled in their browser and those that may have it disabled by using the `<noscript>` tag:

`http://stackoverflow.com/questions/121203/how-to-detect-if-javascript-is-disabled`

Platform/CMS Additional Resources

In the second website hosting scenario, you deployed WordPress, Joomla, and Drupal Content Management Systems. As you deployed the CMS websites you learned that many of them can use AWS S3 as their storage for static and application files. For Drupal, a plug-in is needed to be able to configure it in this manner. More information about the plug-in is available at the following link:

`www.drupal.org/project/s3fs`

AWS Best Practice Documentation/Resources

The resource links below offer more critical information that you should take into consideration when architecting your infrastructure in AWS.

Architecture

Information about best practices in architecture for AWS can be found at the following link:

`https://aws.amazon.com/architecture/well-architected/`

Security

Information about best practices in security within AWS can be found at the following link:

`https://aws.amazon.com/security/`

Training Resources

In this section, I list some of the training resources that you can use to improve your knowledge of working within the AWS platform.

Amazon Web Services

AWS has excellent documentation and you can use these self-paced labs to improve your knowledge:

`https://aws.amazon.com/training/self-paced-labs/`

A Cloud Guru

The following is an excellent training resource for all AWS subjects and AWS certification preparation:

`https://acloud.guru/`

Index

J. Nadon, *Website Hosting and Migration with Amazon Web Services*, DOI 10.1007/978-1-4842-2589-9

Get the eBook for only $5!

Why limit yourself?

With most of our titles available in both PDF and ePUB format, you can access your content wherever and however you wish—on your PC, phone, tablet, or reader.

Since you've purchased this print book, we are happy to offer you the eBook for just $5.

To learn more, go to http://www.apress.com/companion or contact support@apress.com.

Apress®

Printed in the United States
By Bookmasters